A shopper's Guide to Paris Fashion

D0102308

A shopper's Guide to Paris Fashion

ALICIA DRAKE

metro

First published in Great Britain in 1997
by Metro Books (an imprint of Metro Publishing Limited),
19 Gerrard Street, London W1V 7LA

Second edition published in 2000

All rights reserved: no part of this publication may be reproduced,
stored in a retrieval system, or transmitted in any form or by any
means, electronic, mechanical, photocopying or otherwise, without the
prior written consent of the publisher.

© 1997, 2000 Alicia Drake

Alicia Drake is hereby identified as the author of this work in accor-
dance with Section 77 of the Copyright, Designs and Patents Act 1988

British Library Cataloguing in Publication Data. A CIP record of this
book is available on request from the British Library.

ISBN 1 900512 43 2

Illustrations by Jason Brooks, Brighton

Designed by Richard Burgess, London

Printed in Britain by CPD Group, Wales

With thanks to my grandmother, Joan Henderson,
for her originality and expectations.

CONTENTS

PREFACE

Since I first wrote *A Shopper's Guide to Paris Fashion*, the city has changed radically. After years of Gallic depression and cross-Channel envy, Paris has emerged from economic and creative recession and reclaimed its right to be cool.

On the fashion scene the shake-up among the major establishment houses continues, with Marc Jacobs taking design power at the house of Louis Vuitton and transforming the brand from bourgeois predictability to the epitome of contemporary allure. Stella McCartney has given us rock chick at Chloé, while Nicolas Ghesquière has reworked a spare, sculptural silhouette at Balenciaga. Added to that is a new, young generation of independent designers such as Jeremy Scott, Jérôme Dreyfuss, Bless, and Gaspard Yurkievich, who are working in Paris and staking their claim as the new avant-garde.

Indicative of the new energy in town are the fashion stores springing up all over. They have been led by Colette, which opened on rue St-Honoré a couple of years back when the recession was still full on, and has since become a mecca for the Paris fashion crowd.

If Paris has changed, so has this book. We have introduced more detailed maps to try and ease your shopping experience. I've been round and checked out every store, removing those I think are no longer up to scratch as well as those that have closed. I have added 110 new entries – most of which fall into the existing fashion, clothes, accessories and make-up categories. There are more menswear entries than before, and the growing love affair between fashion and home means I have added some key lifestyle and interiors stores as well. Also in terms of new additions I have had a baby, which means that I have got to know both the best pregnancy wear stores (it's extravagant I know, but if there is any way you can get to Paris to buy your pregnancy wardrobe, do it – the clothes here are so much better) and the key children's clothes stores. And there are some eclectic additions – a great stationery store here, a literary wine bar there and not forgetting the flea markets. Overall I have tried to reflect what I love about Paris, namely its cosmopolitan diversity and inimitable chic.

INTRODUCTION

Forget romance, Paris is for shoppers, not lovers. This guide is about how to shop for fashion in Paris, what's hot, what's hip, what's classic French style and where to find it. It's a practical guide to get you to the clothes, shoes, accessories and make-up you desire.

On the fashion atlas Milan may have Gucci, New York slick, commercial clothes and London innovation, but only Paris has both the heritage and international fashion clout. Ever since Englishman Charles Worth moved to Paris in 1845 and set up the city's first ever couture house, Paris has wooed and cooed over its foreign designers.

Today Paris is where Londoner John Galliano has found fortune, first with his own house, then at Givenchy and now at Dior. It is where German Karl Lagerfeld designs for the house of Chanel and where all the Japanese designers from Comme des Garçons' Rei Kawakubo to Yohji Yamamoto choose to show. This combination of imported foreign talent and that of home-grown designers from Christian Lacroix to Martine Sitbon makes Paris fashion unmissable.

The city is divided into 20 arrondissements which spiral out clockwise starting dead centre with the 1st and working out to the 20th in the east. The arrondissements are all-important in Parisian life and they differ widely in terms of atmosphere, architecture, scene and social standing. You are your arrondissement.

To get to grips with Paris retail you've got to start shopping like a Parisian and that means doing it by arrondissement, not subject. So the guide is divided up into the eight crucial fashion areas (all walkable), with a final ninth chapter, Destination Shopping, a round-up of essential boutiques from other arrondissements. Some arrondissements tend to overlap and blur around the edges into the next and you can find one side of a street is officially in, say, the 6th, while the other side is in the 7th. Where this happens or where, for instance, it makes more sense to visit a shop at the edge of the 1st arrondissement while you are walking the 2nd, I have opted for the most logical and easy shopping route, rather than sticking rigidly to arrondissement borders.

The introduction to each chapter gives you an overview of what's on offer in that area. The idea is that wherever you are staying you can start fashion shopping by checking out what's around you first, then figure out which other areas suit your style. For instance, Le Marais is for you if you are looking for a bit of funky, bohemian dressing, whereas the 7th is much more about well-dressed, moneyed Parisian chic.

There are two parts to every shop entry. One is about the style or look of the designer or store, intended so that you can find the store which matches your taste. The other is factual details such as price range, nearest métro stop, opening hours and which credit cards the store takes. Each chapter has a couple of ideas on places to stop for coffee or lunch, as well as suggestions of something else to do like take a steam bath or visit the Museum of Fashion.

Paris fashion still tends to be massively influenced by the French dictates of luxe, bon goût and craftsmanship, but the fashion scene here has loosened up considerably with the increase in the number of international designers and as a result of the recession. For the first time you've got the beginnings of Paris street fashion: clubby urban wear shops, a current obsession with fripe (secondhand retro clothing) and the development of high street retail. All these different strands of fashion, plus the fact that Paris itself is just so dreamy, make shopping here exhilarating.

Shop service can, however, lead to cultural confusion. While we are accustomed to trying on a skirt anonymously in the corner of a communal changing room and then putting all our clothes back on to go and find the size bigger, the French are not. They demand service. This means that when a vendeuse starts trailing you from the moment you walk into the boutique, she doesn't think you're going to nick something, she's just doing her job.

Where French service works well is when you need help with pulling together a look or an outfit. If you find a shop you like and have the confidence, you can walk in, name your budget and say you need an outfit for a wedding, interview, party, work – whatever – and the vendeuse will dress you and do it well. The downside of the Parisian vendeuses or vendeurs is that that they can be breath-takingly rude and pushy. On a cold day during the sales I tried on a pair of shoes that were so big they were falling off. The sales assistant assured me they were the right size – my feet had just shrunk in the cold. If it comes to dispute, don't get nice, get an attitude – it gets results.

The most exciting time to shop for fashion in Paris is when the ready-to-wear fashion shows are on in March and October. The new collections have just arrived in the stores and the city is a slick of mincing models, bottled water and the international fashion pack. Heaven.

PRACTICAL INFORMATION

OPENING HOURS
Shop hours tend to be European in style; very few stores have late night shopping (even some of the department stores don't), but most do stay open until 7pm. A few boutiques still close on Mondays and at lunchtime. Very few stores open on Sunday, with the exception of several in Le Marais. Virgin Megastore, Prisunic and Sephora are a few of the rare shops in central Paris to stay open until midnight.

HOLIDAYS
August is a write-off for shopping as so many boutiques, restaurants

and stores close for a couple of weeks or for the whole month. All the Parisians go on holiday and Paris without the Parisians is just not the same. During the month of May there are three bank holidays and practically all the stores close for them.

SALES (SOLDES)

By law the sales cannot start before the first Monday after Christmas and the last week of June. Nevertheless there are always people holding sales or at least discounting during the run-up to Christmas.

ALTERATIONS

These are part of the service when buying fashion in Paris. How they are dealt with depends on the boutique. If you're buying designer kit you can expect to have it altered for free, but even high street stores will offer alterations, but they are more likely to charge for them. Stores will usually speed through an alteration if you are only in Paris for a limited time.

ETIQUETTE

Every time you walk into a boutique they will say 'Bonjour Madame/Bonjour Monsieur'. It's sincere and polite and you're expected to say 'Bonjour Madame/Bonjour Monsieur' right back.

FOOD AND DRINK

Cafés are mostly used for a simple breakfast, a coffee any time of day and a lunch like steak and chips, omelette or salad. Salon de thé literally means tea room, and these are a good place to get a lunch of a superior quiche-like tarte or tea and fruit crumble in the afternoon. Brasseries are where you go to load up with oysters, onion soup and sauerkraut. You can get alcohol served with your food practically anywhere in Paris – for instance, they'll serve you wine in a tea room or at McDonald's.

COFFEE

Coffee in Paris is served small, black and strong. It's really non-French to ask for a café au lait after 11am. But if you can't stomach a paint-stripping espresso in the afternoon, try a noisette, a small espresso with a dash of milk. It's considered cool and Parisian, so has the added advantage that the waiters will treat you with a little respect.

CIGARETTES AND STAMPS

These are available in the tabac, which is often in a café, and always has a red 'Tabac' sign out front. They sell stamps, cigarettes and phone cards (Télécartes).

TIPPING

A 15% service charge is already included on every restaurant/café bill by law. As a gesture you can leave a couple of francs if you have had coffee, or 10–30FF after dinner, but you are not expected to pay a 10% tip.

PUBLIC TELEPHONES

Practically all public phones are now card-operated; you buy the Télécarte at a post office or tabac. Alternatively you often find a coin-operated phone downstairs in cafés.

TAXIS

As it's hard to hail a cab on the street in Paris, it's best going to a taxi rank, often found by the métro. You have to kick and scream if you want them to take more than three people in the car and they will charge you extra. They also charge extra for bags. A tip of a couple of francs is polite.

MÉTRO

The métro is easy to use, frequent and safe. It's cheapest to buy a car-net, a book of 10 tickets which costs 52FF. It's one ticket for one trip, irrespective of length. The métro runs from 5.30am through to 12.45am.

TOURIST OFFICES

These are extremely helpful for anything from day trips to hotels. Find the main Paris tourist office at 127 avenue des Champs-Élysées, 75008. Tel: 08 36 68 31 12; website: www.paris-touristoffice.com

---

GLOSSARY OF TERMS

HAUTE COUTURE

This is what Paris fashion built its reputation on, but there are now only around eighteen couturiers left. Haute couture is the name for a dress or outfit made to measure by a couturier specifically for you. The couture shows take place every January and July. The couple of thousand women still rich enough to buy haute couture attend the shows, although Middle Eastern clients often prefer to see them by video. They then rush round to Chanel, Ungaro, Dior etc., try on the samples and bagsy their dress. Although the same design can be sold to more than one person, the couture houses are scrupulous in preventing women in the same social scene from choosing the same outfit. After she has chosen her design and intimate measurements have been taken, a toile is made. The client has a couple of fittings using the toile before they even start cutting out the real thing. Then les petites mains in the haute couture atelier get to work, stitching, beading, corseting, embroidering – all by hand. Back for another fitting, this time of the actual dress, still time for tweaking to get it perfect. From show time to finished outfit, the whole process takes around six weeks, and the woman pays a bill of at least £20,000 for an evening dress.

PRÊT-A-PORTER
Ready-to-wear is a term for clothes bought off the peg. Unlike haute couture, designer ready-to-wear is not made by hand but manufactured in a factory. It is in ready-to-wear that the designers make their cash. The ready-to-wear shows get the most hype, publicity and press and take place in March and October, showing clothes that will appear in the stores the following season. There are also huge profits to be made from licensing. A licence can be for anything – scent, sunglasses, shoes – to which the designer sells the right to make a product using his or her name and image.

DIFFUSION LINES
The majority of designers now have 'diffusion' lines as well, which are cheaper – usually priced at around 60% of the designer's own ready-to-wear – and more widely distributed. A diffusion line is usually not designed by the designer him- or herself, but rather is 'inspired' by their style and uses cheaper fabrics and with a lesser quality finish.

DÉPÔTS-VENTES
These are secondhand shops selling recent clothes (as opposed to fripe, see below) ranging from designer to high street. (See 16th arrondissement for secondhand Chanel, Valentino, Ungaro etc. and Le Marais for secondhand more avant-garde designers, from Ann Demeulemeester to Comme des Garçons.) People come in and consign their clothing and accessories to be sold and the shop undertakes to give them a cut. It's a more accessible way of buying designer fashion, some of which may be just a season old.

SOLDERIES
These are sale shops, which can be either permanent sale shops of one store like A.P.C. Surplus in the 6th, or a store which sells off the unsold stock from different designers (see solderies in the chapters on the 2nd, Le Marais and 9th). Prices are usually reduced by 50% or more; the clothes are unused and mostly date from the year previously, i.e., the autumn/winter collection is sold the following autumn/winter.

FRIPE
This is the French word used to describe secondhand clothing from

another decade or era. Fripe is a '50s jacket you pick up at the market, or a '70s nylon blouse you find at a clubwear store. It is fashionable in Paris at the moment, partly because it is so cheap. There are quite a few sources of fripe included in the book (see the 2nd, 9th and Destination Shopping); it's a great way to find unique, wonderful retro clothing.

DIRECTIONAL
This describes leading-edge fashion.

VENDEUR/VENDEUSE
Sales assistant.

SIZE GUIDE

● WOMEN'S CLOTHES

FRANCE	36	38	40	42	44	46
UK	8	10	12	14	16	18
USA	3	5	9	12	14	16

● WOMEN'S SHOES

FRANCE	36	37	38	39	40	41
UK	$3^1/_2$	$4^1/_2$	$5^1/_2$	$6^1/_2$	$7^1/_2$	$8^1/_2$
USA	5	6	7	8	9	10

● MEN'S SUITING

FRANCE	46	48	50	52	54	56
UK/USA	36	38	40	42	44	46

● MEN'S SHIRT COLLAR

FRANCE	37	38	39	40	41	42	43
UK/USA	$14^1/_2$	15	$15^1/_2$	16	$16^1/_2$	17	$17^1/_2$

● MEN'S SHOES

FRANCE	40	41	42	43	$44^1/_2$	46
UK	$6^1/_2$	7	8	9	10	11
USA	$7^1/_2$	8	9	10	11	12

1ST ARRONDISSEMENT

Paris is divided physically and psychologically by the River Seine. North of the river is the Rive droite, or Right Bank, and to the south the Rive gauche, Left Bank. The Rive droite, or at least those arrondissements closest to the Seine, is a heady mix of grand boulevards, splendid mansions, horse chestnut trees and luxe.

The vast Palais du Louvre sets the tone for the 1st arrondissement. It's the largest museum in the world and looking good after radical cleaning to celebrate its 300th year as a museum. The former royal palace is now host not only to the magnificent art collection, but to an underground shopping mall and the Paris fashion shows. The Carrousel du Louvre mall was built in the mid-1990s at a cost of 900 million FF. The federation of couture and prêt-à-porter then decided to have a go at simplifying the Paris fashion calendar by hiring a space in the mall four times a year so that all the designers could show in the same place. Nice idea and it worked for a while, until those fickle designers just got bored with the mammoth space and antiseptic stage at the Louvre and moved out looking for more exciting locations to show. Now it's back to a breakneck schedule with over 80 shows in nine days and locations scattered around nightclubs, television studios, empty swimming pools, vegetable markets and the Louvre. Add to that a wait of around 40 minutes before every show, and no wonder tempers tear and handbags clash.

When you've 'done' the Mona Lisa take a break at the Café Marly, which is situated in the cours Napoléon of the Louvre with a stunning view of the glass pyramids. Or walk across from the Louvre to Richelieu's Palais Royal, which has gardens and benches for a picnic. It's devastatingly beautiful but somehow often gets left off the tourist agenda. It used to be a hang-out for prostitutes and gambling in the 18th century, when just after the Revolution the outrageously dressed dandies, les Incroyables, would strut before les Merveilleuses, the demoiselles in their racy Empire gowns. Nowadays it's more serene and has some of Paris's most highly desirable property, costing five times as much as the rest of the city.

Everywhere you look in the 1st, the glossy black and white packaging of the House of Chanel stalks the streets. The Chanel store in the rue Cambon is the pilgrimage point for anyone wanting to buy into the logo go-go dream. It was in this street that Gabrielle Chanel first opened up as a milliner in 1910. The next road over to the east is rue de Castiglione which leads you to the place Vendôme. This square has high-carat intensity with the haute joaillerie stores of Cartier, Boucheron, Bulgari, Mauboussin, Chaumet and Van Cleef et Arpels. To the south is the rue St-Honoré which has become a key shopping artery for Paris fashion owing to the opening of Colette, a kind of shrink-to-fit department store specialising in all things cool.

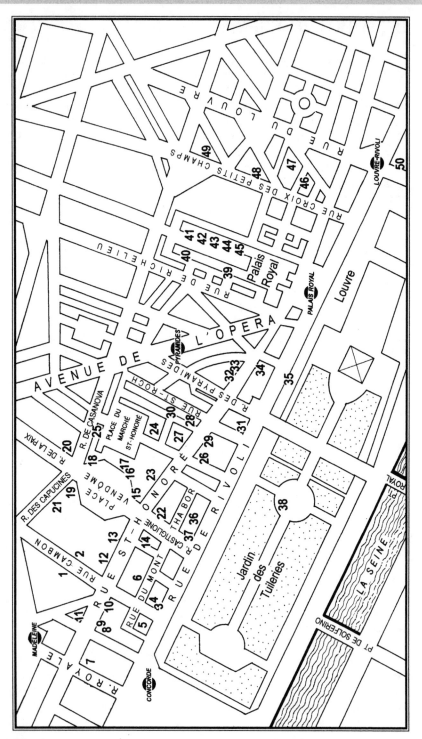

A shopper's Guide to Paris Fashion

1 CHANEL
2 BOB SHOP
3 MARIA LUISA
4 MARIA LUISA ACCESSOIRES
5 W. H. SMITH
6 MARIA LUISA HOMME
7 GEORGES RECH
8 TORAYA
9 VENTILO
10 MAXMARA
11 HERVÉ CHAPELIER
12 INDIES
13 DARYS
14 HÔTEL COSTES
15 GUERLAIN
16 GIORGIO ARMANI
17 TRUSSARDI
18 CHARVET
19 EMPORIO ARMANI
20 JEAN DINH VAN
21 MAÎTRE PARFUMEUR
22 ANNICK GOUTAL
23 GUCCI HOMME
24 LE PAIN QUOTIDIEN
25 PHILIPPE MODEL
26 COLETTE

27 BONPOINT
28 MONIES
29 REGINA RUBENS
30 DAVÉ
31 CABANE DE ZUCCA
32 KARENA SCHUESSLER
33 VERLET
34 CAFÉ RUC
35 MUSÉE DE LA MODE ET DU TEXTILE
36 GALIGNANI
37 ANGELINA'S
38 JARDINS DES TUILERIES
39 DIDIER LUDOT
40 LA MUSCADE
41 DIDIER LUDOT
42 JÉRÔME L'HUILLIER
43 SALONS DU PALAIS ROYAL SHISEIDO
44 ET VOUS & TRACE
45 JOYCE MA
46 BY TERRY
47 CHRISTIAN LOUBOUTIN
48 VICTOIRE HOMME
49 ROBERT CLERGERIE
50 LE FUMOIR

RUE CAMBON

CHANEL: **FRENCH DESIGNER WEAR**

If ever there was a marketing queen before her time, it was Gabrielle Chanel. True she was also a genius of design, taking womenswear to a level of comfort and pared-down chic it had never imagined. But the irrepressible success of the house of Chanel today is still pinned on those key 'branded' items which she invented during her 62-year career. A quick whip round the rue Cambon store leaves you in no doubt. What the women are clamouring for in here are the quilted handbags (first appearance 1955), the braided tweed tailleurs (first appearance 1957), two-tone shoes (first appearance 1917), plus all her favourite accessories – camellia flowers, bows, gilt buttons and lashings of chain. What Lagerfeld has done since he joined in 1983 is to juggle and reinterpret the constants with self-assured daring, so they breathe aspiration once more. Sometimes he teases with jogging suits and nipple bikinis, but mostly he pleases with every new take on the braided tweed jacket. Recently Lagerfeld has pushed the house into the future with a light touch, designing sleek, sculptured jackets, downsizing the logo and pushing a contemporary luxe look.

The rue Cambon store is the historical centre of Chanel with both the couture and ready-to-wear ateliers upstairs as well as the offices and, on the third floor, Chanel's old apartment. This store is the largest in Paris, with make-up, perfume, costume jewellery and the biggest selection of ready-to-wear, bags and shoes, and it stocks sizes from 6 to 20. Downstairs they've opened a VIP lounge where you can sit and drink champagne and spend in private.

CHANEL, 29–31 rue Cambon, 75001
Tel: 01 42 86 28 00
Métro: Madeleine
also at:
42 avenue Montaigne, 75008. Tel: 01 47 23 74 12
Chanel shoes, 25 rue Royale, 75008. Tel: 01 44 51 92 93
Opening Hours: Mon–Fri: 9.30–18.30, Sat: 10.00–18.30
August: open
Credit Cards: Visa, Amex, Diners, MC, JCB
Price Range: Chanel suit 13,000–30,000FF, 1,550FF for a plastic camellia brooch, padded bags 4,950–9,000FF

BOB SHOP: TROUSERS

This store specialises in trousers and is an institution among a certain chic, essentially classic Parisian, aged around 35 and up. They do 15 different styles of trouser, all with an emphasis on femininity and nat-ural fabrics, such as a linen and silk mix for summer and a wool and cashmere flannel in winter. They do a wide range of styles so that everyone can find the cut to suit their figure. Trousers come with great finish and attention to detail such as hand-sewn hems and satin-edged interior waist bands. Alterations are free and if you see a style of trouser you like, but want it in another of the Bob Shop's fabrics, they will make it up for you at no extra cost.

BOB SHOP, 20 rue Cambon, 75001
Tel: 01 40 15 96 55
Métro: Madeleine or Concorde
also at:
14 rue du Four, 75006. Tel: 01 43 54 05 59
Opening Hours: Mon–Sat: 10.30–18.30
August: closed for three weeks, 6th arr. store stays open
Credit Cards: Visa, Amex, MC
Price Range: trousers 950–1,200FF

MARIA LUISA: INTERNATIONAL DESIGNER STORE

An obligatory stop at the beginning of the season for every self-respecting fashion follower, Maria Luisa has a great eye and faultless taste for picking out chic, sharp clothes with a deviant edge. 'Fashion nowadays is multi-trend and I try and sell the best of every trend,' she says, flicking through rails of Marc Jacobs, Balenciaga, Jean Paul Gaultier, Martine Sitbon, Martin Margiela et al. Alongside the big name designers, she sells younger and newer talent such as Olivier Theyskens gothic rock vision and the cool pool-side wear and swim-ming costumes of Tomas Maier.

Not only is this Venezuelan-born Parisian brilliant at buying, but she always considers the clothes in context, as in who will be wearing it and when. This shows when you shop here as the staff are great at helping you pick out pieces that fit your existing wardrobe and look.

Véronique Leroy

MARIA LUISA, 2 rue Cambon, 75001
Tel: 01 47 03 96 15
Métro: Concorde
Opening Hours: Mon–Sat: 10.30–19.00
August: open except Mon
Credit Cards: Visa, Amex, Diners, MC, JCB
Price Range: skirts from 690FF, evening dresses from 4,550FF, knits from 450FF

MARIA LUISA ACCESSOIRES:
DESIGNER ACCESSORIES

Maria Luisa is turning into a fashion empire: she has expanded recently, adding an accessories store and around the corner a menswear boutique. The star of this store is the shoe genius Manolo Blahnik and Maria Luisa starts the season with the store piled high with his shoeboxes. Come the Paris fashion shows, the stock is seriously depleted as the fashion pack sweeps through town and snaps up every available Manolo heel. Shoes-wise she also stocks Marc Jacobs, Ann Demeulemeester and the vaguely kinky heels of Pierre Hardy, a French shoe designer also responsible for the Hermès shoe collection. Alongside are dainty silk handbags by Lulu Guinness and sleek lounging homewear from Italian luxury brand Frette.

MARIA LUISA ACCESSOIRES, 4 rue Cambon, 75001
Tel: 01 47 03 48 08
Métro: Concorde
Opening Hours: Mon–Sat: 10.30–19.00
August: open except Mon
Credit Cards: Visa, Amex, Diners, JCB
Price Range: Manolo's from 2,500FF

W. H. SMITH: BRITISH BOOK STORE

Can't live without *Hello!*? Come here to find it. It's got all the UK press including newspapers and every glossy mag title as well as a great selection of world media. They probably have the best selection of English written literature in Paris with a particularly strong contemporary fiction choice. It's also one of the few places in Paris you can get a decent birthday card.

W. H. SMITH, 248 rue de Rivoli, 75001
Tel: 01 44 77 88 99
Métro: Tuileries or Concorde
Opening Hours: Mon–Sat: 9.30–19.00, Sun: 13.00–18.00
August: open
Credit Cards: Visa, Amex, MC

MARIA LUISA HOMME: DESIGNER MENSWEAR

Maria Luisa has always had a small and superior selection of menswear in the original boutique, but her clientele has simply outgrown the space. So she has opened a store right around the corner selling designers such as McQueen, Ann Demeulemeester, Helmut Lang, Gaultier and Marc Jacobs. 'The idea is to have a totally masculine space where men can drink, smoke and do whatever they want to,' says Maria Luisa. The store is divided into three fashion chambers and high points include cashmere 'sweatshirts' from Marc Jacobs, sharp suits by Timothy Everest and succulent hand-knits from Sarah Dearlove. There are also men's shoes by Manolo and Rodolphe Menudier, plus swimwear by Tomas Maier.

MARIA LUISA HOMME, 38 rue du Mont Thabor, 75001
Tel: 01 42 60 89 83
Métro: Concorde
Opening Hours: Mon–Sat: 10.30–19.00
August: open except Mon
Credit Cards: Visa, Amex, Diners, MC, JCB
Price Range: suits from 4,200FF, shoes 1,300FF, knits from 400FF

RUE ST-HONORÉ

GEORGES RECH: FRENCH CHIC

Classic, groomed and good-looking clothes. If you are a blue-chip exec
or the wife of a blue-chip exec you're going to like Georges Rech. He
started his label in 1960 and has since retired – his former house model
and assistant Danielle Jagot now designs the collection. It is not trend-
setting, it is French commercial style: chic, fairly expensive, perfect finish and will leave you feeling appropriately and well dressed. Lots and
lots of suiting, dresses, trousers and winter coats like a narrow camel
coat with big caramel buttons. Perennial Georges Rech styling
includes frogging on velvet and navy suits with cream braiding. Come
summer the store is jumping with mother of the bride and future
mother-in-law fighting over that outfit. Synonyme is the slightly less
expensive line which is a little sportier in outlook.

GEORGES RECH, 273 rue St-Honoré, 75001
Tel: 01 42 61 41 14
Métro: Tuileries
also at:
23 avenue Victor Hugo, 75016. Tel: 01 45 00 83 19
54 rue Bonaparte, 75006. Tel 01 43 26 84 11
Opening Hours: Mon: 11.00–19.00, Tue–Sat: 10.00–19.00
August: open
Credit Cards: Visa, Amex, Diners, MC, JCB
Price Range: Georges Rech suit 4,000–6,000FF, winter coat 4,000–6,000FF,
Synonyme suit 3,000–4,000FF

TORAYA: JAPANESE TEA ROOM

A Japanese tea room where the look is chilled zen but done with
warmth: plump beige Michelin-man padded banquettes are broken up
by the odd seat in apricot, there is a bonsai-growing garden, birds
tweeting over the sound system and they serve traditional Japanese
patisseries in sugar-spun colours. Toraya jasmine tea tastes like a dive
in the ocean, while the tea room ambience is serene and modern
should you feel like a break from Belle Époque splendour.

TORAYA, 10 rue St-Florentin, 75001
Tel: 01 42 60 13 00
Métro: Concorde
Opening Hours: Mon–Sat: 10.00–19.00
August: open
Credit Cards: Visa, Amex, JCB
Price Range: Japanese tea 16–40FF, patisseries 15–22FF

VENTILO: FRENCH CLASSIC WOMENSWEAR

See 2nd arrondissement for details.
267 rue St-Honoré, 75001. Tel: 01 40 15 61 52

MAXMARA: SLEEK ITALIAN FASHION
See 8th arrondissement for details.
265 rue St-Honoré, 75001. Tel: 01 40 20 04 58

HERVÉ CHAPELIER: SMART NYLON BAGS
See 6th arrondissement for details.
390 rue St-Honoré, 75001. Tel: 01 42 96 38 04

INDIES: ELEGANT WOMENSWEAR
See 6th arrondissement for details.
372 rue St-Honoré, 75001. Tel: 01 42 61 26 03

DARYS: OLD JEWELLERY
Katherine Darys represents the third generation of her family to deal
in old jewellery. These are charming rather than serious jewels and
Darys do every style from 1970s huge chunky bangles and statement
rings to delicate drop earrings with semi-precious stones and strands
of coral or jet. It's a treasure trove – great for finding charm bracelets,
cuff-links and show-off rings from the 1930s. Julia Roberts has been in
and the place is always teeming with jewellery designers and stylists
on the scout for buyable inspiration.

DARYS, 362 rue St-Honoré, 75001
Tel: 01 42 60 95 23
Métro: Madeleine
Opening Hours: Mon–Fri: 10.30–18.00, Sat: 12.00–18.00
August: call to confirm
Credit Cards: Visa, Amex, Diners, MC, JCB
Price Range: from 200FF for silver earrings to 29,000FF for sapphire ring

HÔTEL COSTES: STOP FOR DRINKS/COFFEE/STAY
Behind an understated doorway manned by 'We're just hanging out
rather than collecting your bags' doormen hides a smart and intimate
85-room hotel. Life revolves around the carnation pink Italianate
courtyard with neo-Classical figures perched on a portico, which
somehow avoids looking camp. All the bars and eating areas are
arranged round the courtyard, and in summer you can eat or drink
outside. The hotel is owned by Jean-Louis Costes, who did the Café
Costes in Les Halles which defined 1980s Paris and has since closed.
Decorator Jacques Garcia went for a look of 19th-century-Italian-
palace-meets-Napoleon-III and the effect is elegant luxe with tasselled
kissing sofas and porcelain fireplaces. Hotel guests include Matt
Dillon, Mickey Rourke, Eva Herzigova, Kate Moss, Ann
Demeulemeester and every US fashion glossy during the collections.
Parisians use the hotel to meet up with friends for drinks, business
meetings or dinner after the theatre as the restaurant stays open till
2am. Service can be painfully slow, but at least there is the people-

watching to while away the wait. Downstairs is a high-tech gym with steam baths and inky-blue pool.

HÔTEL COSTES, 239 rue St-Honoré, 75001
Tel: 01 42 44 50 00
Fax: 01 42 44 50 01
Métro: Tuileries
Restaurant/Bar Opening Hours: 7.00–2.00am
Credit Cards: Visa, Amex, Diners, MC, JCB
Price Range: standard room 1,590FF, suite duplex apartment 3,450FF, dinner 250FF per head without wine

PLACE VENDÔME

GUERLAIN: SCENT

See 8th arrondissement for details.
2 place Vendôme, 75001. Tel: 01 42 60 68 61

GIORGIO ARMANI: ITALIAN DESIGNER

The master of Italian restraint, Giorgio Armani is loosening up his act. He has revamped his store on the place Vendôme using London architect Claudio Silvestrin who has made the space warmer with blond stone walls and bronze fittings. The overall effect complements the elegance of Armani. And it is not just in the shop fittings that he has loosened up, but in the clothes. He has taken that same easy elegance he brought to the jacket and translated it to the rest of the wardrobe, while breaking away from his palette of neutrals and introducing soft pastels and fresh blues and greens. And while the suit might not be the only career option for contemporary women, at the end of the day an Armani suit still speaks great taste, authority and considerable purchasing power. Evening wear is supple, feminine and decorated with delicate beading. Also in this store you will find the funky snowsport brand Armani Neve.

GIORGIO ARMANI, 6 place Vendôme, 75001
Tel: 01 42 61 55 09
Métro: Opéra
Opening Hours: Mon: 11.00–19.00, Tue–Sat: 10.00–19.00
August: open
Credit Cards: Visa, Amex, Diners, MC, JCB
Price Range: trousers from 2,000FF, suits from 8,500FF, evening dresses from 20,000FF, bags from 3,500FF

TRUSSARDI: ITALIAN LUGGAGE AND CLOTHES

Italian luxury brands with history are on a roll right now, and leather fashion house Trussardi is cutting in on the action. Its origins are as a family firm of glove-makers founded in 1910. The design concept today is to keep the quality and suppleness of glove leather and put it into clothes and accessories. The bags are chic and pared down to the essential: pale pistachio structured leather with steel handle, or an asymmetrical shoulder bag in big square croc print. But the coolest is a line made from matt neoprene (wet-suit) caught with a polished leather shoulder strap. The clothes style is luxurious, understated and focuses on exquisite leathers. Carla Bruni buys all her friends' wedding presents here, and Mickey Rourke comes for the clothing, as does Donna Karan.

TRUSSARDI, 8 place Vendôme, 75001
Tel: 01 55 35 32 50
Métro: Concorde or Opéra
Opening Hours: Mon–Sat: 10.00–19.00
August: closed for three weeks
Credit Cards: Visa, Diners, Amex, JCB, MC
Price Range: asymmetrical shoulder bag 2,300FF, most bags 1,500–2,000FF, black leather shift dress 3,950FF, soft jersey halter-neck 700FF

CHARVET: GENTLEMAN'S TAILOR

Over 160 years old, Charvet is the bastion of French male sartorial style. Whoever said you cannot buy class had obviously never shopped at Charvet: brilliant woven silk ties, impeccably cut made-to-measure shirts and the softest of leather slippers with matching pochettes are all gentleman's relish. Their past client list reads like a *Who's Who* of French history: Charles de Gaulle, Émile Zola, Charles Baudelaire, Manet and Cocteau as well as John F. Kennedy and the Duke of Windsor, although they're pretty tight-lipped about current customers. They do a Charvet eau de cologne which comes packaged in vaguely kitsch champagne-look miniature bottles and is a favourite of fashion retailer Joseph Ettegdui.

CHARVET, 28 place Vendôme, 75001
Tel: 01 42 60 30 70
Métro: Opéra
Opening Hours: Mon–Sat: 9.45–18.30
August: open except Mon
Credit Cards: Visa, Amex, Diners, MC, JCB
Price Range: woven silk ties from 540FF, leather slippers from 775FF, made-to-measure shirts from 1,750FF

EMPORIO ARMANI: ITALIAN CHIC

See 6th arrondissement for details.
25 place Vendôme, 75001. Tel: 01 42 61 02 34

JEAN DINH VAN: CONTEMPORARY JEWELLERY

Just up the street from Cartier et al, but a world apart, is the boutique of Jean Dinh Van who makes precious contemporary jewellery. Half-Vietnamese, half-French, he spent ten years working for Cartier before cutting loose from the traditional big rock style. His small, slightly squashed gold crosses pierced through the centre and worn on a leather cord are simple but striking and his wide bands of beaten gold are the preferred ring of contemporary Parisiennes.

JEAN DINH VAN, 7 rue de la Paix, 75001
Tel: 01 42 61 74 49
Métro: Opéra
Opening Hours: Mon:10.45–18.30, Tue–Fri: 10.00–18.30, Sat: 10.45–13.00, 14.00–18.30
August: closed for one week around 15 Aug
Credit Cards: Visa, Amex, Diners, MC, JCB
Price Range: small gold crosses from 1,600FF, wide beaten gold band from 12,900FF

MAÎTRE PARFUMEUR: PERFUME HOUSE

See 7th arrondissement for details.
5 rue des Capucines, 75001. Tel: 01 42 96 35 13

RUE ST-HONORÉ CONTINUED
ANNICK GOUTAL: PERFUME HOUSE

A former concert pianist, Annick Goutal started making scents in 1981, since when her company has been bought out by champagne-makers Taittinger, and very sadly she has recently died. The perfumes are floral and subtle. Madonna wears Passion, Prince Charles uses Eau d'Hadrien and when Prince William was born the late President Mitterrand sent him a gift of the baby scent. As well as perfumes, there are eaux de parfum, eaux de toilette and a whole range of soaps, body lotions and body oils. Make the most of all the wonderful things on offer – you are in fail-safe gift-buying country. They also stock scented candles in gold-edged glasses which Parisians are mad about. Every purchase is beautifully wrapped in cream and gold with lashings of gold ribbon.

ANNICK GOUTAL, 14 rue Castiglione, 75001
Tel: 01 45 51 36 13
Métro: Tuileries or Concorde
also at:
12 place St-Sulpice, 75006. Tel: 01 46 33 03 15
Opening Hours: Mon–Sat: 10.00–19.00
August: open
Credit Cards: Visa, Amex, Diners, MC, JCB
Price Range: bars of soap 79FF, scented candles in a glass 290FF, eau de toilette starts at 220FF; all scent bottles are refillable

GUCCI HOMME: DESIGNER MENSWEAR
See 8th arrondissement for details.
350 rue St-Honoré, 75001. Tel: 01 42 96 83 27

LE PAIN QUOTIDIEN: LUNCH/BRUNCH STOP
A farmhouse-style restaurant in the centre of town sounds unlikely, but it works. Le Pain Quotidien is a Belgian chain with several restaurants dotted around Paris; this one has a great terrasse in the shade. Inside the decor is urbanised rustic with huge long tables to sit around and creamy-coloured ceramics, while the food comes fresh and in generous portions. The Mediterranean salad is piled high with grilled aubergines, mozzarella and pesto, all doused in olive oil, while the house speciality is a weekend brunch which includes platefuls of smoked salmon, fresh bread (delivered daily from Belgium), pots of home-made dark chocolate and velvety praline spreads plus limitless cups of coffee.

LE PAIN QUOTIDIEN, 18 place du Marché St-Honoré, 75001
Tel: 01 42 96 31 70
Métro: Tuileries
also at:
18 rue des Archives, 75004. Tel: 01 44 54 03 07
3 rue Bachaumont, 75002. Tel: 01 40 41 98 26
Opening Hours: every day: 7.00–19.00
August: open
Credit Cards: Visa, Amex, Diners, MC, JCB
Price Range: breakfast from 35FF, salads from 60FF, sandwiches 25–52FF,
brunch 115FF

PHILIPPE MODEL: SOCIETY HAT-MAKER

Having slogged it out during the 1980s as the designers' hat designer,
Philippe Model has kicked the catwalk into touch and is now enjoying
the rewards as society hat-maker. He makes serious hats for serious
occasions. Think big, add feathers, then fruit. Or take a massive burnished gold straw and drape it in a load of old gold netting that looks
like it's been dragged from the attic – the result: a Model masterpiece.
Not every hat is extravagant: for a wedding there is a 1940s-style white
straw bandeau or, more beachy, a straggly straw hat with real stable
straw draped from the brim. Clientele is smart: Princess Caroline of
Monaco is a favourite customer and Kristin Scott Thomas bought her
wedding hat here. If you are in town for the the Prix de Diane Hermès
race in June and are stuck without a hat it's good to know that, for this
event only, Model hires them out. Worth checking out if you are a
bride as he also does bridal shoes. There is no longer a Philippe Model
store on the Left Bank.

PHILIPPE MODEL, 33 place du Marché St-Honoré, 75001
Tel: 01 42 96 89 02
Métro: Tuileries or Opéra
Opening Hours: Tue–Fri: 10.00–19.00, Sat: 11.00–19.00
August: closed 4–31 Aug
Credit Cards: Visa, Amex
Price Range: occasion hat 700–3,000FF, sportier beach range 300–700FF

COLETTE: STYLE/DESIGN/ART/FOOD

Ruthlessly hip and indicative of a new energy in town, Colette is a sort
of post-modern, shrink-to-fit department store selling clothes, home
furnishings, accessories, magazines, beauty, CDs and food. What
makes it hot is the store's relentless pursuit of the new, plus an innovative buying policy whereby everything is picked to complement certain store themes for the season. There are three floors, with the
ground floor devoted to lifestyle selling trainers, gadgets, François
Nars cosmetics and Prada Sport shoes and bags. The first floor is fashion which varies widely from season to season but staples include
Jeremy Scott, Véronique Branquinho, Marni, Chloé and Alexander

McQueen, plus for men Yves Saint Laurent Rive Gauche, Raf Simons and for men, women and kids cashmere by Lucien Pellat-Finet. It is a great source for accessories with hand-made, charming bags by Olympia Le Tan, Marie-Hélène de Taillac's cool, elegant jewels and Alain Tondowski's razor-sharp heels. Also on the first floor is an exhibition space for photographic shows plus a media corner with hot magazine titles. Downstairs is the water bar which stocks 30 different kinds of mineral water and is always thick with very thin girls snacking on a glass of H_2O. It is a great stop for lunch (although you cannot reserve) and service is obliging – always a novelty in this city.

COLETTE, 213 rue St-Honoré, 75001
Tel: 01 55 35 33 90
Métro: Tuileries
Opening Hours: Mon–Sat: 10.30–19.30
August: open
Credit Cards: Visa, Amex, Diners, MC, JCB
Price Range: glass of water from 10FF, Marie-Hélène de Taillac's jewels from 2,500FF, François Nars lipstick 175FF, Pucci purse 300FF

BONPOINT: CHILDREN'S WEAR
See 7th arrondissement for details.
320 rue St-Honoré, 75001. Tel: 01 49 27 94 82

MONIES: JEWELLERY
This is chunky statement jewellery with a bohemian feel. Created by Swedish designer Gerda Lyndaard, there are ropes of jade, amethyst, amber, grenadine or peridot, huge rings carved from a rock of amethyst or pink quartz and bangles made from polished horn. The look is ethnic-goes-Bloomsbury-set, that is, jewellery to be worn with a piece of serious Japanese designer clothing, rather than some safari suit.

MONIES, 320 rue St-Honoré, 75001
Tel: 01 40 20 90 01
Métro: Tuileries
Opening Hours: Mon: 14.00–19.00, Tue–Sat: 11.00–19.00
August: closed for three weeks, call for dates
Credit Cards: Visa, Amex
Price Range: pink quartz ring 1,200FF, raw coral necklace 15,000FF, necklaces from 1,500FF

REGINA RUBENS: FRENCH CLASSIC WOMENSWEAR
Regina Rubens prides herself on designing for women in real life. Clothes are for working women, reasonably priced and timeless with a typically French sport-chic look. It is a good place to find wardrobe basics with well-cut trousers and suiting. The Regina Rubens real-life manifesto means she uses a lot of stretch mixed into fabrics for ease of movement and purposefully ensures that even delicate pieces such as

silk knit tops are all washable by hand. Sizes go from 36 to 44 (basically a UK size 16) which is sometimes hard to find in Paris, and they can also make up the clothing in larger or smaller sizes specially for you. It takes 15 days, costs 20% extra and can be sent on to you anywhere in the world at no added cost.

REGINA RUBENS, 207 rue St-Honoré, 75001
Tel: 01 40 20 40 31
Métro: Tuileries
also at:
13 rue du Cherche-Midi, 75006. Tel: 01 45 44 96 95
15 rue de Passy, 75016. Tel: 01 45 20 56 56
Opening Hours: Mon–Sat: 10.00–19.00
August: open
Credit Cards: Visa, Amex, Diners, MC, JCB
Price Range: skirt from 700FF, trousers from 900FF, jacket from 2,000FF, silk knit top 500–800FF

DAVÉ: CHINESE FASHION FOOD

Davé has got to be the most enduring of hip restaurants in Paris. For fourteen years now it's been a fashionable staple diet and it even features in Isaac Mizrahi's fashion docu-movie *Unzipped*. The owner Davé is Chinese and a dandy. The decor is not spectacular, bit of a darkish regular Chinese restaurant actually, with a fish tank and a friendly dog. But take a closer look at the tiny polaroids and snaps and you realise they are all of mind-blowingly famous fashion and art people. A teeny matchstick sculpture by Rebecca Horn, photos from Helmut Newton and 'model corner' with pictures of Helena, Amber and Shalom, Kate, Naomi, Cindy and Claudia – all at Davé and snapped with him. Then over to designer corner: Galliano, Helmut Lang, Gaultier, Jil Sander, Montana, Alaïa, Yves Saint Laurent – all shot chez Davé. When asked why it's so popular, he's modestly coy, describing it as a canteen for the fashion world during the collections. Rather than you choosing, he serves up his selection of Chinese and Vietnamese food and all the fashion editors, photographers, models and designers such as Miuccia, Tom Ford, Karl, Dries and Donna Karan drop by.

DAVÉ, 39 rue St-Roch, 75001
Tel: 01 42 61 49 48
Métro: Pyramides
Opening Hours: 12.00–14.00, 19.30–past 23.00, closed Sat and Mon lunch; book during collections
August: closed for two weeks, call for exact dates
Credit Cards: Visa, Amex, JCB
Price Range: around 200FF a head with wine

CABANE DE ZUCCA: JAPANESE DESIGNER

Another of the new generation of Japanese designers, Zucca is a former assistant to Issey Miyake, who has been his backer and support ever since he went solo in 1988. He recently moved from the Left Bank to open this store in a buzzier part of town. The Zucca style is fashionable basics with a functional, work-wear feel and a slim cut for both men and women. Fabrics and finishes are high-tech with plastified lace or glazed thick cotton, but cutest are the accessories such as bags and the cult Cabane de Zucca plastic watch which comes in juicy fruit colours.

CABANE DE ZUCCA, 8 rue St-Roch, 75001
Tel: 01 44 58 98 88
Métro: Tuileries
Opening Hours: Mon–Sat: 10.00–19.00
August: closed for three weeks
Credit Cards: Visa, Diners, MC, JCB
Price Range: jacket from 2,000FF, trousers 1,200FF, knitwear from 990FF, underwear 350–425FF

KARENA SCHUESSLER: DESIGNER SHOES

A German shoe designer working in Paris, Karena Schuessler has a distinctive style which fuses fashion with fairly masculine styling; in fact part of her collection is unisex. She started out as a fashion designer, having studied at the school of the Chambre Syndicale de la Couture, and she brings a creative, original spirit to her shoes, working on new and funky heel shapes each season.

KARENA SCHUESSLER, 264 rue St-Honoré, 75001
Tel: 01 53 29 93 93
Métro: Pyramides or Palais Royal
Opening Hours: Mon–Sat: 10.00–19.00
August: open
Credit Cards: Visa
Price Range: shoes from 990FF, bags from 1,500FF

VERLET: ESSENTIAL COFFEE HOUSE

Since 1880, Verlet has been roasting coffees that make even Monday morning bearable. Its location, just down the street from the Comédie Française, means actors such as Gérard Depardieu and Sophie Marceau are devoted fans. It's one of Paris's oldest remaining coffee houses; the beans are roasted fresh every day and sold out of enormous hessian sacks.

VERLET, 256 rue St-Honoré, 75001
Tel: 01 42 60 67 39
Métro: Tuileries or Palais Royal
Opening Hours: Tue–Sat: 9.00–18.30
August: closed all month
Credit Cards: Visa
Price Range: 25–45FF for 250g

CAFÉ RUC: CONTEMPORARY BRASSERIE

What was originally an old-fashioned brasserie servicing the Comédie Française has been transformed by the ubiquitous Costes brothers into a contemporary brasserie with a girl-friendly menu servicing a fashionable clientele. Located opposite the Louvre, it has been decorated (as so many of the Costes establishments) by Jacques Garcia who has shown uncharacteristic restraint. Outsize crimson pleated lampshades are one of the few touches of flamboyance, while outside on the terrasse are some fairly superior deckchairs which come padded for comfort. Food is contemporary, simple, mildly international with the emphasis on fish and chicken, while the crowd is mixed from Lionel Jospin to Robert de Niro with acres of model-types in between. A nice spot for an apéritif or dinner.

CAFÉ RUC, 159 rue St-Honoré, 75001
Tel: 01 42 60 97 54
Métro: Palais Royal
Opening Hours: every day: 8.00–2.00am
August: open all year round
Credit Cards: Visa, Amex, Diners, MC, JCB
Price Range: poulet tandoori 90FF, fresh tuna steak with sesame seeds 95FF, grilled prawns 120FF

MUSÉE DE LA MODE ET DU TEXTILE:
COSTUME COLLECTION

The fashion and textiles collection from the Musée de la Mode et du Textile is now housed and presented in a greatly enlarged space which opened in 1997. The idea is to present themed exhibitions with pieces chosen from the permanent collection. The space itself, though large, is fairly grey and uninspiring; however, the costumes and clothes are amazing and include court dress from the 18th century, and outstanding dresses from the golden age of Paris couture including Poiret, Dior, Chanel, Vionnet and Grès, continuing right up to contemporary clothing from Gaultier, Galliano and Yves Saint Laurent.

MUSÉE DE LA MODE ET DU TEXTILE, Union Centrale des Arts Décoratifs, 107 rue de Rivoli, 75001
Tel: 01 44 55 57 50
Opening Hours: Tue–Fri: 11.00–18.00 (Wed until 21.00), Sat/Sun: 10.00–18.00
Entrance Fee: 35FF

GALIGNANI: FRENCH AND ENGLISH BOOKSHOP

A delightful bookshop for both English and French books with particularly good sections on fashion (history, monographs and contemporary writing), art, architecture, photography and interior design. They've got all the international fashion glossies and masses of fiction, with helpful service and a browser-friendly atmosphere.

GALIGNANI, 224 rue de Rivoli, 75001
Tel: 01 42 60 76 07
Métro: Tuileries or Concorde
Opening Hours: Mon–Sat: 10.00–19.00
August: open
Credit Cards: Visa, MC

ANGELINA'S: TEA ROOM

Although this enormous tea room is a Paris guidebook cliché, in a fashion shopping guide it's got to get a mention. Situated in the rue de Rivoli just down from the Louvre, it has been the place for tout Paris to take tea ever since it opened up in 1903. Chanel was a regular, so was Proust, King George V visited, and nowadays it's frequented by Inès de la Fressange, Rei Kawakubo, Gaultier, John Major, Naomi and all the models for lunch between shows. Male supermodel Werner brings his mum. It's big enough to be a little anonymous. Weekends are very busy, but you are soon seated. It has a slightly weathered feel with nicotine-coloured wood panelling and murals of Nice. It's very Parisian, although there used to be a lot of 70-year-old widows who would come, according to the maître d', 'at 3 o'clock and stay till 7 with one cup of tea', but since a change of management there's less of that. A real treat is the 'Africain' hot chocolate made with real chocolate and served with a lump of Chantilly cream and a necessary jug of cold water. More of a chore is the Mont Blanc, a mountainous blob of meringue covered in Chantilly and wrapped in chestnut cream. From the années folles to the cholesterol-free 21st century, this place is still a Paris institution. For the food without the feel, there is a branch on the third floor of the department store Galeries Lafayette.

GUCCI

Hip girl on Rue de Rivoli

ANGELINA'S, 226 rue de Rivoli, 75001
Tel: 01 42 60 82 00
Métro: Tuileries or Concorde
Opening Hours: Mon–Fri: 9.00–19.00, Sat/Sun: 9.00–19.30
August: open
Credit Cards: Visa, Amex, MC
Price Range: L'Africain 36FF, Mont Blanc 35FF, salads around 87FF

JARDINS DES TUILERIES: GARDEN TOUR

The Tuileries gardens have become fashionable again to sit and stroll in, and when you've overdosed on the Louvre or if you just love gardens, you can do a guided tour for free around the Tuileries. They were rebuilt by André le Nôtre in 1664, who also designed the gardens at Versailles and every other famous flower bed of the time. They are in a French formal style punctuated by two ponds and with the most stunning vista off to the west. The tour, in French, is fun and takes you round all the sculptures of mythic testosterone heroes, identifies the 2,680 trees and hams up the history of 600 Swiss guards who were chased and killed in the gardens by revolutionaries. There are lots of cafés that you could try in the gardens, but by far the nicest is Café Véry. It's a casual chic conservatory building and you can sit inside or out in the gardens under trees. They do good, reasonably priced food such as smoked salmon, crème fraîche on toast on a bed of celery galette or a superior croque monsieur with a creamy pepper sauce.

JARDINS DES TUILERIES, rue de Rivoli, 75001
Métro: Concorde or Tuileries
Opening Hours: summer: 7.00–21.00, winter: 7.30–19.30
For the tour, meet inside the gardens at the Arc du Carrousel, a small pink arch at the Louvre end of the gardens. Tel: 01 40 20 90 43. Tour times: Wed/Fri/Sat/Sun at 15.00
Café Véry: Tel: 01 47 03 94 84
Opening Hours: 11.00–24.00 daily
August: open
Credit Cards: Visa, Amex
Price Range: smoked salmon toast with celery galette 39FF, croque monsieur 27FF, chicken and wild mushrooms 42FF

PALAIS ROYAL

DIDIER LUDOT: ANTIQUE COUTURE AND BAGS

Didier Ludot is an ambulance-chaser of the fashion world. He persuades old ladies or their heirs to sell him their wardrobes of haute couture and then he sells it. He started at the age of 23 when all he knew about haute couture, he says, is the fact that his mother dressed in it. Twenty-odd years later he's an expert with his own private collection and dealing in French haute couture from 1925 to 1975. He's a darling of the models who, he explains, 'find it more amusing to dress in Chanel from the end of the 1950s to the 1970s, than from today'. Naomi, Linda and Yasmeen love dressing in old couture and Stephanie Seymour has started her own collection which she wears as well. Miuccia Prada has been dressing in it for years. There are two boutiques; the more interesting has the clothes and is at No. 20 – it's often locked as Didier tends to sit with his two bulldogs in the other, accessories, boutique. He'll open it for you no problem and you can gaze at the suits, dresses, day coats and evening dresses by Dior, Balenciaga, Givenchy, Grès, Chanel, Balmain and Patou. A deep raspberry-pink Chanel coat dress from the early 1960s that was the catwalk model is priced 10,000FF and a little Jean Patou camel shift dress is 4,500FF. Next door in the accessories shop are shoes by Roger Vivier and Perugia, and Hermès crocodile handbags. There is also a selection of secondhand recent accessories like Hermès Kelly bags, Chanel padded bags and costume jewellery, at half the original price.

DIDIER LUDOT, 20/24 galerie Montpensier, 75001
Tel: 01 42 96 06 56
Métro: Palais Royal
Opening Hours: Mon–Sat: 10.30–19.00
August: open
Credit Cards: Visa, Amex, Diners, JCB
Price Range: haute couture 6,000–15,000FF, shoes from 800FF

LA MUSCADE: RESTAURANT AND TEA ROOM

During the summer when you can sit outside on the terrasse this has to be one of the most idyllic spots in Paris. The gardens of the Palais Royal are in flower, fountains froth and kids are kicking footballs in the dust. You can use this restaurant for lunch, tea or dinner and it's a great break point if you've just done the Louvre. They serve simple fresh food, with slight hints of the South of France in, for instance, calamari fried in ginger and lime. The restaurant's claim to fame is that Cocteau lived upstairs, so there are references to him in the decor and the menu. Inside, the sofas are covered in pansy-purple velvet and the table tops, huge mirror and bar are in polished copper. For tea, chocolate macaroons or chocolate and orange tart are favourites and at night there is a prix-fixe menu. For dinner you really need to book to ensure a place on that terrasse.

LA MUSCADE, 67 galerie Montpensier, 75001
Tel: 01 42 97 51 36
Métro: Palais Royal
Opening Hours: every day: lunch: 12.00–15.00, salon de thé: 15.00–19.00, dinner: 19.00–20.30 (21.30 in summer). Doors of the Palais Royal close at 23.00
August: open
Credit Cards: Visa, Amex, MC
Price Range: prix-fixe dinner menu 168FF, tea, toast and jam 44FF, orange and chocolate tart 38FF

Café Marly

DIDIER LUDOT: LITTLE BLACK DRESS

Didier has recently opened a third boutique on the opposite side of Palais Royal to his existing shops in which to house his collection of little black dresses. He mixes stellar little black dresses from couturiers such as Balenciaga, Chanel, Givenchy and Yves Saint Laurent with his own contemporary collection of dresses inspired by the deadly sins and featuring such high-camp names as Coquetterie and Caprice.

DIDIER LUDOT, 125 galerie de Valois, 75001
Tel: 01 40 15 01 04
Métro: Palais Royal
Opening Hours: Mon–Sat: 11.00–19.00
August: open
Credit Cards: Visa, Amex, Diners, MC, JCB
Price Range: Didier Ludot little black dresses 2,700–4,500FF

JÉRÔME L'HUILLIER: FRENCH DESIGNER

French designer Jérôme L'Huillier designs clothes that are fashionable, but safe. They appeal to women who love, rather than live, fashion. His collections are often inspired by movies, such as the Steve McQueen and Faye Dunaway film *The Thomas Crown Affair*. 'You look at the way she was dressed in that movie – and then you look at the way people dress on the streets of Paris today and you despair,' laments Jérôme. He has come up with a girl-about-town roll-neck tunic worn over straight trousers, and a wool crêpe coat dress in colour combinations such as turquoise, khaki and camel or plum, lilac and pink. He's best known for his suits and sexy cut dresses.

JÉRÔME L'HUILLIER, 138–139 galerie de Valois, 75001
Tel: 01 49 26 07 07
Métro: Palais Royal
Opening Hours: Mon–Sat: 11.00–19.00
August: open for most of the month, call for exact dates
Credit Cards: Visa, Amex, MC
Price Range: jacket 2,500FF, trousers 1,300FF, dress 1,200–1,800FF

SALONS DU PALAIS ROYAL SHISEIDO:
                                                      SCENT

In terms of shopping experiences, this is exotic. Serge Lutens has created a dramatic and magnificent salon in which to showcase the family of scents he has created for the Japanese cosmetic and perfume house Shiseido. The decor and ambience are archly dramatic with rosewood panelling, marble floor, purple orchids and lilac walls populated by hand-painted tiny darting figures, insects, flowers and astrological signs. The scents are heady and sensuous, divided into five families: Nouvelles Eaux, Fleurs Nobles, Les Eaux Boisées, Les Sompteux, Les Eaux Anciennes. They can be worn by men and women and bear such names as Muscs Koublaï Khän, described as a 'tawny, animalistic' scent, or Tubéreuse Criminelle, 'a perfume that bewitches'. Before buying you need to ask yourself whether your powers of seduction are up to that of your scent. The fragrances are sold exclusively here and the bottles can be engraved with your initials.

SALONS DU PALAIS ROYAL SHISEIDO, 142 galerie de Valois, 75001
Tel: 01 49 27 09 09
Métro: Palais Royal
Opening Hours: Mon–Sat: 10.00–19.00
August: open
Credit Cards: Visa, Amex, Diners, MC, JCB
Price Range: all scents priced 600FF for 75ml

ET VOUS & TRACE: DESIGNER WOMENSWEAR
This boutique sells both the Et Vous clothes and the personal collection of the talented Japanese designer Koji Tatsuno who excels in both cut and innovative textile design.

ET VOUS & TRACE, 11 rue de Valois, 75001
Tel: 01 40 15 04 43
Métro: Palais Royal
Opening Hours: Mon–Sat: 12.00–18.30
August: call for exact dates
Credit Cards: Visa
Price Range: Trace trousers from 900FF, coat from 5,000FF, dress from 1,300FF

JOYCE MA: GALLERY
The gracious and elegant Joyce Ma, owner of several major department stores in Taiwan and Hong Kong, has her gallery here in the shade of the Palais Royal arches. Exhibitions change every two months and reflect Madame Ma's passions from the monumental blackened bronze vases of Ibu Poilâne to the woven carpets of Brad Davis and Janis Provisor. All exhibitions are selling.

JOYCE MA, 168–173 galerie de Valois, 75001
Tel: 01 40 15 03 72
Métro: Palais Royal
Opening Hours: Mon: 14.30–18.30, Tue–Sat: 11.00–18.30
August: closed
Credit Cards: Visa, Amex, Diners, MC, JCB

BY TERRY: COUTURE COSMETICS
'This is not a make-up bar nor an ordinary beauty salon,' declares the sleek and rosy-lipped Terry de Gunzburg; 'it's much more like a couture house, a kind of creative ideas laboratory set on making women look more beautiful.' After 12 years spent as creative director at Yves Saint Laurent cosmetics (a position she still holds), Terry decided to open By Terry, a salon selling made-to-measure cosmetics. The ground

floor houses the 'ready-to-wear' cosmetic collection with products such as 'éclat' which contains reflector pigment to cover up the after-effects of heavy nights out. If you take the couture option you are ushered upstairs and behind swathes of damson velvet curtains, where you get to meet Terry and her team of colourists and chemists. They take between one week and four to whip up at least five different shades, intensities and finishes of the product you desire, for example a lipstick. You then take the samples home to test and pick out your definitive product which is then dermatologically tested and manufactured for you. Extravagant yes, but tempting particularly when Terry promises, 'I can make a foundation that he won't notice even when you're dining tête-à-tête with your face five inches from his.'

BY TERRY, 21 passage Vero-Dodat, 75001
Tel: 01 44 76 00 76
Métro: Louvre-Rivoli
Opening Hours: Mon–Sat: 11.00–19.00
August: open
Credit Cards: Visa, Amex, Diners, MC
Price Range: ready-to-wear line 430–780FF, refills 130–190FF, couture lipstick with four refills from 2,500FF

CHRISTIAN LOUBOUTIN: DESIGNER SHOES

If you think you've got the lifestyle, Louboutin's got the heels to match. He's the shoemaker by appointment to Cher, Naomi, Elle Macpherson, Princess Caroline of Monaco, Catherine Deneuve and every American heiress and Middle Eastern princess worth her dowry. He's one of those designers who just seems to think beautiful. With others it's all angst and creative turmoil, with Louboutin it's a bit of a gossip and a giggle and a brilliant pair of shoes at the end of it. His creative style tends to veer between the elegant classic and daring fantasy. Past creations have included resin heels with real hydrangeas, Guinness can heels, Wedgwood motifs and giant silk daisy buckles. 'I'm not into comfort,' explains Christian, 'but my shoes do have to serve as something between a weapon and an objet d'art.'

CHRISTIAN LOUBOUTIN, 19 rue Jean-Jacques Rousseau, 75001
Tel: 01 42 36 05 31
Métro: Louvre-Rivoli
Opening Hours: Mon–Sat: 11.00–19.30
August: closed
Credit Cards: Visa, Amex
Price Range: shoes 1,500–2,500FF, boots around 3,500FF

VICTOIRE HOMME: MEN'S SHIRTS
See 6th arrondissement for details.
10–12 rue du Colonel Driant, 75001. Tel: 01 42 97 44 87

ROBERT CLERGERIE: ELEGANT DESIGNER SHOES
See 6th arrondissement for details.
46 rue Croix des Petits Champs, 75001. Tel: 01 42 61 49 24

LE FUMOIR: BAR/RESTAURANT/CAFÉ
One of a new breed of Parisian restaurants, Le Fumoir is done out in
olive-brown walls with battered leather club chairs and a vase of faded
blood-red gladioli. The ambience is nonchalant cool with a room right
at the back of the restaurant designed to look like a library straight out
of a private house. Here you can sit in calm and while away a couple
of hours with a pot of tea and a copy of Camus borrowed from the

bookshelves. The restaurant has 3,000 books, many of which can be
borrowed (you need to leave some sort of deposit rather than just walk
off with some first edition). At night the scene is fashionable, while the
food, it has to be said, went through a fairly erratic starting phase but
is much improved and includes a great Caesar salad and tuna steak.
Still it is a restaurant more for scene than cuisine.

LE FUMOIR, 6 rue de l'Amiral Coligny, 75001
Tel: 01 42 92 00 24
Métro: Louvre-Rivoli
Opening Hours: every day: 11.00–2.00
August: open
Credit Cards: Visa, Amex
Price Range: lunch menu 105FF, cocktails during happy hour (18.00–20.00
every day) 35FF, dinner menu 170FF

Place
des
Victoires

2ND ARRONDISSEMENT

During the 1980s this area was treacherously trendy with black-clad designer shoppers backed up along the rue Étienne Marcel. Then recession hit and it became a kind of fashion ghost town. Now it is happening again with both designer and high street stores springing up all along the rue Étienne Marcel, accompanied by cool cafés, restaurants and bars.

The 2nd arrondissement is dominated to the east by the rag-trade garment district known as the Sentier. In less than a square mile there are over a thousand clothing manufacturers and if you walk north up any of the streets off rue Étienne Marcel you're soon caught up in rolling rails of clothing and barrow boys heaving fabric.

The Sentier is all about running up three thousand pairs of fluorescent lime jeans overnight and the rest of the French high street fashion industry hate it. They whine about Sentier copying, employing illegal workers and shoddy quality. Although often short on original design, the truth is that the Sentier is brilliant at fast production, exploiting trends and cheap prices. Some of France's big success stories like Kookaï, Naff Naff, Morgan and Et Vous started here.

As a quartier, the 2nd is lively and local. The money centre of Paris is here, to the north of place des Victoires with the stock exchange or Bourse and the Bank of France. The mood gets foodie along the rue Étienne Marcel, with specialist shops selling obscure soufflé dishes and oozing cheeses in the gourmet street market of rue Montorgueil.

For fashion there is a whole road of Agnès b. boutiques at rue du Jour, and don't miss other cool French labels such as Gas, Paul & Joe and Barbara Bui. As this is rag-trade land, several companies such as Kookaï, Et Vous as well as designer shoe shop Kabuki all have permanent sale stores selling off old stock. What's new in the area is the enclave of street, club and '70s kitsch kit to be found at Le Shop and Kiliwatch.

Just down the rue Montmartre is Les Halles, which for over 800 years was the site of the massive fruit and veg market of Paris. It was moved out in the 1960s and replaced by an underground shopping precinct. Other than the wonderful St-Eustache church, Les Halles is now pretty grubby and smells of pee and fried onions. It's good for teenage cheap trend, but otherwise don't bother going underground. The rue Étienne Marcel is the main road cutting through this area; everything above it is officially the 2nd, everything below is the 1st. But it's easier to shop both sides of the street in one trip, that's what Parisians do and that's why I've combined them in one chapter.

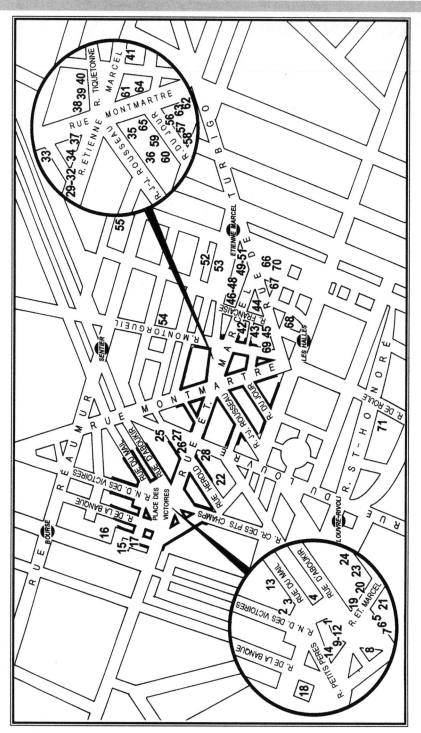

1 VICTOIRE
2 ISLAND
3 BLANC BLEU
4 PLEIN SUD
5 AGATHA
6 CACHAREL
7 KENZO
8 APOSTROPHE
9 STÉPHANE KÉLIAN
10 CLIO BLUE
11 THIERRY MUGLER HOMMES
12 FORMES
13 CHEZ GEORGES
14 MICHEL PERRY
15 JEAN PAUL GAULTIER
16 BONNIE COX
17 A PRIORI THÉ
18 CUTLER AND GROSS
19 ANNE FONTAINE
20 BONPOINT
21 YOHJI YAMAMOTO
22 ZAMPA
23 LE SHOP
24 PANOPLIE
25 VENTILO
26 PAUL & JOE
27 RAW ESSENTIALS
28 Y'S YOHJI YAMAMOTO
29 GAS FASHION
30 GAS JEWELLERY
31 JOSEPH
32 COMME DES GARÇONS
33 M.YXT
34 COMME DES GARÇONS
35 ABSINTHE
36 FIFI CHACHNIL

37 JÉRÔME ABEL SEGUIN
38 KILIWATCH
39 PATRICK COX
40 ANTHONY PETO
41 PATTAYA
42 BARBARA BUI CAFÉ
43 MISS CHINA
44 MISS CHINA TEA
45 MISS CHINA KIDS
46 KABUKI
47 BARBARA BUI
48 KABUKI HOMME
49 KABUKI AFTER
50 ET VOUS STOCK
51 BRUUNS BAZAAR
52 ÉRIC ET LYDIE
53 LE DÉNICHEUR
54 RUE MONTORGUEIL (FRUIT AND VEG MARKET)
55 KOOKAÏ LE STOCK
56 AGNÈS B.
57 INDIES
58 AGNÈS B. ENFANT
59 PÔLES
60 LA DROGUERIE
61 MOKUBA
62 CLAUDIE PIERLOT
63 MON AMI PIERLOT
64 FREE
65 GHOST
66 SCOOTER
67 MOSQUITOS
68 FREE LANCE
69 MONDO SHOP GROUP
70 MARIA
71 RAG TIME

PLACE DES VICTOIRES

VICTOIRE: WOMEN'S DESIGNER FASHION

A designer store once known for selling the cutting edge of fashion, Victoire has now turned to realism dressing. It is still designer wear, but owner Gilles Riboud now concentrates on wearable chic clothes with a wider price range. That said, of the four womenswear Victoire stores in Paris this is the most fashionable. Choosing the clothes for the store, Riboud says, is like choosing a bouquet: 'It's a mix of the big statement flowers, pretty scent, nice vase and lots of back-up greenery.' Big statement flowers here include DKNY and Italian designers Marni, Alberta Ferretti and Dolce & Gabbana. There are fresh understated designs by Mr & Mrs MacLeod and Pucci print dresses from Catherine Malendrino. There is also a good selection of the GR816 collection from Gilles Rosier, one of the younger exciting Parisian designers. For greenery there are less expensive trousers from Regina Rubens and lots of knitwear and shirts under Victoire's own label. If you're looking for a specific outfit, the staff here are good at helping you pull one together and they have all the bags, hats, belts and scarves to do it. Customers are around age 35 and up – Linda Evans, Lauren Bacall and Tina Turner all shop here – and in summer there's a younger customer for the pretty summer dresses. There are two shops here, divided between No. 10 which has all the fold-up clothes and No. 12 which stocks all the hanging clothes.

VICTOIRE, 10–12 place des Victoires, 75002
Tel: 01 42 61 09 02
Métro: Sentier or Les Halles
also at:
1 rue Madame, 75006. Tel: 01 45 44 28 14
16 rue de Passy, 75016. Tel: 01 42 88 20 84
Opening Hours: Mon–Sat: 9.30–19.00
August: open
Credit Cards: Visa, Amex, Diners, MC, JCB
Price Range: trousers from 800FF, suiting 2,000–6,000FF, summer dress 800–2,000FF

ISLAND: CASUAL MEN'S SHIRTING

Island attracts the boys from the Bourse and is best for its shirts. They are mostly non-work styles and what the French describe as sportswear chic with lots of button-down collars and colours like pale aqua.

ISLAND, 4 rue Vide-Gousset (located in place des Victoires), 75002
Tel: 01 42 61 77 77
Métro: Sentier or Les Halles
Opening Hours: Mon–Sat: 10.00–19.00
August: closed week of 15 Aug
Credit Cards: Visa, Diners, Amex, MC, JCB
Price Range: shirts 395–800FF

BLANC BLEU: NAUTICAL WEAR

Blanc Bleu makes clothes for skippers and their mates. The look for men is more seafarer than St-Tropez, with thick cotton cable sweaters and performance jackets with metal snap fasteners. Colours for men are, not surprisingly, mostly navy and white, highlighted with orange, red and yellow. Upstairs is womenswear where the nautical theme is a lot less literal – it's pretty, but safe French weekend chic. There is a fitted French navy cotton ribbed sweater with a row of mother of pearl buttons on the shoulder and for summer long linen cross-over sundresses. For more of a coquette style there are skimpy blue halter-neck T-shirts and tiny white shorts with turn-ups.

BLANC BLEU, 14 place des Victoires, 75002
Tel: 01 42 96 05 40
Métro: Sentier or Les Halles
Opening Hours: Mon: 11.00–19.00, Tue–Sat: 10.00–19.00
August: open
Credit Cards: Visa, Amex, Diners, MC
Price Range: women's cotton T-shirts 170FF, tiny white shorts 335FF, long linen cross-over sundress 1,030FF, cotton ribbed knit sweater 460FF, men's thick cable knit polo-neck 1,200FF, men's performance jackets 1,690FF

PLEIN SUD: TREND DESIGNER WOMENSWEAR
See Le Marais for details.
2 place des Victoires, 75002. Tel: 01 42 36 75 02

AGATHA: COSTUME JEWELLERY CHAIN

This is a chain of costume jewellery stores you'll find all around Paris. They sell masses of Chanel-inspired gilt, chunky earrings, Scottie dogs (their logo), charm bracelets, plastic pearls, paste bangles and jet. It's worth poking around to find the more fashionable pieces, but fairly expensive for what it is, i.e., mass-manufactured metal.

AGATHA, 5 place des Victoires, 75002
Tel: 01 40 39 08 25
Metro: Sentier or Les Halles
Opening Hours: Mon–Sat: 10.00–19.00
August: closed week of 15 Aug
Credit Cards: Visa, Amex, Diners, MC, JCB
Price Range: rings 50–900FF, bracelets 60–300FF, necklaces 250–500FF

CACHAREL: CLASSIC FRENCH LOOK
See 6th arrondissement for details.
5 place des Victoires, 75002. Tel: 01 42 33 29 88

KENZO: FRENCH DESIGNER
See 7th arrondissement for details.
3 place des Victoires, 75002. Tel: 01 40 39 72 00

APOSTROPHE: FRENCH CHIC WOMENSWEAR
See 8th arrondissement for details.
1 bis place des Victoires, 75002. Tel: 01 40 41 91 00

STÉPHANE KÉLIAN: DESIGNER SHOES
Great branch of Kélian, particularly for the more fashion styles; for full details see 7th arrondissement.
6 place des Victoires, 75002. Tel: 01 42 61 60 74

CLIO BLUE: PRETTY JEWELLERY
See 6th arrondissement for details.
8 place des Victoires, 75002. Tel: 01 42 61 51 05

THIERRY MUGLER HOMMES:
FRENCH DESIGNER
See 7th arrondissement for details.
8 place des Victoires, 75002. Tel: 01 49 26 05 02

FORMES: PREGNANCY WEAR
Since I wrote the first edition of this book I have had a baby which involved (among other things) much searching for suitable pregnancy clothes. Trying to reconcile your fashion look with a projectile bump is harder than you might expect, which is why I think French pregnancy brand Formes does a clever job. Their clothes are intended for women who work and have a social life and a vague interest in fashion, and hence are designed to correspond with your pre-pregnancy wardrobe. It is a sort of Agnès b./MaxMara look for pregnant women. The silhouette is flattering and with a major emphasis on cut and, this being France, a healthy dose of sex appeal. They also recognise that realistically you are only going to want to buy a few pieces and wear them day in, day out, so their fabrics are built to last. I bought black trousers and a well-cut sleeveless tunic top which I wore non-stop and have since lent to friends. They do good work suits (skirt or trouser), jeans and for night-time sexy designs such as a long black dress slit up the sides to be worn alone or layered over a pair of trousers.

FORMES, 10 place des Victoires, 75002
Tél: 01 40 15 63 81
Métro: Sentier or Les Halles
also at:
5 rue du Vieux Colombier, 75006. Tel: 01 45 49 09 80
41 rue de Passy, 75016. Tel: 01 46 47 50 05
Opening Hours: Mon–Sat: 10.30–19.00
August: open
Credit Cards: Visa, Amex
Price Range: skirt 250–500FF, jacket 800–1,300FF, dress 450–750FF, trousers from 420FF

CHEZ GEORGES: TRADITIONAL FRENCH BISTRO

A heavenly bistro, serving traditional French food and platefuls of Paris ambience. Opened in 1964 by Georges, it is now run by his son and grandson. However, not much has changed and Georges still nips up to town to see the regulars. It serves classic French cuisine with Lyonnaise influence like a sole au Pouilly, which is sole cooked in crème fraîche, white wine and shallots, or grilled calves' kidneys. This is Paris charm without trying: water served in pewter jugs, heavy silver cutlery, white linen, 'proper' service and a mirrored dining room. During fashion weeks it's madness and you must book. A house trick is to let you drink any of the bottles of wine on the front of the menu au compteur, which means by measure. It's perfect if you are eating alone as you can still choose a good bottle of wine and only pay for what you drink.

CHEZ GEORGES, 1 rue du Mail, 75002
Tel: 01 42 60 07 11
Métro: Sentier or Les Halles
Opening Hours: Mon–Sat: 12.00–14.15, 19.15–21.45
August: closed first three weeks
Credit Cards: Visa, Amex, MC
Price Range: à la carte only, around 300FF a head with wine

MICHEL PERRY: DESIGNER FASHION FOOTWEAR

Michel Perry's shoes stay the fashion side of fetishistic. Hugely innovative, his designs are often exaggerated and heels always sky-high for calf elongation. The clientele is, says his PR, 'très fashion' and the sort of women who have a thing about their shoes: Naomi, Madonna, Jerry Hall, Chrystèle and Cher. It's dominatrix dressing, with narrow satin boots perched on spiky '80s heels. The heel is where Perry really makes his mark. His signature is the thick cylindrical heel, but he creates a new one every season, like a block heel which splays around the sole of the shoe. Even his more classic shoe and boot styles teeter on trend, for example a best-selling knee-high black leather boot which is cut higher in front and has a precariously sliced heel. The shop setting is fabulously stylish with lime chiffon at the windows, clotted-cream

and pale pink shoe boxes and 1940s garden furniture. All the shoes and boots are made in Italy. He's in the process of expanding the menswear line, which at the moment is tame by comparison.

MICHEL PERRY, 4 rue des Petits Pères, 75002
Tel: 01 42 44 10 07
Métro: Sentier or Les Halles
Opening Hours: Mon–Sat: 11.00–19.00
August: open
Credit Cards: Visa, Amex, MC
Price Range: knee-high boots 2,950FF, women's shoes 1,500–3,000FF, men's footwear 1,750–1,950FF

GALERIE VIVIENNE

Galerie Vivienne was opened in 1826 and became a terribly smart place to saunter. Then it fell out of favour and there was talk of demolition until Gaultier's enormous store opened up in the 1980s and catapulted it back into fashion.

JEAN PAUL GAULTIER: FRENCH DESIGNER WEAR
This store, which eats into the galerie Vivienne, was the original Gaultier store to open in Paris at the beginning of 1986. It's massive, with two floors done out in copper that looks as if it's been left out in the rain to turn green, videos in the floor, a massive video projector upstairs and everywhere Greek statues as mannequins. On the ground floor you'll find womenswear and accessories; upstairs, menswear and shoes. The store is larger than the one in rue Faubourg St-Antoine and often has more stock, particularly in menswear. For full details on Gaultier, see Destination Shopping.

JEAN PAUL GAULTIER, 6 rue Vivienne, 75002
Tel: 01 42 86 05 05
Métro: Bourse
also at:
30 rue du Faubourg St-Antoine, 75012. Tel: 01 44 68 84 84
Opening Hours: Mon–Fri: 10.00–19.00, Sat: 11.00–19.00
August: open
Credit Cards: Visa, Diners, Amex, JCB
Price Range: suit from main line 5,000–7,000FF, JPG jacket 1,500–2,200FF, jeans 460–650FF

BONNIE COX: TREND WOMENSWEAR
See Destination Shopping for details.
62 galerie Vivienne, 75002. Tel: 01 42 60 05 00

A PRIORI THÉ: TEA ROOM AND RESTAURANT
A sublime location in the middle of the galerie Vivienne, with the sun

Galerie Vivienne on a rainy Thursday in Paris

streaming through the roof, nice service and great home cooking make this a permanent hot spot. The only seats that count in this place are outside. There you can check out the passers-by at close quarters, even by Paris standards. New Yorker Peggy opened the tea room in 1980 and serves breakfast, lunch, tea and weekend brunches. It's all home-baked muffins, scones, jams and cheesecakes. The menu changes monthly but a long-term favourite is the chicken breast stuffed with citron confit and coriander served with steamed vegetables. During the shows you can't move for designers, buyers and fashion editors. Jean Paul Gaultier, whose shop is just round the corner, is a regular; Donna Karan's been in. At the weekends there are lots of swarthy men in blazers with wrap-around sunglasses and immaculate girls with Yorkshire terriers and perfect highlights, and that's just the dog's hair. You need to book during fashion week.

A PRIORI THÉ, 35–37 galerie Vivienne, 75002
Tel: 01 42 97 48 75
Métro: Bourse
Opening Hours: Mon–Sat: 9.00–18.00, Sun: 13.00–18.00
August: open
Credit Cards: Visa, MC
Price Range: breakfast scone, butter and jam 15FF, coffee 12FF, Saturday brunch 135FF, Caesar salad 82FF

CUTLER AND GROSS: FASHIONABLE SUNGLASSES
English opticians who specialise in sunglasses, Cutler and Gross are consistently fashionable. They opened up in Paris recently with the teeniest of stores and Linda, Amber and Malcolm McLaren have all been in to buy their shades. Their style is glam but wearable, with good-quality plastic lenses. If you're caught at the shows without your dark glasses this is where to come.

CUTLER AND GROSS, 2 galerie Vivienne, 75002
Tel/Fax: 01 40 15 05 33
Métro: Bourse
Opening Hours: Mon: 15.00–19.00, Tue–Sat: 11.00–19.00
August: open Mon–Fri
Credit Cards: Visa, Amex, Diners, JCB
Price Range: 640–880FF

ALONG OR JUST OFF RUE ÉTIENNE MARCEL

ANNE FONTAINE: WOMEN'S WHITE COTTON SHIRTS
If you need white work shirts, go to Anne Fontaine and stock up. They sell only white cotton shirts, which are nice quality and made in France. Styles are fairly classic but feminine, and details like covered buttons, a well-cut collar or crisp poplin add chic. In summer there are more relaxed or party looks too, like a halter-neck cotton piqué top or white organdie bolero which ties over a short white shirt. Every season there are a hundred different styles, most around the same price.

ANNE FONTAINE, 50 rue Étienne Marcel, 75002
Tel: 01 40 41 08 32
Métro: Étienne Marcel
also at:
64–66 rue des Saints-Pères, 75007. Tel: 01 45 48 89 10
Opening Hours: Mon–Sat: 10.30–19.00
August: closed
Credit Cards: Visa, Amex, MC
Price Range: basic collection 395–495FF, organdie bolero with shirt 750FF

BONPOINT: CHILDREN'S CLOTHES
See 7th arrondissement for details.
50 rue Étienne Marcel, 75002. Tel: 01 40 26 20 90

YOHJI YAMAMOTO DESIGNER MENSWEAR
Less poetic than his womenswear but with more humour, Yohji Yamamoto's clothes for men tend to be relaxed, sometimes a little dishevelled, and to be worn by artistes of any kind. His collections are inspired by utilitarian workwear and the photographs of the 19th-century artist August Sander. The big sellers here are the beautifully-

proportioned jackets with ample shoulder and long sleeve in navy or black gabardine, as well as wide-legged black trousers which trail the floor with nonchalant abandon.

YOHJI YAMAMOTO, 47 rue Étienne Marcel, 75001
Tel: 01 45 08 82 45
Métro: Étienne Marcel
Opening Hours: Mon: 11.30–19.00, Tue–Sat: 10.30–19.00
August: open
Credit Cards: Visa, Amex, Diners, MC
Price Range: pair of socks 140FF, wool gabardine blazer 3,360FF, three-piece suit 12,000FF

ZAMPA: DESIGNER HIPPIE CHIC

This is one of a number of stores to have sprung up post-Colette selling a mix of fashion, decor and design. The store concept is about a kind of hippie artisan feel with a loft decor and a fair amount of incense thrown around, but not without the necessary quota of Paris chic. Clothes-wise it is about fluid, easy pieces with bias-cut long dresses, a store staple, also thick knit cardigans by Marc le Bihan, wide-legged trousers in sari fabrics and pretty cashmere sweaters from Madame à Paris. There is cute hippie kids' kit such as tie-dye tops and trousers by Wowo, while for accessories they have leather clogs, hairy ponyskin bags by Marie Bouvero and pale pink cowboy hats from Eugenia Kim. They also stock a skin-care range by Nuxe which includes the deliciously-named crème fraîche moisturiser.

ZAMPA, 10 rue Hérold, 75001
Tel: 01 40 41 11 24
Métro: Louvre-Rivoli or Les Halles
Opening Hours: Mon: 14.30–19.00, Tue–Sat: 10.30–19.00
August: closed first three weeks
Credit Cards: Visa, Amex, MC, JCB
Price Range: dresses from 770FF, crème fraîche Nuxe 190FF, bags from 700FF

LE SHOP: CLUB AND STREETWEAR

As the club and streetwear look has moved on, so Le Shop has slightly lost its edge and monopoly on the market in Paris. It still sells a fusion of music and clothes trends with DJs jostling for space alongside designers such as Poulbox, Fresh Jive, Combo and Split. There are two floors of forty stalls selling clothes from young designers, vintage, clubwear, snowboarding kit, urban brands such as Carhaart, skateboards and shoes. On the ground floor is a DJ site featuring 24 different DJs a week. It is still a great place to pick up a funky something to make an outfit: David Ackerman kinky camouflage boots, flash sunglasses or a '70s black nylon ski-jacket. But rather than appealing to a wide range of ages and looks, now I'd say it is pitched at a young, hard-core urban customer.

LE SHOP, 3 rue d'Argout, 75002
Tel: 01 40 28 95 94
Métro: Sentier or Étienne Marcel
Opening Hours: Mon–Fri: 11.00–19.00
August: closed for middle two weeks, call for exact dates
Credit Cards: Visa, Amex, Diners, MC
Price Range: trainers 300–600FF, nylon shirts 100–500FF, skateboards
700–1,000FF, cup of coffee 5FF

PANOPLIE: AVANT-GARDE DESIGNER MENSWEAR

Its discreet address (as in tucked away at the back of a courtyard)
means you don't exactly stumble across Panoplie, but fashion boys
seek it out for its strong selection of designer menswear. Owner Jean-
Louis Beaumont opened his first menswear store at the age of 17, then
went on to direct the Gaultier store on rue Vivienne, before opening
here. He stocks suiting and casual wear divided between designer
fashion look and a more urban street feel, although he admits to a
strong taste for a 1950/1960s shape and feel. For designer kit there are
clothes by Ann Demeulemeester, Helmut Lang, Kostas Murkudis and
Vivienne Westwood and Martine Sitbon's new and cool menswear,
while on the urban front he sells Mandarina Duck (the clothes, not the
bags) and Vexed Generation. Some designers get a bit precious about
him mixing their clothes with other designers', but Beaumont advo-
cates mixing brands with abandon. The look and cut of the clothes
tend to be for a slim-set or smallish man who is fashion-aware.

PANOPLIE, 7 rue d'Argout, 75002
Tel: 01 40 28 90 35
Métro: Sentier or Étienne Marcel
Opening Hours: Mon: 13.00–19.00, Tue–Sat: 11.00–19.00
August: closed for week of 15 Aug
Credit Cards: Visa, Diners, MC, JCB
Price Range: trousers 700–2,500FF, suit 4,500–6,300FF

VENTILO: FRENCH CLASSIC WOMENSWEAR

This is a French vision of American sportswear meets colonial India.
On the ground floor it's fairly casual, with cotton safari jackets, Mid-
west chambray dresses and a lot of cotton jodhpurs with buttons up
the calf (which can look frumpy). What works best here is the more
formal Ventilo look on the first floor, which offers a woman who likes
easy dressing a smart alternative. For example, there is a fuchsia silk
organdie shirt worn over a full-length linen dress or a cream wool
crêpe trouser suit with a three-quarter length Nehru jacket. During the
summer months Ventilo is past master at doing that whole well-bred
well-dressed French look, that means great white shirts (which French
women never seem to get grubby), dead simple long linen dresses, little cardigans and pastel-coloured tennis pumps. The store decor is
very New England and built for husband-and-wife retail with big

sofas in the middle of the shop floor. On the third floor is a squeaky-clean tea room which is about as far removed from a smoky Paris bistro as you can get. On the ground floor is a pretty home interior section which has some rather lovely white organdie curtains with appliqué leaf detail from India.

VENTILO, 27 bis rue du Louvre, 75002
Tel: 01 42 33 18 67
Métro: Étienne Marcel or Sentier
also at:
59 rue Bonaparte, 75006. Tel: 01 43 26 64 84
267 rue St-Honoré, 75001. Tel: 01 40 15 61 52
10 rue des Francs Bourgeois, 75003. Tel: 01 40 27 05 58
96 avenue Paul Doumer, 75016. Tel: 01 40 50 02 21
Opening Hours: Mon: 12.00–19.00, Tue–Sat: 10.30–19.00
August: closed for first two weeks
Credit Cards: Visa, Amex, MC
Price Range: jodhpurs 600FF, organdie shirt 895FF, full-length linen dress
1,290FF, crêpe wool suit 3,000FF; tea room: pot of tea 25FF, salad of gua-
camole and tortillas 68FF

PAUL & JOE: TREND WOMENSWEAR
Paul & Joe is hot right now with Paris designer Sophie Albou tapping
into that whole sexy girl, hippie-luxe mood and the Paris girls are
queuing up at the door to snap up her fashionable pieces. Check out
one of her two stores while you're in town. The shop in the Left Bank
is more for basics, while the Right Bank has got all the groovy pieces
from cute appliquéd handbags and sexy halter-neck dresses to pretty
print and embroidered skirts. Whatever the season's trend, Sophie has
got it taped.

PAUL & JOE, 46 rue Étienne Marcel, 75002
Tel: 01 40 28 03 34
Métro: Étienne Marcel
also at:
40 rue du Four, 75006. Tel. 01 45 44 97 70
Opening Hours: Mon–Sat: 10.00–19.00
August: closed first three weeks
Credit Cards: Visa, Amex, Diners, MC, JCB
Price Range: skirts from 800FF, trousers 1,000FF

RAW ESSENTIALS: UNISEX WORKWEAR
Dutch brand G Star sells a kind of urban workwear based on US military themes. It's a macho look with funky intentions. There is cement
on the floor, well-toned boys to serve you and come Saturday the store
is pumping. Jeans are the big sellers here with four different cuts and
deep dark denims. For men Elwood, an extreme baggy style with knee
pads, has turned cult, while women choose the slimmer fit Low Waist.
There are also plenty of ribbed T-shirts, cotton fitted tops and button-
shouldered sweaters. Think Top Gun for the new millennium.

RAW ESSENTIALS, 46 rue Étienne Marcel, 75002
Tel: 01 42 21 44 33
Métro: Étienne Marcel
Opening Hours: Mon: 11.30–19.00, Tue–Sat: 10.30–19.00

August: closed for three weeks
Credit Cards: Visa, Amex, Diners, MC, JCB
Price Range: jeans 450–790FF

Y'S YOHJI YAMAMOTO: DIFFUSION LINE

This store features a less expensive collection designed by Yohji Yamamoto for men and women. See 6th arrondissement for details.
25 rue du Louvre, 75002. Tel: 01 42 21 42 93

GAS: DELUXE HIPPIE FASHION

A major hit with the model community, this tiny store does Indian souk meets Moroccan bazaar meets St-Tropez pool-side. There are clothes by loads of different designers but basically the look is sexy

bohemian in jewel colours to be worn with a hot body and perma-tan. New stock arrives every two weeks throughout the season and there are always plenty of one-off pieces such as a stiff, almost Provençal-style skirt with orange, purple and gold braiding that undulates round the body or a gorgeous emerald-green paisley dressing-gown coat lined in scarlet silk. They always have a cute selection of accessories such as diamanté bindis, plastic beaded mules, silk printed head-scarves or fringed gypsy shawls.

GAS, 44 rue Étienne Marcel, 75002
Tel: 01 42 33 36 04
Métro: Étienne Marcel
Opening Hours: Mon–Fri: 10.30–19.00, Sat: 11.00–19.00
August: call for exact dates
Credit Cards: Visa, Amex, MC
Price Range: Indian plastic bangles 10FF, shawls 2,800FF, silver crochet top 280FF

GAS: PRETTY COSTUME JEWELLERY
Some French costume jewellery still looks very Trump Towers; the jewellery at Gas does not. They like to call it baroque but it's far too dainty for that. There are earrings, bracelets and necklaces which are in simple shapes like a square or abstract flower and filled with small coloured crystals and semi-precious stones. It's feminine rather than fashionable, although they do work with fashion colours like grena-dine, amethyst, violet, orange and lime. They have a great choice of earrings and in summer there are fun pieces like a silver daisy chain hipster belt. They have their own workshops down in Marseille mak-ing all the jewellery, so stock changes all the time.

GAS, 44 rue Étienne Marcel, 75002
Tel: 01 45 08 49 46
Métro: Étienne Marcel
Opening Hours: Mon–Fri: 10.30–19.00, Sat: 11.00–19.00
August: closed 15–23 Aug
Credit Cards: Visa, Amex, MC
Price Range: rings 600–1,500FF, bracelets 300–600FF, earrings 180–700FF, chain belt 290FF

JOSEPH: CONTEMPORARY WOMENSWEAR
See 8th arrondissement for details.
44 rue Étienne Marcel, 75002. Tel: 01 42 36 87 83

COMME DES GARÇONS: DESIGNER WOMENSWEAR
Rei Kawakubo has often said if you want to know what she's feeling, take a look at her clothes. Something must be ecstatic in her life right now, as after years of black absolute rule, her recent collections have been superb blasts of colour and print. She continues to push her

design further into architectural dimensions with a level of cutting that leaves you mystified but deeply impressed, like her rose-petal formations and layered dresses which are cut like an exposed wound to reveal the layer beneath.

The combination of her extreme talent, severe appearance and well-publicised lack of interest in talking to the press has made Kawakubo into a sort of high priestess of the fashion industry. But after the ecstasy of press and buyers over the intellectualism of her collections has subsided, let's not forget that in reality it's a little more commercial than that. She produces eleven lines, sells to or in 33 countries and her annual turnover is around 700 million FF, which is twice that of either Yamamoto or Miyake. In Japan, where Comme des Garçons is a way of life rather than a fashion, she has 389 stores. She works in Tokyo, but has shown in Paris ever since her first appearance in 1981 when she effectively ripped up fashion convention and challenged it to start again. Her two stores here (womenswear and menswear) are not as aggressively minimalist as they once were. In fact, it's getting a little cluttered in there, what with all those socks, perfumes, dry body oils, balms – and even a scented candle. Prices are expensive, but every fabric is created exclusively for each collection and then never used again. There is a second line designed by Kawakubo herself and manufactured in Italy which is called Comme des Garçons, Comme des Garçons and is around 50% or so less expensive than the main line. Downstairs you will find the collection of Junya Watanabe, Kawakubo's brilliant assistant, who has plunged back into black with structured suiting and intricate cut-leather dresses.

One tip: save the sales assistants the laugh – there is a button to the right of the electric door, which you need to press to get in.

COMME DES GARÇONS, 42 rue Étienne Marcel, 75002
Tel: 01 42 33 05 21
Métro: Étienne Marcel
Opening Hours: Mon–Sat: 11.00–19.00
August: closed weekend of 15 Aug
Credit Cards: Visa, Amex, Diners, MC, JCB
Price Range: cape coat 12,000FF, dévoré velvet jacket 6,000FF, layered dress 7,000FF

M.YXT: PROFESSIONAL MAKE-UP

Damien Dufresne was a make-up artist for 15 years before he decided to set up shop here. He chooses what he reckons to be the best products from his favourite brands, be that Longcils Boncza mascara (kind of magic powder you apply with a wet brush), eye-shadow from Il Makiage or a lip-gloss from Viseart, and then he displays the lot in a vast artist atelier. This shop is a real find for all obsessive eyebrow pluckers: not only does he sell the best 'laser' tweezers I've come across (says the owner of at least ten pairs of tweezers), but he will also

pluck your eyebrows into great shape (no appointment necessary, cost 50FF). His make-up and the look he advises are fashion-aware, as in bare minimum. 'I like a blush that makes you look as if you've just done two hours' fresh-air mountain biking,' says Damien, rather than two hours with your head in your vanity case. He's just started a 'maquillage express' whereby you drop by on your way out at night and they'll do you a slick fresh face for around 150FF.

M.YXT, 11 rue de la Jusienne, 75002
Tel: 01 42 21 39 80
Métro: Étienne Marcel
Opening Hours: Mon–Fri: 10.00–19.00, Sat: 12.00–19.00
August: open
Credit Cards: Visa
Price Range: brushes 46–120FF, mascara 80FF, Il Makiage eye-shadow 82FF, lip-gloss 65FF

COMME DES GARÇONS: DESIGNER MENSWEAR

Next door to her womenswear store Rei Kawakubo has her menswear. As well as the main line there is the shirting which has some lovely relaxed looks like cotton jersey front panels against a stripe, or striped shirts which have been overprinted. The Comme des Garçons shirt is the essential buy for every architect, artist or media man earnestly seeking career recognition.

COMME DES GARÇONS, 40 rue Étienne Marcel, 75002
Tel: 01 42 36 91 54
Métro: Étienne Marcel
Opening Hours: Mon–Sat: 11.00–19.00
August: closed week of 15 Aug
Credit Cards: Visa, Amex, Diners, MC, JCB
Price Range: shirting 700–1,200FF

RUE JEAN-JACQUES ROUSSEAU

ABSINTHE: DESIGNER WOMENSWEAR

Marthe Desmoulins' buying aesthetic is all about retro. She looks as though she's walked straight out of the 1920s with jet-black cloche haircut, palest make-up and rows of long beads. Her taste is for clothes with a similarly retro sensibility so she sells designers like Dries Van Noten, Julie Skarland, Sami Tilouche and Humbert. She loves what she calls colours from the past – faded lilacs, dusty greens and dun browns – the sort of shades you'd find in Virginia Woolf's house is how she describes them. She has a great eye for jewellery and accessories and sells shoes from the '20s and antique-looking jewels.

ABSINTHE, 74–76 rue Jean-Jacques Rousseau, 75001
Tel: 01 42 33 54 44
Métro: Les Halles or Étienne Marcel
Opening Hours: Mon–Sat: 11.00–19.30
August: closed part of the time
Credit Cards: Visa, Diners, MC, JCB
Price Range: accessories from 80FF, shoes 1,200FF, clothes 600–3,000FF

FIFI CHACHNIL: KITSCH AND FLIRTY WOMENSWEAR

Outside in a windowbox is a row of blooming peach plastic azaleas. Inside is a doll's house of a shop full of baby-doll dresses and breathy nylon nighties. Designer Delphine Véron did all the clothes for the Pierre & Gilles photographs and has been designing cutesy kitsch for years. Dresses are flirty, often empire line, in ginghams, sugary shades or plastified tartan and built to show off 'your bosom, waist and hips' – what else is there left? Most of the styles are flared to flatter and come with a built-in bustier to prop up your bosom. There are also some really pretty knit tops in cashmere and angora, like a pale pink sweater with stripes of bordeaux. She's also got a line of underwear called Fifi which is suitably dizzy with the sort of peach-melba knickers women wore at Wimbledon in the '70s and a poached-salmon nylon negligée with black ruffles – very Cicciolina. All bras are push-up balconnet and come in size B only.

FIFI CHACHNIL, 68 rue Jean-Jacques Rousseau, 75001
Tel/Fax: 01 42 21 19 93
Métro: Les Halles or Étienne Marcel
Opening Hours: Mon–Sat: 11.00–19.00
August: sometimes closed for a couple of days, call for exact dates
Credit Cards: Visa, MC
Price Range: fake-fur heart key ring 50FF, bed jackets 900FF, bras 420FF, frilly knickers 225FF, nylon nightie 885FF

BACK ON TO RUE ÉTIENNE MARCEL

JÉRÔME ABEL SEGUIN: OBJETS D'ART

Sculptor Jérôme Abel Seguin leads a peachy life of six months in Sumbawa, Indonesia, and the rest of the year in Paris. New York fashion store Barneys has one of his enormous sculpted screens and *World of Interiors* magazine recently ran a feature on his house in Indonesia. His shop in Paris sells Indonesian objets which are mostly pieces from everyday life, like a long teak offering plate or wooden boxes for storing betel leaves. There are small black and cream horn statues of kings which unscrew to keep your medicines in, and what Jérôme describes as the Indonesian vanity case – a stone plinth and rolling pin to crush powders. Downstairs is his own work which includes undulating monumental screens made from Kalongo wood and branch bas-relief.

True, as gifts to take home they don't exactly scream 'Made in France', but what a perfect excuse just to buy something for yourself.

JÉRÔME ABEL SEGUIN, 36 rue Étienne Marcel, 75002
Tel: 01 46 81 64 25
Métro: Étienne Marcel
Opening Hours: Mon–Sat: 10.30–19.00
August: closed for part of month, call for exact dates
Credit Cards: Visa, MC
Price Range: betel-leaf boxes 180FF, horn statues 160FF, offering plate 3,600FF, undulating screen 45,000FF

KILIWATCH: SECONDHAND AND NEW FASHION
For a walk on the wild side, try Kiliwatch. It's another key mover on the Paris young fashion scene and since it opened, all the fashion establishment from Christian Lacroix to Calvin Klein have been in to see what the fuss is about. They sell two types of product: their own clubby fashion label and, much more exciting, lots and lots of second-hand clothing, or fripe. They buy up secondhand clothing for men and women by the tonne, sort it, clean and chemically disinfect it, sort it again, iron it and put it in the shop. What's on display depends on what's in fashion, but there is a corner for most urban styles from nylon football-terrace Ellesse tracksuits to 1950s prom dresses. It's fantastic for party wear with spangled lurex jumpsuits, nylon nighties in tinned-salmon pink and a black lurex halter-neck dress with chevron stripes of pink, green and electric blue. For daywear there are suburban '50s golfing trews, suede shirts and polyester slacks. All the stylists and design teams come here looking for inspiration and prints during the collections, so Kiliwatch know in advance which look is going to be hot and they either make it themselves or find it in fripe.

KILIWATCH, 64 rue Tiquetonne, 75002
Tel: 01 42 21 17 37
Métro: Étienne Marcel
Opening Hours: Mon: 13.00–19.00, Tue–Fri: 10.30–19.00, Sat: 10.00–19.30
August: closed for part of month, call for exact dates
Credit Cards: Visa, Amex, MC, JCB
Price Range: halter-neck dress with chevron stripes 350FF, polyester slacks 350FF, suede shirt 300FF, golfing trews 250FF

PATRICK COX: DESIGNER SHOES
Now that the Wannabe loafer has sold a million, it's no longer quite so wannabe and shoe wizard Patrick Cox has had to come up with other designs for your feet. He's squared off the toe on the loafer and made it in forest green or purple, moc-croc or suede. For the main line it's Granny shoe dressing with antique-look leathers in mustard yellow, rust and aubergine. For disco nights there are strappy glitter sandals which are a big hit with Paris drag queens.

PATRICK COX, 62 rue Tiquetonne, 75002
Tel: 01 40 26 66 55
Métro: Étienne Marcel
also at:
21 rue de Grenelle, 75007. Tel: 01 45 49 24 28
Galeries Lafayette (1st floor), 75009. Tel: 01 42 82 10 21
Opening Hours: Mon–Sat: 10.00–19.00
August: open
Credit Cards: Visa, Amex, MC, JCB
Price Range: Willbe loafers 850–1,300FF, main line 1,100–1,800FF

ANTHONY PETO: GENTLEMEN'S HATS

An Englishman in Paris, Anthony Peto is married to hat designer
Marie Mercié, which is how he fell into hats. Former editor of *The Art
Magazine,* he only started designing hats several years ago when customers kept asking Marie for men's hats and she replied she wasn't
interested. His look is kind of kooky gentleman. Best sellers are the
superior Montecristi panamas but there are also canvas sailor cap
shapes and cotton knitted bonnets. Top hats made from dun brown
and cream straw are popular with French summer bridegrooms. For
winter the look is rather dandy with felt trilbies, chapeaux melons
(bowler hats) and floppy fedoras.

ANTHONY PETO, 56 rue Tiquetonne, 75002
Tel: 01 40 26 60 68
Métro: Étienne Marcel
Opening Hours: Mon–Sat: 11.00–19.00
August: closed
Credit Cards: Visa, Amex, Diners, MC, JCB
Price Range: sailor cap 300FF, straw top hat 650FF, superior Montecristi
panama 1,900FF

PATTAYA: THAI RESTAURANT

Lots of Chinese restaurants in Paris do a sideline in Thai dishes, but
they often turn out disappointingly tasteless. Here is a restaurant
which cooks fresh and fragrant Thai food. When you need a break
from baguettes, try a starter of steaming fish and lemon grass soup,
then chicken sautéed in ginger or chilli mussels cooked in basil. The
restaurant backs on to a pedestrian cobbled street and during the summer you can eat out there. Prices are reasonable but the loo is for body
contortionists. Booking essential.

PATTAYA, 29 rue Étienne Marcel, 75001
Tel: 01 42 33 98 09
Métro: Étienne Marcel or Les Halles
Opening Hours: every day: 12.00–14.30, 19.00–23.00, closed Sun lunch
August: open
Credit Cards: Visa only
Price Range: per head with wine or beer 100FF lunch, 150FF dinner

BARBARA BUI CAFÉ: FASHIONABLE CAFÉ

Decor-wise this is done out in the ubiquitous beige/greige minimalism which makes it appear a bit of an insipid take on the Emporio Armani caffè over on the Left Bank, but that said it's actually a pleasant place to stop for lunch and they do great coffee. For lunch try grilled prawns served with mango and fresh pasta, honey-roasted chicken or red mullet served with a coriander-spiked puréed potato. Service is friendly and in summer the windows open out and there's a nice terrasse where you can sit sheltered from the traffic by the huge pots of bamboo plants. Clientele is a mix of glossy shoppers and the local rag-trade magnates who come wielding medallions and mobiles.

BARBARA BUI CAFÉ, 27 rue Étienne Marcel, 75001
Tel: 01 45 08 04 04
Métro: Étienne Marcel or Les Halles
Opening Hours: Mon–Sat: 12.00–19.00, 20.00–23.30
August: open
Credit Cards: Visa
Price Range: starter from 55FF, main course from 70FF, pudding 40FF

MISS CHINA: CHINA GIRL FASHION

For China girl fashion, come here. Owner Bonnie Tchien Hy is Chinese and runs her own style bureau in Paris as well as the Miss China and Miss China tea store opposite. She mixes elements of traditional Chinese costume like the Mao jacket and cheong-sam long dress with a dose of French styling and trend. The cheong-sam dress is basically the same, but recut to fit the Western figure and comes full length or to the knee in traditional red or gold embossed silk satin, as well as lilac or pale almond. The shop is a three-floor summer palace of Chinese kitschery – candy-floss-pink satin quilts, mini rice cookers and propaganda booklets. There are also Miss China accessories like a satin bag which is young and fun, but check on the seams before you buy; I always seem to find one fraying. She also does a wedding cheong-sam in white and gold with an enormous train, which can be made to measure and costs around 4,650FF.

MISS CHINA, 3 rue Française, 75001
Tel: 01 40 41 08 92
Métro: Les Halles or Étienne Marcel
Opening Hours: Tue–Sat: 11.00–19.00
August: closed
Credit Cards: Visa, Amex
Price Range: satin bags 195FF, short cheong-sam 1,250FF, black satin shirt with buttons down side 955FF, full-length cheong-sam 1,995FF

MISS CHINA TEA: TEA SALON

Directly opposite is the Miss China tea room. It's a doll's-house decor mixing battered leather seats with red tinselly table cloths and dainty chinese crockery. Open all day for green and black Chinese tea, they also do a light, guilt-free lunch such as noodle soup. You can buy loose tea and there are tea accessories such as a wicker picnic hamper containing a teapot and two cups.

MISS CHINA TEA, 4 rue Française, 75001
Tel: 01 40 41 69 84
Métro: Les Halles or Étienne Marcel
Opening Hours: Mon–Sat: 11.00–19.00
August: closed
Credit Cards: Visa, Amex
Price Range: tea 35–45FF

MISS CHINA KIDS: CHILDREN'S WEAR

This is a scaled-down version of Miss China clothes with sweet little kung-fu suits, mini Mao jackets in cotton, and adorable red silk slippers with beaded and sequinned flowers. There are also great big bloomers which come in bright silks and loud prints and are intended to hide bulky nappies.

MISS CHINA KIDS, 3 rue Française, 75001
Tel: 01 40 41 05 33
Métro: Les Halles or Étienne Marcel
Opening Hours: Mon–Sat: 11.00–19.00
August: closed
Credit Cards: Visa, Amex
Price Range: bloomers 125FF, reversible silk jackets from 250FF

KABUKI: DESIGNER WEAR
Kabuki bills itself as a designer shop specialising in accessories as the priority with the clothes to match. It is owned by William Halimi, husband of designer Barbara Bui, who has her own store practically next door, and his idea is to bring a bit of designer action to this end of the street and create their own competition. As the years go by the two of them have practically monopolised this end of the street what with Barbara Bui plus café and now three Kabuki stores, this one for womenswear, one further along the street for menswear and another small store selling the shoes from past collections.

Halimi is interested in one woman only and she is, he says, 'informed, élitist, looking for fashion with luxury'. He makes his buying selection in terms of product rather than designer, selling a look he describes as 'chic, modern, urban'. The ground floor is for accessories with handbags and luggage by Prada, Sergio Rossi and Miu Miu and shoes by Martine Sitbon, Rodolphe Menudier and the Italian pack – Prada, Sergio Rossi, Costume National and Miu Miu. Upstairs for womenswear there is slick fashion by Prada, Miu Miu, Helmut Lang, Martin Sitbon and Costume National and of course wardrobe staple pieces by Barbara Bui.

KABUKI, 25 rue Étienne Marcel, 75001
Tel: 01 42 33 55 65
Métro: Étienne Marcel
Opening Hours: Mon: 13.00–19.30, Tue–Sat: 10.30–19.30
August: open
Credit Cards: Visa, Amex, Diners, MC, JCB
Price Range: shoes from 1,000FF, bags from 1,200FF, trousers from 850FF, top from 800FF

BARBARA BUI: FASHIONABLE WOMENSWEAR
See 8th arrondissement for details.
23 rue Étienne Marcel, 75001. Tel: 01 40 26 43 65

KABUKI HOMME: DESIGNER MENSWEAR
Based on much the same concept and look as the womenswear Kabuki store, this shop has the men's accessories and clothes going from a casual sporty look through to smart suiting. The ground floor has nylon and leather bags, also travel bags, plus shoes, boots and trainers by Prada, Costume National, DKNY and Prada Sport. Upstairs there

are clothes by Prada, Miu Miu, Calvin Klein, Helmut Lang Jeans for men and women, Martine Sitbon and the phenomenally successful Prada Sport for both men and women.

KABUKI HOMME, 21 rue Étienne Marcel, 75001
Tel: 01 42 33 13 44
Métro: Étienne Marcel
Opening Hours: Mon: 13.00–19.30, Tue–Sat: 10.30–19.30
August: open
Credit Cards: Visa, Amex, Diners, MC, JCB
Price Range: trousers from 1,000FF, shoes from 1,200FF, suits 5,300–8,700FF

KABUKI AFTER: DESIGNER SHOE SALE SHOP

This is a great store for shoe bargains as it sells off all the unsold shoe stock from the Kabuki stores and is a bit of a bazaar stocking the previous season's footwear from Prada, Miu Miu, Martine Sitbon, Costume National and Rodophe Menudier for women, while for men there are shoes, boots and trainers from Calvin Klein, Prada, Michel Perry et al. Prices are reduced by 50% to 60%.

KABUKI AFTER, 13 rue de Turbigo, 75002
Tel: 01 42 36 44 34
Métro: Étienne Marcel
Opening Hours: Mon: 13.00–19.30, Tue–Sat: 10.30–19.30

August: open
Credit Cards: Visa, Amex, Diners, MC, JCB
Price Range: shoes from 800FF

ET VOUS STOCK: PERMANENT SALE SHOP

The sale shop for Et Vous is a little-known bargain spot selling Et Vous's men's and women's wear designed by Koji Tatsuno. The stock here is one year old and sold at 50% off. At the front are womenswear and accessories. It's the sort of place where if you're lucky, you'll pick up a pair of Cutler and Gross sunglasses at a third of the price. There are lots of basics like trouser suits, stretch jeans and knitwear as well as more seasonal pieces such as tweed coats, hooded tops and ponyskin jackets. There are shoes by Michel Perry and Patrick Cox. At the back of the shop you'll find Et Vous menswear which is much more classic jeans, linen jackets, Nehru suits (house special), ties and T-shirts. It is a good place to pick up men's casual shirts which are all priced at 200FF. At the end of May and December, they sell off all the press samples and prototypes from that season. The stock changes regularly every two weeks and the service is very friendly.

ET VOUS STOCK, 15–17 rue de Turbigo, 75002
Tel: 01 40 13 04 12
Métro: Étienne Marcel
Opening Hours: Mon–Sat: 12.00–19.00
August: closed 15–31 Aug
Credit Cards: Visa
Price Range: Patrick Cox loafers 400FF, women's brown suede jeans 800FF, jeans for men or women 200FF, pure wool men's suit 1,500FF

BRUUNS BAZAAR:
CASUAL MEN'S & WOMEN'S WEAR

Brothers Bjorn and Tais Bruuns are apparently fashion stars in their home town of Copenhagen; over here they are building a niche clientele of women who like their clothes layered, loose and casual. It's kind of bohemian Northern-style with apron dresses worn layered over satin trousers, pale prints, wide-legged trousers, ruffled skirts over visible petticoats. In winter things get cosy to withstand the Danish elements with thick felt trousers with wide turn-up hem, soft knits and floor-length coats. Woolly bonnets, knitted bags and padded coats could cause melt-down in an air-conditioned environment.

BRUUNS BAZAAR, 13 rue de Turbigo, 75002
Tel: 01 42 36 29 29
Métro: Étienne Marcel
Opening Hours: Mon: 13.00–19.00, Tue–Sat: 11.00–19.00
August: open
Credit Cards: Visa, Amex, Diners, MC, JCB
Price Range: from 300 to 2,000FF, trousers 1,195FF, padded satin skirt 995FF

ÉRIC ET LYDIE: FASHIONABLE JEWELLERY

Partners in love and life, Éric and Lydie make girly and fashionable jewellery. They launched at the end of 1994 by doing work for designer GR816 and since then have designed all the jewellery for Christian Lacroix's couture shows. Éric describes their style as slightly Victorian with hints of Italian Renaissance and they work a lot with stained antique-look metals in delicate designs. The result is contemporary with touches of retro – all the earrings, for example, are screw-on. There is a seriously pretty theme of snowflakes with clusters of small stones in orange, purple, copper or white which come in earrings, bracelets, necklaces and rings. Fashion-wise, what's popular are the skinny pink metal chokers which are lined with a smattering of red crystal and tie at the back with a slim red ribbon. Also available in green or turquoise, they look brilliant at night. The best seller is a set of five rings set with coloured crystal which twist around to fit together, price 330FF.

ÉRIC ET LYDIE, 7 passage du Grand Cerf, 75002
Tel/Fax: 01 40 26 52 59
Métro: Étienne Marcel
Opening Hours: Mon–Sat: 14.00–19.00
August: closed for part of month, call for exact dates
Credit Cards: Visa
Price Range: skinny metal choker with crystals 350FF, starlet hairgrip 40FF, prices tend to be under 1,000FF

LE DÉNICHEUR: KOOKY CAFÉ

A couple of years ago Frank Besegher was working as an undertaker at Père Lachaise cemetery. Now he owns this tiny and kooky café where you can buy not only a goat's cheese and basil omelette, but the vase that's displayed on a shelf or the plastic '50s knick-knack hanging on the wall. Food is fresh and simple, with all produce purchased that day from the nearby rue Montorgueil market. Frank's grandmother's recipes steal the show, such as a banana, honey and almond cake ('Everyone kept saying "mmmm this is good", so we called it "C'est bon",' shrugs Frank modestly), apricot crumble, double chocolate tart or creamy Saint Marcellin cheese on Poilâne toast. The place is kitted out in his flea-market finds and there are regular themed selling exhibitions, such as a riot of plastic snowflake paper weights. A little offbeat and raw, the place is hopping with rappers and Nike-shod shoppers. You need to book at lunch.

LE DÉNICHEUR, 4 rue Tiquetonne, 75002
Tel: 01 42 21 31 01
Métro: Étienne Marcel
Opening Hours: Mon: 19.00–2.00, Tue–Sun: 12.00–16.00, 19.00–2.00
August: closed for two weeks
Credit Cards: Visa
Price Range: weekend brunch 80FF, lunch menu 55FF, dinner menu 72FF

RUE MONTORGUEIL: FRUIT AND VEG MARKET

Les Halles food market is long dead, but rue Montorgueil lives on. More open-air shops rather than stalls, the cobbled street is always a highway for shoppers and chefs who come for the fresh fruit and veg. Delicious cheeses, fish, seafood, fresh pasta, wine, exotic florists, this is what Parisian lifestyle is all about. It was once the city's oyster market and it is a great old-fashioned Paris street with a complete mix of people. There are the stall-holders: butchers in bloody aprons, newspaper sellers and the sausage man; and the fashion PR and photographer set who laze around on the cafés' terrasses. And then there are all the gentle oddies who always come with a market, like one old clochard who turns up to sing to you as you sit outside. What claims to be the oldest bakery in Paris, Stohrer's, is at No. 51, stop at Little Italy for a serious coffee and for lunch try Le Centre Ville at No. 57. It serves a tasty toasted bruschetta at any time of the day. It's a wonderful lunch or pick-me-up snack for around 40FF.

KOOKAÏ LE STOCK: PERMANENT SALE SHOP

This is the permanent sale shop for Kookaï in Paris and it is gratifyingly cheap. It used to be the Kookaï headquarters before they moved out of the Sentier a couple of years ago and hence the store is massive. It is stocked with all the unsold clothing, shoes and accessories from the same season the previous year. Before you run screaming from your hotel for Kookaï kit: if you are British, it is not the same clothes you find back home. France and Britain have different collections and the French Kookaï look is much younger, often teenage with less of the trend pieces. That said, it is still a great place to stock up on T-shirts, knit tops, Capri pants, stretch jeans and tennis shoes. The tops are the best thing, with white V-neck T-shirts with satin-edging collars and great cotton and viscose ribbed crop sweaters. There are rows of print dresses which may be a bit adolescent-looking. There is no warehouse sale madness, it's well displayed and all the clothes are folded, but it does get packed on Saturdays. There is an incentive system for multiple purchases.

KOOKAÏ LE STOCK, 82 rue Réaumur, 75002
Tel: 01 45 08 93 69
Métro: Réaumur Sébastopol
Opening Hours: Mon–Sat: 10.00–18.30
August: open
Credit Cards: Visa, Amex, Diners, MC, JCB
Price Range: mostly 40–80FF, three 40FF pieces for 100FF, three 80FF for 200FF

AROUND LES HALLES

ST-EUSTACHE

This church at the bottom of rue Montmartre is one of Paris's most beautiful, and the city's second largest church after Notre-Dame. It is where Molière was christened and buried and where Louis XIV took his first communion. When the market was just in front, it was the church of the stall-holders and inside is a chapel with a lovely frieze in celebration and memory of the people of the market. If you are around on Sunday there are short organ recitals at 5.30pm and you can come and go as you like.

AGNÈS B.: QUINTESSENTIAL FRENCH WOMENSWEAR

Agnès b. epitomises a certain French look – it's timeless but of the moment, it's classic yet somehow very cool (witness the whole cast of *Pulp Fiction* dressed in Agnès b.). She is to basics what Lacroix is to lace. The womenswear store here is enormous with all the Agnès b. essentials for life, the neat grey wool gabardine trouser suit, the fab cut black leather jeans (she wears them all the time), silk satin shirts and delicate print dresses. They are clothes meant for a modern, working woman, which is exactly what Agnès b. herself is, with five children and an annual turnover of $247 million when last disclosed.

Now in her mid-fifties, Agnès likes to play down her design process and says it's all instinct, that she never goes into a clothes shop, never sees what other designers are up to. If that's the case she must have some extra-sensory device for picking up on fashion, because she's got all the trends every season. But she's smart enough to offer more than just trend – she does skirts in every length from short to maxi, trousers in every shape from cigarette cut to palazzo. That way, her clothes appeal to a wide range of women. One common denominator across the women's collections is that the cut is lean. She has kept her left-wing philanthropic principles, still hands out condoms for free, and is a major patron of contemporary French and international art. Agnès b. stores in this street can kit out the whole family: menswear is at No. 3, children's wear at No. 2 and a travel/decor store at No. 10.

AGNÈS B., 6 rue du Jour, 75001
Tel: 01 45 08 56 56
Métro: Les Halles or Étienne Marcel
also at:
6 rue du Vieux Colombier, 75006. Tel: 01 44 39 02 60
Opening Hours: Mon–Sat: 10.00–19.30
August: open
Credit Cards: Visa, Amex, MC
Price Range: T-shirt 160–240FF, knitwear 460–820FF, black leather trousers 3,600FF, jackets from 1,400F, knee-length skirts from 780FF, cigarette-cut trousers 680FF

INDIES: ELEGANT WOMENSWEAR
See 6th arrondissement for details.
4 rue du Jour, 75001. Tel: 01 40 13 91 27

AGNÈS B. ENFANT: FRENCH CHILDREN'S WEAR
Basically this is Agnès b. scaled down to fit babies and kids up to the age of 16. She uses the same fabrics and prints as the main collection, although shapes are obviously different and one can't help noticing the prices aren't particularly scaled down. The clothes are cute: popper sweatshirts in sugary shades, chic white cotton canvas rompers and, most adorable, the white fleecy baby-gros with b. b. written across the front, as in bébé.

AGNÈS B. ENFANT, 2 rue du Jour, 75001
Tel: 01 40 39 96 88
Métro: Les Halles or Étienne Marcel
Opening Hours: Mon–Sat: 10.00–19.00
August: open
Credit Cards: Visa, Amex, MC, JCB
Price Range: baby pyjamas 320FF, popper sweatshirts 280–320FF, girl's dress from 280FF

PÔLES: CHIC KNITWEAR
See 6th arrondissement for details.
17 rue du Jour, 75001. Tel: 01 45 08 93 67

LA DROGUERIE: HABERDASHERY AND WOOL
You know all those handy hints in magazines about changing buttons on a cheap jacket to make it look smarter, or buying an inexpensive unlined jacket and then lining it? French women actually do all that. And they come here to indulge their haberdashery habit. The shop has the best selection of stylish buttons and braiding. There's a crazy variety of jewellery beads, from bubble-gum glass bits to wooden olives, as well as feathers of every colour for hat trimming. They also sell reams of wool, angora, silk and cotton for knitting and there are sweaters hanging up that the atelier has knitted up to show new techniques or yarns, like a chainmail knit sweater in pewter viscose. The store is always packed in the afternoons.

LA DROGUERIE, 9–11 rue du Jour, 75001
Tel: 01 45 08 93 27
Métro: Les Halles
Opening Hours: Mon: 14.00–18.45, Tue–Sat: 10.30–18.45
August: Tue–Sat: 13.00–18.45
Credit Cards: none
Price Range: buttons 1FF–120FF for marble buttons, beads 50 centimes–30FF each

MOKUBA: RIBBONS

More haberdashery – this Japanese store sells 37,000 different kinds of ribbons including iridescent, palest metallic organzas, pleated taffetas, wide velvet and ridged silk ottoman. There is also lots of frogging, lace, leather fringing and silk cording. All the Paris hat-makers come here, as do the couture teams from fashion houses like Dior, Chanel and Lacroix. If you're into making your own clothes and accessories you're going to love it.

MOKUBA, 18 rue Montmartre, 75001
Tel: 01 40 13 81 41
and there's a smaller Mokuba boutique just along the road at No. 26
Métro: Les Halles
Opening Hours: Mon–Fri: 9.30–18.30
August: closed
Credit Cards: Visa
Price Range: 75 centimes–15FF a metre

CLAUDIE PIERLOT: COOL FRENCH FASHION

Claudie Pierlot is what the French call Titi Paris dressing. The look is pure Robert Doisneau – clothes to be worn at a bar in Montmartre with a bottle of Bordeaux and an accordion playing. It's not trendy, but it hints at all the trends. If you're looking for clothing which is oh-so-Paris and at high street prices, come straight here. The cut is petite, which works OK for the tops and coats, but suiting and trousers come out narrow. In summer there are always print swing skirts and plain and pretty shift dresses with maybe a halter neck to make the difference. Stripy ribbed knits in apple green, navy and white are teamed with white Capri pants. There's always a retro taste to the collections whether in the prints, which can be inspired by a scrap of fabric Claudie found at the puces (flea market), or in the colours she uses, like a moss green or deep burgundy. She believes in keeping the outfit simple, but taking it from day to night by changing the hair, shoes and jewellery – rule number one in the essential Parisian dress code.

CLAUDIE PIERLOT, 1 rue Montmartre, 75001
Tel: 01 42 21 38 38
Métro: Les Halles or Étienne Marcel
also at:
23 rue du Vieux Colombier, 75006. Tel: 01 45 48 11 96
Opening Hours: Mon–Sat: 10.30–19.00
August: closed first three weeks, call for exact dates
Credit Cards: Visa, Amex, MC
Price Range: T-shirt 190FF, coat 3,000FF, dresses 800FF, suit 1,200–1,500FF

MON AMI PIERLOT: WEEKEND LINE

More of the same but this time cheaper basics or holiday clothing. At the front of the store is womenswear with the Pierlot classic marin sweater in tomato-red and cream stripes. There are African batik print sundresses, zip-up navy wool cardigans and quirky odds and ends like clogs or moped goggles. There is a little section of kiddies' wear, then right at the back is the menswear.

MON AMI PIERLOT, 3 rue Montmartre, 75001
Tel: 01 40 28 45 55
Métro: Les Halles or Étienne Marcel
Opening Hours: Mon–Sat: 10.30–19.00
August: closed first three weeks, call for exact dates
Credit Cards: Visa, Amex, MC
Price Range: T-shirts 45FF, stripy marin sweater 410FF, zip-up cardigan 500FF, men's cord jacket 975FF

FREE: FUNKY WOMENSWEAR

See 8th arrondissement for details.
8–10 rue Montmartre, 75001. Tel: 01 42 33 15 52

GHOST: FASHIONABLE WOMENSWEAR

Tanya Sarne makes whimsical dresses which speak sexy in an undone way; it's a look to be worn with a rough chignon and lip-gloss (see Helena Christiansen or Jemima Khan for details). The keys to Ghost's success are several: first the fabric (a soft viscose which is put through a lengthy production process including being shrunk, dyed and then reshaped) which moves and flatters when on the body; second the fact that Ghost can be worn just as easily by a teenage girl as by a mother of four. Styles are always kept simple: bias-cut slip dresses and cardigans, skirts, little tops with ruffled detail at the sleeve or full-length djellabas. Colours for summer are Caribbean shades of aqua, white, pink and oyster, while for winter colours are deeper and darker ranging from plum through to black. There are always several more 'fabulous' pieces with added detail such as embroidery or georgette insets.

GHOST, 33 rue du Jour, 75001
Tel: 01 44 82 01 13
Métro: Les Halles or Étienne Marcel
Opening Hours: Mon–Sat: 10.30–19.00
August: closed for ten days
Credit Cards: Visa, Amex
Price Range: tops from 500FF, basic dress 1,000FF

SCOOTER: TREND JEWELLERY

Cheap teenage junky jewellery – check it out. Avoid the lightweight ethnic look which really is cheap and go for the kitsch. There are

identity bracelets as worn in Photo Love teenage magazines and you can pick your dedication of 'Sexy', 'Bébé' or 'Only You' on a baby-blue or sugar-pink background. Also cool are nylon crocheted shopping bags in custard yellow or deep purple, and heaps of coloured paste and pretty crystal jewellery. Scooter is also available at stands in the major Paris department stores.

SCOOTER, 10 rue de Turbigo, 75001
Tel: 01 45 08 50 54
Métro: Étienne Marcel
also at:
12 rue Guichard, 75016. Tel: 01 45 20 23 27
Opening Hours: Mon–Fri: 10.00–19.00, Sat: 11.00–19.00
August: call for details
Credit Cards: Visa, Amex, MC, JCB
Price Range: rings 45–395FF, crocheted shopping bag 165FF

MOSQUITOS: FUNKY FOOTWEAR
See 6th arrondissement for details.
19 rue Pierre Lescot, 75001. Tel: 01 45 08 44 72

FREE LANCE: FASHIONABLE FOOTWEAR
See 6th arrondissement for details.
22 rue Mondétour, 75001. Tel: 01 42 33 74 70

MONDO SHOP GROUP: SLINKY CLUBWEAR
Club girls only need apply. No matter what the trends, designer Tim Bargeot does Bardot meets Bond girl: custard-yellow feather bras, red vinyl shift dresses with strategic gaps, holograms, neoprene – think daring, think diet. It opens on Saturday afternoon and is soon packed with boys handing out flyers and party girls out to blow their cash.

MONDO SHOP GROUP, 3 rue de Turbigo, 75001
Tel: 01 42 21 31 77
Métro: Les Halles or Étienne Marcel
Opening Hours: Mon–Fri: 11.00–19.30, Sat: 12.30–19.30
August: open
Credit Cards: Visa, Amex
Price Range: vinyl shift dress 500FF, towelling T-shirts 100FF, gold sequin
hot-pants 295FF

MARIA: SKIMPY TOPS AND DRESSES

It's an uninspiring shop front, but inside are body-beautiful cotton and viscose knit tops, bikinis, cache-coeurs and dresses. It's a sexy look, but not tacky. You need a tan and upwardly mobile breasts to get away with some pieces and according to Maria's mum she designs for 'young, pretty, well-made women'.

MARIA, 28 rue Pierre Lescot, 75001
Tel: 01 40 13 06 00
Métro: Étienne Marcel
Opening Hours: Mon–Sat: 10.00–20.00
August: open
Credit Cards: Visa, Amex, MC
Price Range: all tops 290–390FF, halter-neck dress 690FF

RAG TIME: ANTIQUE FRENCH FASHION

On the other side of the gardens of Les Halles you will find Rag Time where in a crush of a boutique, Françoise Auguet sells antique French clothing. Some is couture, some is not and the earliest pieces date from the end of the 19th century although she tends to specialise in the '20s through to the '50s. All cleavage and fag ash, Françoise sits on the phone in the tiny shop organising the annual auction of haute couture at the Hôtel Drouot salesroom. She saves the best couture pieces she finds for museums and private collectors, the rest comes to the shop. You need to poke around to find pieces, but Françoise is very relaxed about that. You can pull out a Balenciaga summer dress in raspberry satin façonnée or a Chanel 1950s silk suit in stripes of pink and red. If you are slimmish it's a brilliant place to find evening dresses. Françoise adores the 1930s, so there are always plenty of bias cut silk satin dresses which look very Galliano. There are hat boxes and hats from cruising lurex turbans to a Givenchy dashing black velvet number. And then there are the cardboard boxes of gloves, shawls, underwear and swimming costumes (one box full of 1940s costumes she calls the 'Ralph Lauren' box). She is known for having a great selection of wedding dresses and Saturday afternoon is always blooming with brides-to-be. She works with an alterations team who, depending on the piece, can make things slightly bigger, as well as smaller.

RAG TIME, 23 rue du Roule, 75001
Tel: 01 42 36 89 36
Métro: Louvre-Rivoli or Châtelet
Opening Hours: Mon–Sat: 14.30–19.30
August: sometimes open, sometimes closed – call her
Credit Cards: none
Price Range: hats 200–1,500FF, Balenciaga summer dress 3,500FF, Chanel couture silk suit 3,000FF, wedding dresses 1,500–15,000FF, suiting 900–1,500FF

LE MARAIS
(3RD AND 4TH ARRONDISSEMENTS)

The Marais couple are artsy with cash. Together they walk the cobbled streets dressed in his-and-hers Issey Miyake and looking for fashion which is off the conventional wall, slipping in a museum or four between stores. An idyllic setting of crammed streets and secret courtyards, the Marais is full of artists, writers, film-makers, painters and architects; designers Azzedine Alaïa and John Galliano are both residents.

Stretching across the 3rd and 4th arrondissements, the Marais is long on intimate charm, with a clutch of 17th-century town mansions like the fabulous Hôtel de Sully on the south side of Paris's oldest square, place des Vosges. A heartachingly romantic square built by Henri IV at the beginning of the 17th century, place des Vosges attracts the kind of buskers who turn up in a string quartet and play Chopin. The streets are overdosed with bars, salons de thé and restaurants. When the weather is fine check out the secluded and beautiful Marché Ste-Catherine where you can sit in the sun and sip kirs. At night-time, try Anahï on rue Volta, an Argentinian restaurant which is wall-to-wall fashion with regulars like Helmut Lang and Rei Kawakubo, or Italian restaurant L'Osteria on rue de Sévigné for a buzzy scene and heavenly risotto.

The area, cut through by the main rue St-Antoine, is about a ten-minute walk from Notre-Dame. Culturally, it's dynamic, with some fifteen museums ranging from the Musée Picasso to the museum of hunting and nature. What makes it exciting is its people-mix, with the old Jewish area of rue des Rosiers and rue des Écouffes situated adjacent to the new gay Paris, which is based around rue Saint Croix de la Brettonerie and has a friendly, happening bar scene. To the north is the 3rd arrondissement which is where Paris cutting-edge contemporary art galleries meet shamelessly tacky bag and belt wholesalers, between the Centre Pompidou and the Musée Picasso. Everything is close in the Marais, so it means you can shop, eat and culturally achieve all in one session.

Rue des Francs Bourgeois is a main Marais artery and lined with stores, a lot of them selling stylish kit for the home, but don't be afraid to break away into the streets off it and don't miss rue des Rosiers – a destination fashion zone. Along this narrow cobbled road, between kosher butchers and Jewish delis is L'Éclaireur, a great source for designer clothing. Come Sunday the street reclaims its right as thoroughfare of the Jewish community and the place is buzzing. Stop at any of the cafés for a great snack of falafel or pickled herring. Unlike the rest of Paris, the Marais is one of the few areas where many of the stores stay open on Sunday.

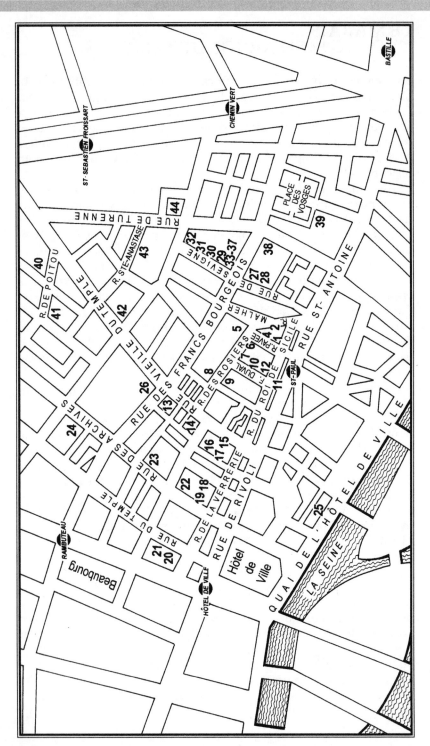

A shopper's Guide to Paris Fashion

1 CARAVANE
2 SISSO'S
3 PAULE KA
4 LE LOIR EST DANS LA THÉIÉRE
5 ICB
6 PLEATS PLEASE
7 L'ÉCLAIREUR
8 MARTIN GRANT
9 MILLER ET BERTAUX
10 EXTREM ORIGIN
11 L'AMATCHI
12 ALTERNATIVES
13 ORDNING & REDA
14 LA BELLE HORTENSE
15 LE MOUTON A CINQ PATTES
16 ANATOMICA
17 FREE LANCE POUR HOMMES
18 AZZEDINE ALAÏA
19 LE PAIN QUOTIDIEN
20 GAMMES DE
21 LA BOUTIQUE
22 CLOÎTRE DES BILLETTES

23 LES BAINS DU MARAIS
24 LES ARCHIVES DE LA PRESSE
25 GALERIE 88
26 NICKEL
27 PLEIN SUD
28 DEVANA
29 CHRISTOPHE LEMAIRE
30 LA LICORNE
31 ATSURO TAYAMA
32 COMPTOIR DE L'IMAGE
33 AUTOUR DU MONDE
34 ANNE FONTAINE
35 VENTILO
36 HOME AUTOUR DU MONDE
37 ET VOUS
38 CAMPER
39 ISSEY MIYAKE
40 L'HABILLEUR
41 DOMINIQUE PICQUIER
42 JOSÉ LÉVY A PARIS
43 FRÉDÉRIC SANCHEZ
44 ADELINE ANDRÉ

ON AND AROUND RUE DES ROSIERS

CARAVANE: STYLISH INTERIORS

This is a stylish interiors and textiles store which does a great line of giant, oversized sofas. Now obviously if you're over for the weekend on Eurostar you might not fancy lugging a sofa home (although they do deliver), but it is also a source for gifts and furnishings. As the name suggests there is a definite ethnic feel with pieces bought from India, Morocco, Vietnam, Uzbekistan, although the store never slips into folk-land, but is rather cosmopolitan with urban polish. There are chunky leather poufs in hot pink or burnt orange, creamy rice-paper lanterns, cross-dyed silk velvet cushion covers and billowing organdie curtains. Gift ideas include silk sleeping-bag sheets (brilliant for travelling on trains or staying in that slightly peeling hotel) and hand-embroidered Suzani throws from Central Asia, which make wonderful throws over furniture.

CARAVANE, 6 rue Pavée, 75004
Tel: 01 44 61 04 20
Métro: St-Paul
Opening Hours: Tue–Sat: 11.00–19.00
August: closed for one week
Credit Cards: Visa, MC
Price Range: leather pouf 750FF, silk sleeping-bag sheets 200FF

SISSO'S: ACCESSORIES

See 6th arrondissement for details.
20 rue Mahler, 75004. Tel: 01 44 61 99 50

PAULE KA: SMART CHIC WOMENSWEAR

Serge Cajfinger's look for Paule Ka label is all about the Parisian take on style – that means sexy, not tarty, glamorous, not mutton dressed as lamb. His inspiration is 1960s and the inevitable 'Jackie O, Audrey Hepburn, Grace Kelly' triumvirate which shows in cotton piqué summer dresses and graphic black and white shifts. For daywear there are fitted trouser suits or skirts chopped the obligatory above-the-knee French length which are intended for the trim figure aged 30 to 50 and a wealthy urban lifestyle. Store director Madame Puibaraud knows her customer and can put together a working wardrobe which will take you through from ballroom to boardroom with the emphasis on getting the whole kit there – hat, bag, shoes, jewellery – rather than spending a day running round Paris trying to make up an outfit.

PAULE KA, 20 rue Malher, 75004
Tel: 01 40 29 96 03
Métro: St-Paul
also at:

192 boulevard St-Germain, 75007. Tel: 01 45 44 92 60
Opening Hours: Mon–Sat: 10.30–13.00, 14.00–19.00 (Sat open over lunch)
August: open
Credit cards: Visa, Amex, MC
Price Range: knitwear from 600FF, suiting 4,500FF, cocktail dress from 3,500FF

LE LOIR EST DANS LA THÉIÈRE: TEA ROOM

Scoring high on scruffy charm, this is where you can flake into a busted leather armchair and sip a cup of thyme infusion or real hot chocolate, depending on your calorie control. Cool, laid back and spacious salon de thé with a sideboard of cakes to choose from; they serve great chunks of walnut cake or tarte salée (a superior kind of quiche) like courgette and goat's cheese or crab and sorrel. Friendly mix of clientele from shoppers to writers and you can hang out for as long as you like during the week reading their newspapers and mags – at weekends you tend to get moved on more quickly as the place is often packed. Weekend brunch is a very popular meal and priced at 110–130FF.

LE LOIR EST DANS LA THÉIÈRE, 3 rue des Rosiers, 75004
Tel: 01 42 72 90 61
Métro: St-Paul
Opening Hours: 12.00–18.30
August: closed for two weeks, call for exact dates
Credit Cards: none
Price range: omelette 30FF, coffee 20FF, tarte salée 45FF

ICB: FASHIONABLE BASICS

Conceived as the own label of Japanese fashion group Kashiyama, this line was always intended as a collection of fashionable basics. At the outset it was designed by American Michael Kors but since he left to head up Céline, ICB is now in the hands of a team of stylists in Japan who seem to be taking the word basic a little too literally. Nice knitwear.

ICB, 2 bis rue des Rosiers, 75004
Tel: 01 49 96 61 00
Métro: St-Paul
Opening Hours: Mon–Fri: 11.00–19.00, Sat: 10.00–19.00
August: open except Mon
Credit Cards: Visa, Amex, Diners, MC, JCB
Price Range: trousers 1,000FF, jacket 2,000FF, skirt 600FF, knitwear 390-1,000FF

PLEATS PLEASE: ISSEY MIYAKE'S SECOND LINE

See 7th arrondissement for details.
3 bis rue des Rosiers, 75004. Tel: 01 40 29 99 66

L'ÉCLAIREUR:

FASHION AND INTERIORS

For international designer fashion, L'Éclaireur is a key destination. Owner Armand Hadida has three stores in Paris and he prides himself on selling the avant-garde of fashion and design or, as he puts it, 'We consider fashion and design as an artistic movement rather than a business.' That's as may be, but come collection time this store resembles more of a store check-out than a museum, with the fashion crowd swarming round to buy the season's key pieces.

The Marais store has both womenswear on the ground floor and menswear in the basement. Hadida's taste is eclectic and includes for women clothes by Margiela, Dries Van Noten, Ann Demeulemeester, Marni, Yohji and Junya Watanabe as well as newer talent such as Josephus Thimister, Kostas Murkudis, Maharishi and Carol Christian Poell. For menswear there is Margiela, Dries and Ann again, as well as Prada and Prada Sport, Jil Sander, Helmut Lang and Mandarina Duck who have diversified from bags and now do a clothes collection as well.

L'Éclaireur is for you if you are reasonably self-assured about your look, as in you are not searching for advice, but rather you've seen the piece and want to buy it.

L'ÉCLAIREUR, 3 ter rue des Rosiers, 75004
Tel: 01 48 87 10 22
Métro: St-Paul
also at:
24 rue de L'Échaudé, 75006. Tel: 01 44 27 08 03
26 avenue des Champs-Élysées, 75008. Tel: 01 45 62 12 32
Opening Hours: Mon: 14.00–19.00, Tue–Sat: 10.30–19.00
August: closed 3–26 Aug
Credit Cards: Visa, Amex, Diners, MC, JCB
Price Range: suiting 4,000–5,000FF, men's suiting 4,000–5,000FF

L'Éclaireur · Rue des Rosiers

MARTIN GRANT: DESIGNER WOMENSWEAR

For some time Australian designer Martin Grant's boutique was kept a closely guarded secret among the Paris fashion cognoscenti. But ever since American Vogue fashion titan André Leon Talley turned up to Martin's show bringing along Naomi as 'house' model, things have heated up. Cate Blanchett has been in to pick out a beautifully cut cherry-red wool dress and both his ready-to-wear and his made-to-measure service are in demand. Grant has lived in Paris for over six years and it shows – his clothes are a cool take on contemporary Paris chic. He makes structured women's wear using sophisticated cutting techniques to render simple, strong silhouettes with, in his words, 'very little decoration'. What detail there is tends to come in the cut and structure of the clothes, for instance a 'Napoleon' winter coat with brilliant horizontal seaming. He is also a favourite with brides looking for alternative glamour for whom he comes up with original dresses such as an organic wedding dress featuring a growing green lawn train.

MARTIN GRANT, 32 rue des Rosiers, 75004
Tel: 01 42 71 39 49
Métro: St-Paul
Opening Hours: Tue–Sat: 13.00–19.30
August: closed for two weeks, call for dates
Credit Cards: Visa, Amex
Price Range: skirts from 700FF, trousers from 800FF, jackets from 2,500FF, winter coats from 4,100FF

MILLER ET BERTAUX: ZEN LIFESTYLE/CLOTHES

Tinkling new-age music on the sound system and seriously disciplined shop display reflect the Zen sentiment of this lifestyle store. Patrick Bertaux and Francis Miller have an eclectic, at times off-beat and humorous taste and their product ranges from clothes and jewellery to ceramics and CDs. Displayed on scrubbed wooden tables are necklaces made from huge baubles of grey felt, sugar-free home-made jams, ceramics by Jonathan Adler and resin chunky rings bearing the message 2000. On the walls hang words such as 'Spirit', 'Imagination', 'Silence', while on the rails hang linen, cotton and felt clothes – drawstring trouser and loose dresses – ideal wear in which to practise your Tai Chi.

MILLER ET BERTAUX, 17 rue Ferdinand Duval, 75004
Tel: 01 42 78 28 39
Métro: St-Paul
Opening Hours: Mon: 14.00–19.00, Tue–Sat: 11.00–13.30, 14.00–19.00
August: closed
Credit Cards: Visa, Diners, Amex, MC
Price Range: 30–2,000FF, trousers from 1,200FF, dress from 2,500FF

EXTREM ORIGIN: STYLISH HOMEWARE

Natural and ethnic-influenced interiors are forever fashionable in Paris and here is a shop that does it beautifully without ever slipping into the relentlessly beige. There are pots, vases, bowls and boxes which are in simple, round, organic shapes. Designer Carine Tontini likes to work with modest woods, making them desirable through redesign. She spends six months a year in Burma, Vietnam and Thailand sourcing wood like the mango, then working with artisans abroad and in France who turn and finish the wood by hand. All the objects are made from one piece of wood and are stained and polished from a light brown to deepest ebony colour. There are also lamp stands made from paper or bamboo roots and ceramics. The ceramics come mostly in tan and cream with vases, pots and a candle cushion – which is a plain cream pad of ceramic with a little spike for a candle.

EXTREM ORIGIN, 10 rue Ferdinand Duval, 75004
Tel: 01 42 72 70 10
Métro: St-Paul
Opening Hours: Tue–Sat: 11.00–19.30, Sun: 14.30–19.30
August: closed for two weeks, call for exact dates
Credit Cards: Visa, Amex, MC, JCB
Price Range: ceramic vase 200FF, set of hand-made paper and envelopes 60FF, thick paper photo albums 120FF

L'AMATCHI: SMART UNDERWEAR

Tucked away in a quiet street, L'Amatchi is where you go for discreet underwear shopping. Owner Denise sells just a few brands and for women the look is pretty, sexy or sporty with a splash of colour. There is lingerie by Spanish brand André Sardà, tights by Philippe Matignon and in the winter luxury silk and wool mix vests by Hanro. During the summer you will find swimming costumes and bikinis by Capucine Puerari. For men Denise sells underwear by Hanro, Abella and British designer John Crummay.

L'AMATCHI, 13 rue du Roi de Sicile, 75004
Tel: 01 40 29 97 14
Métro: St-Paul
Opening Hours: Mon: 14.30–19.30, Tue–Sat: 11.30–19.30
August: closed for two weeks, call for dates
Credit Cards: Visa, Amex
Price Range: knickers from 150FF, bras from 300FF, swimming costumes from 695FF

ALTERNATIVES: SECONDHAND DESIGNER WEAR

This is a dépôt-vente store which means it sells used clothes. The dépôt-vente is a well-known Paris system for picking up designer wear and there are lots around, but they vary massively in standard and style. Alternatives specialises in more avant-garde designer wear for men and women and is one of the best for not only range, but also the condition of the clothes. Prices are around a third of the original price and a piece may be from the current collection or more likely date from a couple of seasons ago. For women there is always a good selection of Miyake's Pleats Please line as well as bits from his main collection, also Prada, Gucci, Yamamoto, Comme des Garçons, Ann Demeulemeester, Dries Van Noten and Martin Margiela. There is the odd work suit by Irié and Agnès b., and sometimes a leather jacket or skirt from A.P.C. Designers change according to what people bring in, but that is the basic stable of names. For men it is good for suiting and jackets from designers like Sonia Rykiel, Paul Smith, Kenzo, Armani and Gaultier. There is a small selection of shoes from Kélian, Clergerie and a rare pair of Manolo's.

ALTERNATIVES, 18 rue du Roi de Sicile, 75004
Tel: 01 42 78 31 50
Métro: St-Paul
also at:
130 rue du Bac, 75007. Tel: 01 42 22 73 66
Opening Hours: Tue–Sat: 11.00–13.00, 14.30–19.00
August: closed 20 Jul–20 Aug
Credit Cards: Visa
Price Range: Ann Demeulemeester strappy silk dress 660FF, Miyake jacket from main line 1,300FF, A.P.C. leather mini skirt and jacket 1,300FF, men's suit 1,500–2,000FF

RUE VIEILLE DU TEMPLE AND WEST

ORDNING & REDA: STATIONERY

Swedish store Ordning & Reda brings out the stationery fetishist in you. Reasonably priced and well designed, their stationery range aims to be stylish but practical. They are great for notebooks, diaries with understated toile cover and a brilliant range of photo albums with thick black paper pages. Ordning & Reda colours used to be just a little too primary, but they are getting more daring and adding lilacs and purples. Mindful of the stationery fetishist's sensitive nature, they pledge continuity (so you won't have your favourite A5 dove-grey bound notebook with plain white sheets discontinued before your very eyes) and they are p.c. about using lots of recycled products to make paper. Wide selection of well-priced fountain pens.

ORDNING & REDA, 53 rue Vieille du Temple, 75004
Tel: 01 48 87 86 32
Métro: St-Paul or Hôtel de Ville
Opening Hours: Tue–Sat: 11.00–19.30, Sun/Mon: 14.00–19.30
August: open
Credit Cards: Visa, Amex, MC, JCB
Price Range: photo album 75–425FF, pen from 15FF, notebooks from 20FF

LA BELLE HORTENSE: LITERARY WINE BAR

Only in France could you open a literary wine bar selling books along-side bottles of Bordeaux. Effortlessly cool, La Belle Hortense is either a nice hang-out for sipping a glass of Saint Martin de la Garrigue while perched at the bar or a local bookshop for picking up your fill of contemporary French fiction – depending on your angle. There are over 2,000 titles, with poetry readings every Wednesday night at 20.00 and regular book signings. Above all there is something terribly civilised about being able to cruise the bookshelves and pick out your titles with glass of wine in hand.

LA BELLE HORTENSE, 31 rue Vieille du Temple, 75004
Tel: 01 48 04 71 60
Métro: St-Paul
Opening Hours: every day: 13.00–20.00
August: open
Credit Cards: Visa, MC
Price Range: glass of wine from 16FF, bottle of wine to take away from 39FF, books from 6.50FF

LE MOUTON A CINQ PATTES: SALE SHOP

Probably the most overrated designer sale shop in Paris. Some people swear by it, but frankly unless you're lucky it's the sort of shop you have to visit every lunch hour for a year before you find the designer dream of a bargain in just your size. Set up nearly 40 years ago in St-Germain, it was the original designer sale shop in Paris and for many a way of life. Whichever fab designers it may once have sold, now you're more likely to find a load of obscure middle-market Italian, German and Belgian beige brands rather than some illustrious design-er label.

LE MOUTON A CINQ PATTES, 15 rue Vieille du Temple, 75004
Tel: 01 42 71 86 30
Métro: St-Paul
Opening Hours: Mon: 14.00–19.30, Tue–Sat: 10.30–14.00, 15.00–19.30 (Sat until 20.00)
August: open
Credit Cards: Visa, Amex
Price Range: 50–1,200FF, prices are usually reduced by a third

ANATOMICA: BODY-FRIENDLY DRESSING

Dressed in a sailor's cap and dungarees, Pierre Fournier talks in rid-dles about his store Anatomica: 'We're the specialists in speciality, nothing is "new" and we're non-designer.' High on eccentricity, Fournier sells essential and 'body-friendly' clothes for men and women. His real obsession is with shoes and selling 'shoes in the shape of feet, to avoid making your feet into the shape of shoes'. He stocks the biggest selection of Birkenstock in Paris, also Blundstone, vegetable-dyed Trippen shoes and Berkemann chunky soles. Then there are the clothes (if you like Muji, you'll love this), which include French workman cotton canvas trousers, a copy of those worn by carpenters at the turn of the century.

ANATOMICA, 14 rue du Bourg-Tibourg, 75004
Tel: 01 42 74 10 20
Métro: Hôtel de Ville
Opening Hours: Mon–Sat: 10.30–19.00, Sun: 14.30–19.00
August: open
Credit Cards: Visa, Amex, MC
Price Range: shoes around 640FF, worker's linen jacket 540FF

FREE LANCE POUR HOMMES:
DESIGNER FOOTWEAR
See 6th arrondissement for details.
16 rue du Bourg-Tibourg, 75004. Tel: 01 42 77 01 55

AZZEDINE ALAÏA: DESIGNER WOMENSWEAR
Ever since his arrival in Paris from Tunisia in 1957, Azzedine Alaïa has always had wealthy, glamorous women with designs on his designs. He studied sculpture at the École des Beaux-Arts in Tunisia and it shows. His clothes have a depth of research, cut and volume which set him apart. Everyone screams that his curvaceous kit is for supermodel proportions only, but he's too talented for just that – Alaïa knows

how to flatter a woman's shape and designs for real figures. Those elasthane dresses may be curve-conscious, but they can look fabulous on a 15- or 50-year-old. Tina Turner wears Alaïa and he not only designed Stephanie Seymour's wedding dress but also hosted the reception at his home/studio in the Marais. For a while now he has opted out of the designer calendar, not doing fashion shows but showing his collection privately and a lot later than anyone else, although word is that he is working to get back into the rhythm.

He has converted an enormous 19th-century steel building, once the warehouse for the department store BHV, into his home, boutique and atelier. So discreet is the Alaïa sign – and not a shop window in sight – that at least once a week some poor darling has to get her chauffeur to drive round the block several times before she finds it. Buzz for admittance (the welcome is sub-zero) and there you are in an enormous space decorated by painter Julian Schnabel. It is one of those stores where you find the clothes rails are in fact one-off Schnabel bronze sculptures. The changing room is big enough to hold a drinks party. In a courtyard round the back of the store is the permanent sale shop of Alaïa which sells all the samples, old stock and odds and ends.

AZZEDINE ALAÏA, 7 rue de Moussy, 75004
Tel: 01 42 72 19 19
Métro: Hôtel de Ville
also at:
18 rue de la Verrerie, 75004 (sale shop). Tel: 01 42 72 19 19
Opening Hours: Mon–Sat: 10.00–19.00
August: open
Credit Cards: Visa, Amex, Diners, MC
Price Range: leather jacket 13,000FF, leather skirt 6,000FF, wool knit dress 4,900FF, short knit skirt 1,800FF

LE PAIN QUOTIDIEN: LUNCH/BRUNCH STOP
See 1st arrondissement for details.
18 rue des Archives, 75004. Tel: 01 44 54 03 07

GAMMES DE: DESIGNER SALE SHOP
A sale shop selling off the previous year's Guy Laroche stock. The fact that there has been rapid turnover in the Guy Laroche design job over the last few years means that you never know quite what to expect in here. On the whole you're looking at a fairly classic, French chic style for a woman aged 35 and up and it's a good place if you're looking for suits. Prices are reduced by 60% and sizing goes from 8 to 18. All labels are ignominiously cut out at the till.

GAMMES DE, 17 rue du Temple, 75004
Tel: 01 48 04 57 57
Métro: Hôtel de Ville
Opening Hours: Mon–Sat: 10.00–19.00
August: open
Credit Cards: Visa, MC
Price Range: Guy Laroche suits from 2,000FF

LA BOUTIQUE: YOUNG DESIGNERS' COOPERATIVE
La Boutique is a cooperative shop for young designers based in Paris. It usually stocks clothes by about nine different designers who are not completely new but have done five or more collections. The designers all hire a space to sell their collection and take turns coming in to work as the sales assistant. It's a funky, laid-back atmosphere with swathes of calico hanging from the ceiling, a low-slung steel chaise longue in the middle of the room with a setter dog asleep on it. Designers and their styles vary dramatically, from slinky Lycra by Erotokritos to more structured padded clothes by Japanese Yoshi Kondo and Hannoh's

97

modern simplicity. It's a good place to find something that's not on every other high street, but it's fairly inconsistent – some days are great, some days you find nothing.

LA BOUTIQUE, 39 rue du Temple, 75004
Tel: 01 42 77 34 74
Métro: Hôtel de Ville
Opening Hours: Mon–Sat: 11.00–19.30 (also Sun in December)
August: closed
Credit Cards: six of the designers accept Visa
Price Range: from 350FF for a Lycra dress to 1,400FF for an overcoat

CLOÎTRE DES BILLETTES: EXHIBITIONS

A wonderful church cloister, this is now used for temporary, often unusual, exhibitions. They can be anything from bits of Moroccan furniture and doors to pages and pages of sketches and poetry on lengths of hessian hanging from the ceiling. All the exhibitions are for selling but there is no problem with just wandering in to look around. Just north up this road at the next junction on the corner of rue des Francs Bourgeois you'll find Le Muffin, a sweet local café where you can drop in for a simple breakfast of coffee and toasted tartine.

CLOÎTRE DES BILLETTES, 24 rue des Archives, 75004
Métro: Hôtel de Ville

LES BAINS DU MARAIS: STEAM BATHS

If you want to take a break from retail for beauty restoration, try the new hammam in the Marais. Steam baths used to be everywhere in Paris but over the last few years many have been closed down and turned into nightclubs or cafés, so it's exciting to find one that has recently opened up. Les Bains du Marais combines the sauna and steam room with Moroccan massage, hairdresser (for men and women), beautician and restaurant. The decor is a whole lot more exotic than the usual health club scene, with exposed brick walls, huge abstract oil paintings and mosaic tiling, and fans include Simply Red's Mick Hucknall and photographer Dominique Isserman. Monday, Tuesday and Wednesday are reserved for women only, Thursday, Friday and Saturday are for men and Sunday is mixed bathing.

LES BAINS DU MARAIS, 31–33 rue des Blancs Manteaux, 75004
Tel: 01 44 61 02 02
Métro: Rambuteau or Hôtel de Ville
Opening hours: Mon: 11.00–20.00, Tue/Thur/Sun: 11.00–23.00, Wed: 10.00–19.00, Fri/Sat: 10.00–20.00
August: closed 12–26 Aug
Credit cards: Visa, Amex
Price Range: 180FF for a day's access to the hammam, sauna and relaxation room

LES ARCHIVES DE LA PRESSE: MAGS

This is a fascinating store dealing in old magazines and catalogues from sports to cinema with a great section on fashion. Stock is mostly the French fashion press from 1900 to 1940, then after the war it gets international with Italian *Vogue*, *Vogue USA* and *Harper's Bazaar*, as well as masses of French titles. Over half the clientele for the fashion mags are in the industry – photographers, designers, stylists – all of them in search of inspiration, wanting to copy a technique or a certain look and in some cases go so far as to use the actual patterns contained in the sew-it-yourself fashion mags. Fashion titles go up to the early 1990s.

LES ARCHIVES DE LA PRESSE, 51 rue des Archives, 75003
Tel: 01 42 72 63 93
Métro: Rambuteau
Opening Hours: Mon–Sat: 10.30–19.00
August: open
Credit Cards: none
Price Range: fashion magazines 50–150FF

SOUTH OF RUE ST-ANTOINE

GALERIE 88: MOROCCAN CAFÉ

Still in the 4th, but down towards the quai on the other side of the Hôtel de Ville, is a great Moroccan-feel café. It's ideal for a break from steak and frites and also happens to be very beatnik and low-key fashionable. Turkish coffee is served in heavy silver pots, with cardamom pods on brass trays. For lunch try an Assiette 88 which is fresh and salady with guacomole, tapenade, aubergine caviar, served with corn chips and caraway bread. Their chocolate fondant tarts are delicious. It is an intimate space in exposed stone and hung with dusty leather pony bags and silver bangles. Service can be painfully slow. In the summer you can sit outside on yellow plastic woven chairs and admire the Seine and the traffic.

GALERIE 88, 88 quai de l'Hôtel de Ville, 75004
Tel: 01 42 72 17 58
Métro: Hôtel de Ville
Opening Hours: 12.00–1.00am
August: open
Credit Cards: none
Price Range: salads and pasta dishes 35–50FF, Assiette 88 50FF, mint tea 20FF, Turkish coffee 15FF

ON AND AROUND RUE DES FRANCS BOURGEOIS

NICKEL: MALE BEAUTY

'Imagine you are a man and you want your shoulders waxed, so you head off to a female salon,' says Philippe Dumont; 'they begin by asking you why you want them waxed in the first place. Next you find yourself dressed in a pale pink gown and standing in a line behind a crowd of staring women. Men need their own beauty space.' And they've got it, thanks to Dumont who has opened the Nickel male beauty salon which specialises in the traditional razor shave as well as less traditional beauty treatments for men including eyelash tinting, facials and body-hair waxing. The clientele is young, fashionable and 30% gay. As well as toning body treatments such as 'Love Handles' and 'Double Chin', Nickel also sells skin-care products and perfume by Acqua di Parma, Payot and their own Nickel brand which includes face-savers such as the 'morning after rescue gel'. Dumont has also opened a Nickel salon in the basement of the Printemps men's department store.

NICKEL, 48 rue des Francs Bourgeois, 75003
Tel: 01 42 77 41 10
Métro: Hôtel de Ville or Rambuteau
Opening Hours: Mon/Tue/Fri: 11.00–19.30, Wed/Thu: 11.00–21.00, Sat: 10.00–19.30
August: closed last two weeks
Credit Cards: Visa, Amex, MC
Price Range: shoulder wax 90FF, facial 280FF, Love Handles, 280FF

PLEIN SUD: TREND WOMENSWEAR

Built for the pert and perfect – that's Plein Sud. It's unrelenting glamour for day and night, and models Karen Mulder, Carla Bruni plus Vanessa Paradis are all customers. Designer Fayçal Amor makes his suiting a nipped and tucked take on the double-breasted suit worn with cigarette trousers and spiky heels. At night, the Plein Sud girl turns rock chick with a Hendrix/Joplin mix of stretch velvet jumpsuit worn under a trailing fake-leather coat and huge fake-fur collar. Even on holiday she won't take a break from those eyelash tongs; she wants diamanté triangle bikinis and sexy little tunics in hot shades that are slit in all the right places. Around November, Plein Sud has a special collection of party and evening dresses. For women who dress for men.

PLEIN SUD, 21 rue des Francs Bourgeois, 75004
Tel: 01 42 72 10 60
Métro: St-Paul
also at:
14 place des Victoires, 75002. Tel: 01 42 36 75 02
70 bis rue Bonaparte, 75006. Tel: 01 43 54 43 06

Opening Hours: Mon–Sat: 11.00–19.00, Sun: 14.00–19.00
August: afternoons only (14.00–19.00)
Credit Cards: Visa, Amex, MC
Price Range: full-length suede coat 6,900FF, knit sweater 800FF, trouser suit 4,500FF

DEVANA: CONTEMPORARY JEWELLERY

Devana sells contemporary, stylish jewellery in a dramatic setting of scarlet walls, church candles and moody music. Most dramatic of all is the great big live royal python lying beneath glass in the middle of the shop. Both the snake and the store belong to Jacob Thage-Jorgensen, who is Danish, and shows a range of stylish jewellery from several designers, many of whom are also Danish. Devana's own line is slightly ethnic without being earnest and is inspired by the links and designs of Rajasthan jewellery, but made in Denmark from heavy sterling silver. Marlena Juhl-Jorgensen's work is more medieval, jewelled and looks like it belongs in a church treasury – crosses and stunning rings in thick matt gold and semi-precious stones. There are designs here for men, women, any age and a variety of tastes, from a massive garnet and twisted silver ring by Alan Faye to the most delicate gold-plate link bracelet.

DEVANA, 30 rue de Sévigné, 75004
Tel: 01 42 78 69 76
Métro: St-Paul
Opening Hours: Tue–Sat: 12.00–19.00, Sun/Mon: 14.00–19.00
August: open
Credit Cards: Visa, Amex, MC
Price Range: rings 50–4,500FF, bracelets 300–6,800FF, necklaces 400–11,000FF

CHRISTOPHE LEMAIRE:
YOUNG FRENCH DESIGNER

Lemaire's clothes are clean-cut and confident – silk shirt-dresses and crisp check shirts – intended for the easy-listening girl. The guy has lost his heart to the 1960s/70s and it shows in his clothes. For men it's an early Jean-Luc Godard feel, with fitted velvet jackets over slim cut polo-necks, while for women 'It's cool, comfort, chic,' says Lemaire, who describes himself as 'very much of a beatnik'. Trained under Lacroix and Yves Saint Laurent, Lemaire DJs in his spare time, hence the record player centre store where he plays his favourite '70s beat.

CHRISTOPHE LEMAIRE, 36 rue de Sévigné, 75003
Tel: 01 42 74 54 90
Métro: St-Paul
Opening Hours: Tue–Fri: 10.30–19.00, Sat: 10.30–20.00, Sun: 14.00–19.00
August: closed for two weeks
Credit Cards: Visa, Diners, Amex, MC, JCB
Price Range: dress from 790FF, jacket from 2,200FF

LA LICORNE: 1920s/1930s COSTUME JEWELLERY

This funny old-fashioned shop is a mine of costume jewellery from the 1920s onwards. For over sixty years La Licorne manufactured costume jewellery just down the road, but with the tarting up of the Marais in the late '70s, they got squeezed out of their premises. Now they sell all their old stock from the 1920s and '30s as well as more recent decades. The glass cases are stuffed with jewellery in black jet, paste, pearls, bakelite and jade. Sift through the tat and there are wonderful tortoiseshell blob earrings, exotic lime-green plastic bracelets, jade pendants, silver-grey pearls and multi-strand jet chokers. They also do repairs.

LA LICORNE, 38 rue de Sévigné, 75003
Tel: 01 48 87 84 43
Métro: St-Paul
Opening Hours: Mon–Sat: 9.00–18.30
August: usually closed from 15 Aug for a week
Credit Cards: Visa, Amex, Diners, MC
Price Range: jet chokers from 250FF, earrings 35–500FF, bracelets 200–700FF

ATSURO TAYAMA: JAPANESE DESIGNER

See 6th arrondissement for details.
40 rue de Sévigné, 75003. Tel: 01 40 29 15 07

COMPTOIR DE L'IMAGE:
PHOTOGRAPHY, FASHION BOOK SHOP

Prime hunting ground for fashion designers is the Comptoir de l'Image, a compact shop selling fashion and photographic books plus back issues of the fashion glossies such as *Vogue, W, Officiel* and *Bazaar*. It is owned by Michel Fink, himself a photographer and one-time assistant to Richard Avedon during the 1960s, who has a great eye and manages to source old titles many of which are downright rare, such as Diana Vreeland's seminal *Allure*. There are of course also current fashion and photography titles (Mario Testino through Juergen Teller). Great display and expert advice make this store a breeze to shop at. Galliano, Marc Jacobs and Raf Simons are all regulars.

COMPTOIR DE L'IMAGE, 44 rue de Sévigné, 75003
Tel: 01 42 72 03 92
Métro: St-Paul or Chemin Vert
Opening Hours: Mon–Sat: 11.00–19.00, Sun: 14.00–19.00
August: open
Credit Cards: Visa, Amex, Diners, JCB
Price Range: 300–10,000FF

AUTOUR DU MONDE: CASUAL WEAR
See 6th arrondissement for details.
12 rue des Francs Bourgeois, 75003. Tel: 01 42 77 16 18

ANNE FONTAINE: WHITE SHIRTS
See 2nd arrondissement for details.
12 rue des Francs Bourgeois, 75003. Tel: 01 44 59 81 59

VENTILO: FRENCH CLASSIC WOMENSWEAR
See 2nd arrondissement for details.
10 rue des Francs Bourgeois, 75003. Tel: 01 40 27 05 58

HOME AUTOUR DU MONDE:
LIFESTYLE/INTERIORS

The home collection to complement Autour du Monde clothes, this used to be all a trifle too Amish-at-home verging on the quaint. It has smartened up its act considerably with a fresh, simple, pared-down home collection and a look that works well with Paris parquet and white walls. Great place for buying gifts – for yourself or others, and particularly good for finding wedding presents which are contemporary stylish, rather than relentlessly trendy and therefore dated in six months. They do a wide selection of vases including those of florist Christian Tortu, also ceramics such as salad and pasta bowls in simple cream with patches of duck-egg blue. There are slightly faded linen cushions, paper lampshades and enough incense and scented candles to burn the house down. Downstairs for furniture and bed-linen.

HOME AUTOUR DU MONDE, 8 rue des Francs Bourgeois, 75003
Tel: 01 42 77 06 08
Métro: St-Paul
Opening Hours: Mon–Sat: 10.00–19.00, Sun: 14.00–19.00
August: open
Credit Cards: Visa, Diners, Amex, MC, JCB
Price Range: vases from 300FF, cushions from 180FF, incense from 40FF

ET VOUS: CONTEMPORARY WOMENSWEAR
See 8th arrondissement for details.
6 rue des Francs Bourgeois, 75003. Tel: 01 42 71 75 11

CAMPER: CULT CASUAL SHOES
See 6th arrondissement for details.
9 rue des Francs Bourgeois, 75004. Tel: 01 48 87 09 09

ISSEY MIYAKE: JAPANESE DESIGNER WEAR
Issey Miyake is an original. One of the first of the Japanese designers
to conquer Paris with his début show in 1973, he has pushed the
boundaries of fashion ever since. His techniques of folding, heat-pleat-
ing and creasing literally changed the shape of the way people dressed
in the late 1980s. His perfume, L'Eau d'Issey, launched in 1992, became
one of the most copied scents and packaging of the '90s. His launch of
a second line, Pleats Please, a collection of permanently pleated, bril-
liantly coloured clothes (see 7th arrondissement), was followed by an
acute case of fashion creasing everywhere, even at Marks & Spencer.

The store here sells mostly the main line for men and women and a
few doors along is his Paris office, where twice a year he and the collection arrive to be shown and sold to the buyers and press. For the
rest of the year, Miyake, born in Hiroshima just before the Second
World War, lives and works in Tokyo. The main-line clothes are innovative, comfortable, expensive and sculptural. They lie flat on a shelf
or hang on a hanger like art work in a gallery, waiting to be brought
alive and let loose on the body. Tina Turner, Grace Jones and Emma
Thompson are all Miyake disciples and come here to shop. Love those
Pleats Please yellow curtains in the changing rooms.

ISSEY MIYAKE, 3 place des Vosges, 75004
Tel: 01 48 87 01 86
Métro: Bastille or St-Paul
Opening Hours: Mon–Sat: 10.00–19.00
August: closed for ten days, call for dates
Credit Cards: Visa, Amex, Diners, MC
Price Range: coat 10,000FF, trousers 2,500FF, raincoat 3,770FF, men's jacket
6,770FF

TO THE NORTH OF THE MARAIS

L'HABILLEUR: DESIGNER SALE SHOP

This is designer sale shopping at its most pleasurable. Colombian John Crawley has built himself a salon rather than a bargain basement, with last year's designer clothes for men and women displayed alongside painting exhibitions. Prices are reduced by 50% to 70% and there are clothes for women from Plein Sud, Vivienne Westwood, Paul & Joe, Dice Kayek and John Richmond and shoes for men and women by Patrick Cox and Robert Clergerie. It's the hippest designer sale shop in town and clientele is made up of John's glam mates and others just in the know. For men there is suiting, weekend wear, sweaters and coats from So, Dolce & Gabbana, Patrick Cox, Vivienne Westwood and Yohji Yamamoto. What's good about L'Habilleur is you're never made to feel a cheapskate shopper – you can buy a fab pair of Patrick Cox moc-croc chestnut high heels for 490FF and they are sold still in their original box and with shoe horn.

L'HABILLEUR, 44 rue de Poitou, 75003
Tel: 01 48 87 77 12
Métro: St-Sébastien Froissart
Opening Hours: Mon–Sat: 11.00–20.00
August: open
Credit Cards: Visa, MC
Price Range: jackets 1,000–1,700FF, trousers 400–600FF, winter coat 1,500–3,00FF, shoes from 495FF

DOMINIQUE PICQUIER:
TEXTILES INTERIORS/ACCESSORIES

This is the boutique of textile designer Dominique Picquier whose designs are mostly plant forms and flowers but executed in a bold, contemporary and graphic way: blown cowslips in olive green, looping petals in faded lilac on linen cotton. You can either buy her fabric by the metre or choose from her range of home furnishings such as poufs, cushions, curtains. There are also fashion accessories in Dominique Picquier fabrics such as tote bags, espadrilles, wallets and wraps which are well-priced and make pretty gifts.

DOMINIQUE PICQUIER, 10 rue Charlot, 75003
Tel: 01 42 72 39 14
Métro: Filles du Calvaire or St-Sébastien Froissart
Opening Hours: Mon–Fri: 10.00–13.00, 14.00–19.00, Sat: 14.30–19.00
August: closed for three weeks
Credit Cards: Visa
Price Range: cushion cover 190FF, pouf 960FF, wallets 185FF, fabric 380FF per metre

JOSÉ LÉVY A PARIS:

DESIGNER MEN'S & WOMEN'S WEAR

French designer José Lévy has had a busy couple of years. He has moved his store to a bigger, higher-profile space in the Marais, broken into womenswear and landed the design director job at hunting, shooting and fishing brand Holland & Holland (owned by the Chanel family, the Wertheimers, who are pushing for a more fashionable identity for the brand). Lévy's own look is sharp tailoring with retro inclinations from the 1940s and '50s. There's something almost schoolboyish to a three-button jacket or wide-legged pants with satin-edged hem. Womenswear is still maturing and at the moment looks pretty much like his menswear, give or take the odd dress and different sizing, but a close-fitting shirt with darting details looks chic.

JOSÉ LÉVY A PARIS, 70 rue Vieille du Temple, 75003
Tel: 01 48 04 39 16
Métro: St-Paul
Opening Hours: Mon: 13.00–20.00, Tue–Sat: 12.00–20.00
August: open
Credit Cards: Visa, Amex, Diners, MC, JCB
Price Range: men's suit 3,500–4,000FF, women's shirt 600–700FF

FRÉDÉRIC SANCHEZ: MUSIC STORE

'This is not the kind of music store where people come running in off the street asking for the latest Mariah Carey album,' insists Fred Bladou. 'No, this is a store for curiosity, discovery, enjoyment.' Frédéric Sanchez and Fred Bladou – known in the fashion business as 'the Freds' – create the soundtracks for some of the hippest runways around, from Prada and Jil Sander to Marc Jacobs and Calvin Klein, and they recently opened a retail space selling music with a fashion spin. For years they've been getting calls and requests from friends, models and clients wanting to buy their runway soundtracks and, although they still can't sell the actual soundtracks (artist rights make that impossible), they can at least supply the individual tracks and the music of the moment. 'It is a totally personal and eclectic selection,' says Sanchez about the 1,000 titles in stock which change daily and range from dance and techno to opera and avant-garde Japanese. And whereas most music stores would have, say, 15 versions of *La Traviata*, they have just the one, 'But it's the one that we love,' says Sanchez – read the *right* one.

FRÉDÉRIC SANCHEZ, 5 rue Ste-Anastase, 75003
Tel: 01 44 54 89 54
Métro: St-Sébastien Froissart or Chemin Vert
Opening Hours: Tue–Fri: 13.00–19.00, Sat: 11.00–19.00
August: closed 7–23 Aug
Credit Cards: Visa, Diners, Amex, MC, JCB
Price Range: 35–800FF

ADELINE ANDRÉ: DESIGNER WEAR

For a couturier, Adeline André is something of an oddity. Her collections are not about voluminous taffeta skirts at 200,000FF a whack, her shows are not held in the Ritz and there is not a bony bottom on a little gilt chair in sight. The most expensive piece in her couture collection is 30,000FF, her ready-to-wear is considerably less.

André makes contemporary, sensous and inventive clothes for men as well as women. She studied at the Chambre Syndicale de la Couture, before working as assistant to Marc Bohan for Christian Dior couture in 1969. For the last fifteen years she has done her own thing, and is best known for inventing the trois armatures jacket, which has three armholes so you wrap the jacket around you one and a half times. For women she does both couture and off-the-peg with a smallish collection of utterly feminine designs like an ethereal organza bias-cut dress which is two layers but made from just one piece of fabric. Her style is an any-age elegance. For men there are thick Cousteau hand-knit sweaters with matching scarves and the trois armatures jacket in flannel. Adeline makes all the stage outfits for Ray Charles and her atelier and boutique are in a small stone building at the back of place des Vosges.

ADELINE ANDRÉ, 5 rue Villehardouin, 75003
Tel: 01 42 77 72 56, call for appointment
Métro: Chemin Vert
Opening Hours: Mon–Fri: 9.30–19.30, Sat: 14.00–19.30
August: closed for one week, call for dates
Credit Cards: Visa, Amex, Diners
Price Range: ready-to-wear 1,500–7,000FF, men's suit 6,500FF, sweaters 800–1,500FF, haute couture dress 20,000–30,000FF

6TH ARRONDISSEMENT

The Left Bank is every cliché of Paris rolled into reality – chain-smoking philosophers, beautiful people, bookshops, bad parking, jazz bars, learning and lovers. It is magical. Historians say that in medieval times the residents of the Left Bank never crossed the river but stayed put on their own side. The habit still holds true today, for the most part.

Every couple of years in Paris one shopping area rises to supremacy and right now it's the area of St-Germain-des-Prés. Traditionally it's been a quartier of bijou little boutiques, interior decorators, galleries and Left Bank free thinkers like Yves Saint Laurent, so people got quite a fright recently when the big luxe boys from over the river started moving in. Die-hard Rive droite institutions like Louis Vuitton, Christian Dior, Emporio Armani and Cartier have all opened up here. Property prices have trebled. Initially there were all sorts of rash rumours including one that Hermès was going to take over the famous bookshop La Hune (turned out false), which had the French press and residents seething. So much so that the mayor of the 6th, Monsieur Lecoq, was forced to make a soothing statement pledging the safety of the three cornerstones of the St-Germain village: Les Deux Magots, Café Flore and the Brasserie Lipp.

If you are only in Paris for a short time, the 6th is the perfect place to get your bearings. It breathes rarefied chic. There are few of the big Paris sights, but wander into the small streets both sides of the boulevard St-Germain and you will discover antique shops, galleries specialising in late-19th-century and 20th-century art, acres of interior fabrics, expensive jazz bars down the rue St-Benoît and a pretty open-air fruit and veg market at Carrefour de Buci.

For fashion shopping it's the best area in town for shoes and accessories in every price range. Designer-wise, Prada and Yohji Yamamoto are here, while the recently renovated Onward (formerly Kashiyama) has a great selection of international avant-garde fashion. Make sure you check out Paul & Joe and Vanessa Bruno for cool fashion clothes, and there are also lots of speciality, one-off boutiques such as Liwan, a great source for lounging kit, and Marie Mercié for stylish hats.

But don't even think about shopping before you have taken your seat in or outside at the Café Flore (Les Deux Magots is plastered in tourists), ordered your morning petit noir and croissant and experienced the spirit of the Left Bank. The Café Flore is just gorgeous – Sartre, de Beauvoir, Brigitte Bardot, Belmondo and Givenchy have all sat here. Inside it's claret-coloured banquettes and racing waiters, while outside on the terrasse glossy girls pause between purchases and discreet lovers meet wrapped in sunglasses. The Flore terrasse is proof that, in Paris, staring is considered an acceptable pastime.

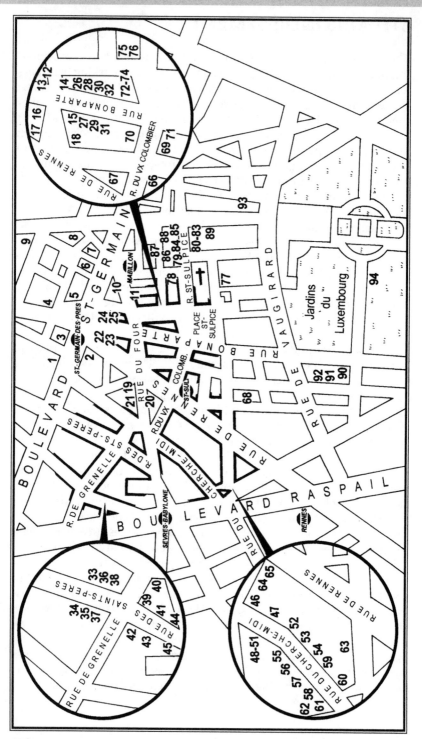

1 SHU UEMURA
2 EMPORIO ARMANI
3 LOUIS VUITTON
4 CHRISTIAN DIOR
5 ONWARD
6 COSMOS
7 L'ÉCLAIREUR
8 AUTOUR DU MONDE
9 LAGERFELD GALLERY
10 BOB SHOP
11 MOSQUITOS
12 TARA JARMON
13 BOOT SHOP
14 MANDARINA DUCK
15 MAXMARA
16 FREE LANCE
17 FREE
18 BURBERRY
19 PAUL & JOE
20 SUPERGA
21 CI DESSOUS
22 APOSTROPHE
23 GEORGES RECH
24 GUERLAIN
25 MARY QUANT
26 TIKI TIRAWA
27 CACHAREL
28 VENTILO
29 JOSEPH
30 INDIES
31 PLEIN SUD
32 COMPTOIR DES COTONNIERS
33 CAPUCINE PUERARI
34 ANNE FONTAINE
35 VERSUS
36 Y'S YOHJI YAMAMOTO
37 ÉTIENNE BRUNEL
38 SABBIA ROSA
39 PRADA
40 YOHJI YAMAMOTO
41 ATSURO TAYAMA
42 SPORTMAX
43 ALAIN MIKLI
44 ANTEPRIMA
45 M.A.C.
46 CAMPER
47 ROBERT CLERGERIE
48 MARE

49 ERÈS
50 GINKGO
51 FAUSTO SANTINI
52 YVES SAINT LAURENT SHOES
53 GROOM
54 REGINA RUBENS
55 CUISINE DE BAR
56 MIU MIU
59 MYMA
58 CLIO BLUE
59 LUNDI BLEU
60 J FENESTRIER
61 CHERCHE-MIDI
62 JOYCE AND CO
63 PEGGY HUYNH KINH
64 CLAUDIE PIERLOT
65 MARCEL LASSANCE
66 VICTOIRE HOMME
67 VICTOIRE
68 JEAN-CHARLES DE CASTELBAJAC
69 FORMES
70 AGNÈS B.
71 HERVÉ CHAPELIER
72 YVES SAINT LAURENT RIVE
   GAUCHE HOMME
73 ANNICK GOUTAL
74 CAFÉ DE LA MAIRIE
75 YVES SAINT LAURENT RIVE
   GAUCHE
76 CHRISTIAN LACROIX
77 SÉVERINE PERRAUDIN
78 SANDRA SERRAF
79 MUJI
80 MAISON DE FAMILLE
81 SISSO'S
82 VANESSA BRUNO
83 MARIE MERCIÉ
84 LA CHAMBRE CLAIRE
85 LIWAN
86 CHRISTIAN TORTU
87 OCTÉE
88 PIERRE SAMARY
89 AU NOM DE LA ROSE
90 A.P.C.
91 A.P.C. GENERAL
92 A.P.C. SURPLUS
93 PÔLES
94 JARDINS DU LUXEMBOURG

BOULEVARD ST-GERMAIN

SHU UEMURA: JAPANESE DESIGNER MAKE-UP

Colour is the key to the Shu Uemura make-up collection. It's another of those lines that started professional then went public as women discovered the beauty of the brand. There are over 100 eye-shadow colours and 120 lipstick colours which, the manageress explained, they do not chop and change as 'it's just too traumatic for the customer to lose her lipstick colour'. There are six different finishes of foundation (the UV liquid foundation is matt and marvellous). Clients include make-up artists Kevyn Aucoin and Stéphane Marais plus designer Karl Lagerfeld, who comes in twice a year for a mega-shop as he does all his fashion sketches in Shu Uemura colours. In between there are a lot of normal people too, who come for the cosmetics and advice, as each sales assistant is a trained make-up artist, so they can help with choosing the right type and shade of foundation or size of false eyelash. There is a good selection for Asian skin, but more limited for black skin. You can book in advance to have a 20-minute free make-up look here at the shop. For more detailed tuition (but no products on sale) there is a Shu Uemura school where you can book in for a three-hour individual lesson (900FF) or share a lesson with two or three others (550FF). The Shu Uemura collection is also sold at Galeries Lafayette.

SHU UEMURA, 176 boulevard St-Germain, 75006
Tel: 01 45 48 02 55
Métro: St-Germain-des-Prés
School: 12 rue de la Paix, 75002. Contact Carla on 01 42 61 19 39
Opening Hours: Mon: 11.00–19.00, Tue–Sat: 10.00–19.00
August: open
Credit Cards: Visa, Amex, Diners, MC

EMPORIO ARMANI: CLOTHES, CAFFÈ

The Italian master who taught us beige elegance and self-restraint opened up in St-Germain on the site of the former Drugstore a couple of years back. In order to butter up the St-Germain anti-retail lobby he had to donate a pile of cash (one million FF) to the St-Germain-des-Prés church window restoration and he also pledged to make his store into a cultural hang-out (as in not just flogging clothes). So on the ground floor is a fashion, art and photography book and magazine section, while downstairs there is a cool selection of house, hip-hop and dance CDs. What's hot here is the caffè which is linen-looking and discreet, serving saffron risotto, plates of gambas and reviving espressos. Come lunchtime the place is knee-deep in PRs, friends and fashion girls. Clothes-wise you can find everything from underwear to evening dresses, and the store stocks the sportier Emporio Armani for men and women, Emporio jeans and, for the aspirational child, Armani junior.

EMPORIO ARMANI, 149 boulevard St-Germain, 75006
Tel: 01 53 63 33 50
Métro: St-Germain-des-Prés
Opening Hours: Mon: 11.30–22.00, Tue–Sat: 10.30–22.00
August: open
Credit Cards: Visa, Amex, Diners, MC, JCB
Price Range: trousers from 650FF, suits from 3,500FF, evening dresses
2,900–6,000FF, bags from 1,000FF

LOUIS VUITTON: LUXURY CLOTHES, LUGGAGE

Louis Vuitton caused an unseemly dash for property on the Left Bank
when they opened their store here early in 1996. Always considered a
Right Bank luxury mover, they stole the march on the competition by
opening up right next door to Les Deux Magots and milking all those
marketable myths of Left Bank intelligentsia and café society. See 8th
arrondissement for details.
6 place St-Germain-des-Prés, 75006. Tel: 01 45 49 62 32

CHRISTIAN DIOR: FRENCH DESIGNER FASHION

See 8th arrondissement for details.
16 rue de l'Abbaye, 75006. Tel: 01 56 24 90 53

ONWARD: INTERNATIONAL DESIGNER FASHION

Kashiyama has been a Left Bank fashion institution for years but has recently undergone much-needed and radical renovation (making it easier to shop) and a name change to Onward. The overall buying policy favours the avant-garde and Left Bank sensibility. 'That means I'm trying to get away from the Right Bank tradition of couture,' explains store director Christine Weiss, 'instead keeping the Left Bank identity of a woman's own sense of style: less structuring, longer skirts, more freedom, more mixing – a little more existentialist.'

There are three floors for retail divided up with ground floor for accessories such as Jamin Puech pretty sequin bags and Alain Tondowski's vampy stilettos. Downstairs the basement is devoted to one designer per season; upstairs trawl your way through rails and rails of designer kit. Clothes range from more established avant-garde talent, such as Gaultier, Demeulemeester, Margiela and Helmut Lang, to new blood such as Thimister and Olivier Theyskens, a Belgian young designer who shot to fame on the back of his gothic black dress worn by Madonna to the Oscars a couple of years back. The only criticism of Onward is that at the beginning of the season the rails are so jam-packed with clothes it can be daunting even to start looking. That said, staff are helpful without cramping your style.

ONWARD, 147 boulevard St-Germain, 75006
Tel: 01 55 42 77 55
Métro: St-Germain-des-Prés
Opening Hours: Mon/Sat: 11.00–19.30, Tue–Fri: 10.30–19.30
August: closed Mon
Credit Cards: Visa, Amex, Diners, MC, JCB
Price Range: trousers 1,200–3,500FF, shoes 1,000–4,000FF, bags 1,000–4,000FF, suits 3,000–6,000FF

COSMOS: CHEAP AND TREND WOMENSWEAR

A friend who worked for American *Vogue* and Galliano in Paris recommended this store for lookalike designer kit. From the outside the store looks pretty cheap and inside there's a sea of seasonal trends – heavily Prada-inspired prints, shamelessly 'Dolce & Gabbana' tops and trousers that should read 'care of Gucci'. Do what the Parisians do and restrict an outfit to just one of these pieces; that way it doesn't look so fake. They stock about fifteen different brands and the emphasis in fabrics is on man-made.

COSMOS, 154 boulevard St-Germain, 75006
Tel: 01 43 26 29 11
Métro: Mabillon or St-Germain-des-Prés
Opening Hours: Mon–Sat: 10.00–19.00
August: open
Credit Cards: Visa, Diners, Amex, MC, JCB
Price Range: trousers from 335FF, T-shirts 150FF

L'ÉCLAIREUR: INTERNATIONAL DESIGNER WEAR

Same ownership and concept as L'Éclaireur over in Le Marais, but this place has more of a focus on casual wear for men and women. The four-floor store has been done out in an industrial style with girders, concrete chunks, exposed floor and some lovely 17th-century wooden beams left poking out. Armand Hadida doesn't go for super-young new talent, he deals in the established avant-garde.

Reflecting fashion, Hadida has opted for more of an urban sports-wear feel for this boutique selling Helmut Lang for men and women, Prada Sport, Maharishi funky embroidered combat trousers and Martin Margiela for men. There are also scents by Comme des Garçons and leather bracelets by Maria Rudman. This is the sort of store where you find fashion editors fighting over the last Helmut Lang dress. It is for people who know their designers and what they want. Eighty per cent of the clientele is foreign and it's quite an industry shop, full of photographers, fashion editors plus all the stars – Cher, Harrison Ford, Johnny Depp and Lenny Kravitz.

L'ÉCLAIREUR, 24 rue de L'Échaudé, 75006
Tel: 01 44 27 08 03
Métro: Mabillon
also at:
3 ter rue des Rosiers, 75004. Tel: 01 48 87 10 22
26 avenue des Champs-Élysées, 75008. Tel: 01 42 89 26 29
Opening Hours: Mon: 14.00–19.00, Tue–Sat: 11.00–19.00
August: closed for part of month, call for dates
Credit Cards: Visa, Amex, MC, JCB
Price Range: T-shirts from 400FF, shoes from 800FF, trousers from 1,200FF, jeans from 600FF

AUTOUR DU MONDE: CASUAL WEAR

Serge Bensimon started out by buying job lots of uniforms from the army which he titivated up and sold on. Now he's taken the concept to a higher plane; he still does a little of the military stock, but concentrates mainly on his own line for both sexes, which is more voyage-inspired. It's about basics in natural fabrics which work best for the summer with slim safari dresses, towelling tops, and dark denim clam-diggers. The shop classic is the consummate French girl en vacances – wide-legged navy trousers and striped cotton mariner top. It's not fashion, it's lifestyle. Menswear has photographer's jackets and the perfect pair of knee-length white shorts straight out of the 1950s Royal Navy. There is never any black in the collections. Serge has three shops in Paris – this Left Bank store has the best selection for clothes. He also has a great lifestyle and interiors store in the Marias.

AUTOUR DU MONDE, 54 rue de Seine, 75006
Tel: 01 43 54 64 47
Métro: Mabillon
also at:
12 rue des Francs Bourgeois, 75004. Tel: 01 42 77 16 18
8 rue des Francs Bourgeois, 75004.
Opening Hours: Mon–Sat: 10.30–19.00, Sun 14.00–19.00
August: open
Credit Cards: Visa, Amex, Diners, MC
Price Range: men's white shorts 455FF, sweatshirts 350FF, photographer's jacket 490FF, towelling polo tops 195FF, linen shirts 470FF, winter wool wide-legged sailor pants 575FF

LAGERFELD GALLERY: PHOTOGRAPHY, CLOTHES

When his signature line folded a couple of years back, Karl Lagerfeld decided to create his own store in St-Germain. The fact it is intended principally as a gallery means the place is not exactly heaving with merchandise; on the ground floor is a round table displaying fashionable magazines, while on the walls hang his distinctive photographs of Paris people including Carole Bouquet, Gérard Depardieu and Olivier Martinez plus hyper-beautiful men and women. There are also Fendi baguette and croissant bags (Karl designs the Fendi womenswear) while downstairs is his new line of clothing for men and women.

LAGERFELD GALLERY, 40 rue de Seine, 75006
Tel: 01 55 42 75 50
Métro: Mabillon
Opening Hours: Tue–Sat: 10.00–19.00
August: closed first two weeks
Credit Cards: Visa, Amex, Diners, MC, JCB
Price Range: cashmere sweater 2,900FF, wool winter coat 13,500FF, Fendi bag 1,900–16,000FF, photographs 15,000–60,000FF

RUE DU FOUR

BOB SHOP: TROUSERS
See 1st arrondissement for details.
14 rue du Four, 75006. Tel: 01 43 54 05 59

MOSQUITOS: FUNKY FOOTWEAR
People usually assume Mosquitos is the second line to Stéphane Kélian, but apparently it's not, it's just made by the same group. The feel is younger, clubbier with loads more colour and aimed at the 15- to 35-year-old. Their summer shoes are always wild, for example, a patent plastic clog in daffodil yellow lined with towelling. But the year-round best sellers are still the chunky suede moccasins in turquoise, jade or magenta on a high white rubber heel. If you are bored of trainers, but still want casual comfort, their E-Mail line is a range of street sneakers, for men and women, in leather with rubber padding protection round the ankle. Mosquitos' production is in Italy, Spain and Portugal rather than France which makes the prices cheaper.

MOSQUITOS, 25 rue du Four, 75006
Tel: 01 43 25 25 16
Métro: Mabillon or St-Germain-des-Prés
also at:
19 rue Pierre Lescot, 75001. Tel: 01 45 08 44 72
99 rue de Rennes, 75006. Tel: 01 45 48 58 40
12 rue Gustave Courbet, 75016. Tel: 01 45 53 36 73
Opening Hours: Mon–Sat: 10.00–19.30
August: open
Credit Cards: Visa, Amex, MC
Price Range: E-Mail shoes from 395FF, boots 800–1,000FF, men's shoes 595–895FF

TARA JARMON: FASHIONABLE WOMENSWEAR
Tara Jarmon is great at getting the look, the price and the quality right. She describes her clothes as 'any age, modern, feminine, uncomplicated and affordable'. A Canadian from Vancouver, Tara came to Paris fourteen years ago to study political sciences and never left. Her store is where you'll find a fashionable and sophisticated high street look rather than high trend or basics. She's good for suiting with plenty of choice in jacket shape from short and boxy to the longer coat-jacket and she always offers two lengths of short skirt. Her Canadian roots show in the cocktail party dresses which are pert and prom-night with fitted bustier and tulip skirts in shantung silk or water mark taffeta. The store is a pleasure to shop in, light and sunny with bleached wooden floors and cut flowers to complement the collections. It's been a hit here since she opened in 1995; Parisians girls love it, but, according to Tara, insist on buying everything oh-so tight: 'That's because they like their rear ends to show,' she reveals.

TARA JARMON, 18 rue du Four, 75006
Tel: 01 46 33 26 60
Métro: Mabillon
also at:
73 avenue des Champs-Élysées, 75008. Tel: 01 45 63 45 41
51 rue de Passy, 75016. Tel: 01 45 24 65 20
Opening Hours: Mon–Sat: 10.30–19.15
August: open
Credit Cards: Visa, Amex, MC
Price Range: wide range of skirts 300–450FF, jackets 900–1,300FF, dresses
500–900FF

BOOT SHOP: TREND FOOTWEAR

This high street shoe shop is great at 'doing' the designer look at a
good price. Shapes, styles and colour may owe a lot to Gucci, Prada,
Chanel and Sergio Rossi, but they've been manufacturing shoes themselves since the 1960s, so as far as retro fashion goes they've lived
through it. Styles include cherry-red strappies on narrow cork wedges,
square-toe peacock-blue shoes and sleek calf boots with snaffle bit.
There's always heaps of colour and lots of the styles are the Boot
Shop's original designs from the 1970s and '80s.

BOOT SHOP, 20 rue du Four, 75006
Tel: 01 46 33 60 73
Métro: Mabillon or St-Germain-des-Prés
Opening Hours: Mon–Sat: 10–19.00
August: open
Credit Cards: Visa, Diners
Price Range: shoes 500–900FF, boots from 1,200FF, short boots 700–900FF

MANDARINA DUCK:
CONTEMPORARY BAGS, LUGGAGE

Mandarina Duck is yet another brand rethinking its image. During the
'80s its brightly-coloured bags were the last word in trend, by the '90s
they were looking decidedly over-designed. They have reacted by
introducing a new line of body bags called 'Task' which are to be worn,

rather than carried. They do everything from suitcases and garment bags to wallets and vanity cases and one of their best sellers is still the sturdy Tank trolley which is waterproof and comes with 'cannelloni-look' padding to avoid damage in transit. A new store selling their clothes and bags is scheduled to open at the end of 2000 on rue St-Honoré.

MANDARINA DUCK, 51 rue Bonaparte, 75006
Tel: 01 43 26 68 38
Métro: Mabillon or St-Germain-des-Prés
Opening Hours: Mon–Sat: 10.00–19.00
August: open
Credit Cards: Visa, Amex, Diners, MC, JCB
Price Range: small trolley 950FF, Task bag from 450FF

MAXMARA: SLEEK ITALIAN FASHION
See 8th arrondissement for details.
37 rue du Four, 75006. Tel: 01 43 29 91 10

FREE LANCE: TREND FOOTWEAR
Reigning naughty boys of French footwear, brothers Guy and Yvon Rautureau make shoes under the label Free Lance. They make trend, they break trend, with kitsch, clumpy, sometimes dainty, styles which don't come cheap at 1,000FF for a pair of moccasins. Whatever they design, their minds don't seem to stray far from the inspiration of sex. Their collections are always massive and a mix of multi-trends. Fantasy is what they do best with ponyskin in acid brights of orange and yellow or patchwork suede stitched into calf boots. For night-time, there are shot-satin party mules and the strappiest of summer sandals. All the shoes are made up in a factory in the Vendée where their grandfather first started in 1870.

FREE LANCE, 30 rue du Four, 75006
Tel: 01 45 48 14 78
Métro: St-Germain-des-Prés
also at:
22 rue Mondétour, 75001. Tel: 01 42 33 74 70
(men's) 16 rue du Bourg-Tibourg, 75004. Tel: 01 42 77 01 55
24 rue de Grenelle, 75007. Tel: 01 45 49 95 83
Opening Hours: Mon–Sat: 10.00–19.00
August: varies, call for dates
Credit Cards: Visa, Amex, Diners, MC
Price Range: 700–2,000FF, boots 2,000–3,000FF

FREE: FUNKY WOMENSWEAR
See 8th arrondissement for details.
32 rue du Four, 75006. Tel: 01 45 44 23 11

BURBERRY: BRITISH DESIGNER LABEL
See 8th arrondissement for details.
55 rue de Rennes, 75006. Tel: 01 45 48 52 71

PAUL & JOE: TREND WOMENSWEAR
See 2nd arrondissement for details.
40 rue du Four, 75006. Tel: 01 45 44 97 70

SUPERGA: TENNIS SHOES
When it comes to getting dressed, Paris girls live by certain sartorial
rules and one of them concerns summer pumps – they've got to be
Superga. Before the Italian shoe brand opened a store here that meant
life was tough, fighting it out at Printemps with every other Parisian
chick for the last pair of size 6 white Supergas. But it's easier now they
have their own boutique which sells the whole collection, both for
women and for men, and in colours ranging from écru through denim
dark blue.

SUPERGA, 51 rue du Four, 75006
Tel: 01 42 84 80 30
Métro: Sèvres-Babylone or St-Sulpice
Opening Hours: Mon–Sat: 10.00–19.00
August: open
Credit Cards: Visa, Amex, MC, JCB
Price Range: summer shoes 300–400FF, winter shoes 500–600FF

CI DESSOUS: PRETTY LINGERIE AND SWIMWEAR
Lingerie and swimming costumes with the emphasis on pretty, soft
and natural rather than racy and lacy. They are cut for the smaller bust
and svelte figure – not all styles go up to a C cup. A typical Ci Dessous
look is a pale mint gingham cotton balconnet bra with a teeny bow in
the middle. Swimming costumes are often lined, with seaming and
darting for shape. You can mix and match bikini sizes and colours.

CI DESSOUS, 48 rue du Four, 75006
Tel: 01 42 84 25 31
Métro: Sèvres-Babylone
Opening Hours: Mon: 12.30–19.00, Tue–Sat: 10.00–13.30, 14.30–19.00
August: open
Credit Cards: Visa, Amex, Diners, MC
Price Range: bras 200–250FF, knickers 130–150FF, one-piece swimming cos-
tume 400–450FF, bikini 300–400FF

RUE BONAPARTE

APOSTROPHE: FRENCH CHIC WOMENSWEAR
See 8th arrondissement for details.
54 rue Bonaparte, 75006. Tel: 01 43 29 08 38

GEORGES RECH: FRENCH CHIC
See 1st arrondissement for details.
54 rue Bonaparte, 75006. Tel: 01 43 26 84 11

GUERLAIN: SCENT
See 8th arrondissement for details.
47 rue Bonaparte, 75006. Tel: 01 43 26 71 19

MARY QUANT: MAKE-UP
The ultimate Chelsea girl, Mary Quant has recently opened in Paris. The store sells mostly her make-up with its revamped packaging. She has the best selection of nail polish, in colours including violet, almond and a new, divine daffodil yellow inspired by the Beatles, called Help! Quant's greatest fan is make-up artist of the moment Pat McGrath.

MARY QUANT, 49 rue Bonaparte, 75006
Tel: 01 43 25 03 96
Métro: St-Germain-des-Prés
Opening Hours: Mon/Thu/Fri/Sat: 10.00–19.00, Tue/Wed: 10.00–18.00
August: open
Credit Cards: Visa, Amex, MC, JCB
Price Range: nail polish 70FF, eye-shadow 57FF, lipstick 110FF

TIKI TIRAWA: SOPHISTICATED KNITWEAR
Tiki Tirawa sells only knitwear. Sophisticated, well-bred plain knits in viscose, linen, merino wool, cotton, silk or cashmere, they are the sort of pieces which, once bought, you can't believe you got dressed without. Shapes are simple: little zipper cardigans, a sleeveless turtleneck dress, straight-cut trousers or slim V-neck cabled sweater. The main thrust of the collection is in écru, golds, nougat tones, black and masses of white, punctuated with navy and bordeaux for the winter and hot-house colours for the summer. Rather than prints or flash trimmings, designer Brigitte Mabe creates interest through ribs, cables, chain-mail knit, transparency and strips of colour like violet next to khaki in a vertical rib.

TIKI TIRAWA, 55 rue Bonaparte, 75006
Tel: 01 43 25 80 28
Métro: Mabillon or St-Sulpice
Opening Hours: Mon–Sat: 10.15–19.00
August: open
Credit Cards: Visa, Amex, MC
Price Range: long-sleeved merino wool sweater 550FF, jacket 1,500FF

CACHAREL: CLASSIC FRENCH LOOK
Having wandered in the wilderness of pretty Liberty print shirts for long enough, Cacharel got back their original designer, Corinne Sarrut, and as a result are looking much stronger. They have updated their

image, reduced their prices by 20% and opened a massive new store here in the 6th for men, women, teenagers and children. This label is for you if you are petite-ish with a good set of collar-bones, any age and you like a feminine, romantic and fairly classic style of dressing. It's very Parisian style for summer with skinny ribbed cardigan worn slightly unbuttoned and teamed with a flirty skirt, or shift dresses with floral green sprigs on cream. In winter you'll find more of the basic Paris working woman wardrobe – cashmere twinsets, above-the-knee skirts and fitted slightly waisted jackets. For men it is a relaxed feel even in their suiting, which for summer tends to be far more linen and casual-continental than British men are used to.

CACHAREL, 64 rue Bonaparte, 75006
Tel: 01 40 46 00 45
Métro: St-Germain-des-Prés
also at:
34 rue Tronchet, 75009. Tel: 01 47 42 12 61
5 place des Victoires, 75001. Tel: 01 42 33 29 88
Opening Hours: Mon–Fri: 10.00–19.00, Sat: 10.00–19.30
August: open
Credit Cards: Visa, Amex, Diners, MC
Price Range: trousers 490–890FF, jackets from 1,200FF, skirts from 450FF, silk/cashmere cardigan 795FF, men's suiting from 2,250FF

VENTILO: FRENCH CLASSIC WOMENSWEAR
See 2nd arrondissement for details.
59 rue Bonaparte, 75006. Tel: 01 43 26 64 84

JOSEPH: CONTEMPORARY WOMENSWEAR
See 8th arrondissement for details.
68–70 rue Bonaparte, 75006. Tel: 01 46 33 45 75

INDIES: ELEGANT WOMENSWEAR
Indies is for the woman who laughs in the face of fashion fads and is looking for career-minded clothing. It sets itself apart from trends and instead produces grown-up, elegant clothing, mostly for the work-place. Suits are plain, classic cuts, never too fitted, with jackets cut long and over the bottom. Nehru collars and trouser suits are Indies clas-sics. What makes the clothing more interesting is the detail: a bronze organza lining to a navy jacket, pieces of slate or carved wooden ele-phant heads as buttons. For the winter, steel-grey boiled wool is their signature with skirts, jackets and coat dresses. Indies is popular with women who are looking for an interesting alternative to the neat little Parisian suit.

INDIES, 59 bis rue Bonaparte, 75006
Tel: 01 46 33 39 28
Métro: St-Germain-des-Prés
also at:
4 rue du Jour, 75001. Tel: 01 40 13 91 27
Opening Hours: Mon–Sat: 10.30–19.00
August: open
Credit Cards: Visa, Amex, MC
Price Range: skirts from 800FF, suits from 3,000FF

PLEIN SUD: TREND WOMENSWEAR

See Le Marais for details.
70 bis rue Bonaparte, 75006. Tel: 01 43 54 43 06

COMPTOIR DES COTONNIERS: BASICS

No surprises here design-wise, but sharp prices pull the girls. Try here for weekend daywear or basic wardrobe fillers like cotton jeans, gingham stretch Capri pants, or longish wrap-around dresses which Paris girls wear with T-shirt and tennis shoes. Relaxed and easy look.

COMPTOIR DES COTONNIERS, 59 ter rue Bonaparte, 75006
Tel: 01 43 26 07 56
Métro: St-Germain-des-Prés
Opening Hours: Mon–Sat: 10.30–19.00
August: open
Credit Cards: Visa, Amex, MC
Price Range: jeans 390FF, trousers 400FF, dresses 600FF

RUE DES SAINTS-PÈRES

CAPUCINE PUERARI: LINGERIE AND SWIMWEAR

Capucine Puerari started off doing underwear before she diversified into clothes. It shows – what looks pretty and girly in lingerie can end up looking fussy in her women's clothes. Apparently French women don't think so, as clothing is what sells best. Swimming costumes are well cut and in bold colours like fuchsia or deep-sea blue with a border of white zig-zag braiding. Lingerie is in faded 1950s tones with Lolita slips in floral prints, delicate bras and low-cut bodies. It's more underwear for a date than for every day and the bad news is the bras come in a B cup only. Emmanuelle Béart, Vanessa Paradis and Helena are all Puerari girls.

CAPUCINE PUERARI, 63 rue des Saints-Pères, 75006
Tel: 01 42 22 14 09
Métro: St Germain-des-Prés or Sèvres-Babylone
Opening Hours: Mon–Sat: 10.00–19.00
August: closed for one week from 15 Aug
Credit Cards: Visa, Amex, Diners, MC
Price Range: one-piece swimming costume 600FF (two-piece 650FF), stretch evening dress 1,200–1,400FF

ANNE FONTAINE:
WOMEN'S WHITE COTTON SHIRTS
See 2nd arrondissement for details.
64–66 rue des Saints-Pères, 75007. Tel: 01 45 48 89 10

VERSUS: YOUNGEST LINE BY VERSACE
This is the youngest in spirit of the Versace lines and it's the one where Donatella Versace gets to let rip. Styled and with all the right models on the catwalk, it may look like it breaks every rule, but by the time it makes it to the shop it can look fairly cheap and trashy. It is not, however, cheap to buy, and for the suiting you're looking at 5,370FF for a viscose nylon slightly western-look jacket with straight short skirt. The jeans are better value and sell well; with a classic cut of high waist and narrow leg they're priced from 500 to 1,810FF. They come in all the indigo shades as well as bright Opal Fruit colours. There is an alterations service which is great if you're petite or thin as they can take in jeans perfectly. Helpful staff.

VERSUS, 64–66 rue des Saints-Pères, 75007
Tel: 01 45 49 22 66
Métro: St Germain-des-Prés or Sèvres-Babylone
Opening Hours: Mon: 11.00–19.00, Tue–Sat: 10.00–19.00
August: open
Credit Cards: Visa, Amex, Diners, MC, JCB
Price Range: suiting 5,000–6,000FF, satin jeans 1,000FF

Y'S YOHJI YAMAMOTO: DIFFUSION LINE
This is not really pitched as a second line in as much as Yohji Yamamoto launched his career with Y's in 1972 and still designs it. There is a Y's line for men and women and in Japan it accounts for 75% of the total Yamamoto turnover. It's still quite an unknown entity here as it's been available in Europe for only three years and is sold only in the Yamamoto own stores. It's a much more everyday look for Yohji and worth exploring if you've always found the main line too designerish for your lifestyle or just too pricey. Everything is made in Japan and it is about half the price of the main line. For women there are beautifully cut trouser suits which work well with a light cotton top which has one hesitant pleat sewn in. And for men there are the Yohji signature three-button, wool, slightly destructured jackets, or sweeping black overcoat. The fact that Yamamoto regards Y's as more than just a diffusion line shows and makes it creative in its own right, rather than a pallid imitation of the real thing.

Y's YOHJI YAMAMOTO, 69 rue des Saints-Pères, 75006
Tel: 01 45 48 22 56
Métro: St-Germain-des-Prés or Sèvres-Babylone
also at:

25 rue du Louvre, 75002. Tel: 01 42 21 42 93
Opening Hours: Mon–Sat: 10.30–19.00
August: open except for three days around 15 Aug
Credit Cards: Visa, Amex, Diners, MC
Price Range: men's and women's suits 3,900FF, shirt 600FF, men's overcoat
6,000FF

ÉTIENNE BRUNEL: DESIGNER WOMENSWEAR

In the words of the designer and store owner Mireille Brunel, this shop
is 'une bordelle'. It's a bit of a mad-house and Mireille is both kooky
and talented. She trained at the Chambre Syndicale de la
Couture and she couldn't care less about trends, she just does her own
thing and the Left Bank woman loves it. There are two lines – one off-
the-peg, the other made-to-measure which involves just one fitting
and five days' wait and is the same price. Round the corner in rue de
Grenelle she's recently opened up for evening and bridal (see Mercerie
d'un Soir), but in this shop it is more about cocktail wear, wedding
outfits (not for the bride), suits and corsets which French women just
love – give them any excuse and they'll get strapped into a corset for
the night. If you are looking for freedom to choose your fabric, and for
something well cut and alternative to wear to a party, come here.

ÉTIENNE BRUNEL, 70 rue des Saints-Pères, 75007
Tel: 01 45 44 41 14
Métro: St-Germain-des-Prés or Sèvres-Babylone
also at:
37 rue de Grenelle, 75006. Tel: 01 45 48 26 13
Opening Hours: Mon–Sat: 11.00–19.00
August: depends, call for details
Credit Cards: Visa, Amex, Diners, MC
Price Range: dress 1,500–2,000FF, jacket 2,000–3,000FF, corset 1,800FF

SABBIA ROSA: SEXY LINGERIE

Sabbia Rosa underwear is what a woman is talking about when she
says, 'Bring me something back from Paris.' For twenty years this
Tunisian Parisian has been making luscious lingerie in silk satin and
hand-made Calais lace. It's a supermodel knicker shop – Kate,
Claudia, Linda and Stephanie are all customers. Madonna goes for
violet and purple underwear and when Naomi turns up 'I lock the
door and she goes through every drawer,' reveals Sabbia. All the bras,
knickers, corsetry, petticoats, slips and camisoles come in 25 different
colours which include exotic shades of jade, tomato red, lime and
rouge cardinal. There is also a range of prints – the sort you would not
normally find on underwear: Sabbia goes for dog's-tooth check or
wild poppies. Prices are serious (800FF for a pair of knickers), but it's
all hand-made – and those fluffy marabou mules are just perfect for
putting the milk bottles out in the morning.

SABBIA ROSA, 71–73 rue des Saints-Pères, 75006
Tel: 01 45 48 88 37
Métro: St Germain-des-Prés or Sèvres-Babylone
Opening Hours: Mon–Sat: 10.00–19.00
August: closed for one week, call for dates
Credit Cards: Visa, Amex
Price Range: skirt slip 2,000FF, marabou mules 1,400FF

PRADA: ITALIAN DESIGNER WEAR AND ACCESSORIES

This is the original Prada location, with three boutiques, although there are two larger stores to be found in the 8th arrondissement on avenue Montaigne and rue du Faubourg St-Honoré. Here you'll find shoes, bags, leather accessories and the women's clothes collection.

PRADA, 3, 5, 9 rue de Grenelle, 75006
Tel: 01 45 48 53 14
Métro: Sèvres-Babylone
also at:
10 avenue Montaigne, 75008. Tel: 01 53 23 99 40
6 rue du Faubourg St-Honoré, 75008
Opening Hours: Mon–Sat: 10.00–19.00
August: closed for four days around 15 Aug
Credit Cards: Visa, Amex, Diners, MC, JCB
Price Range: pea-coat 4,000–5,000FF, knitwear in silk and cashmere 2,000–4,000FF, belted gabardine jersey stretch coat 7,000–8,000FF, shoes 1,200–2,000FF, boots 2,200FF, nylon bags 1,500FF, leather 3,500–4,500FF

YOHJI YAMAMOTO: JAPANESE DESIGNER

Always at fashion's cutting edge, Yohji Yamamoto has returned to its hot-seat with a series of collections which are both poetic in their elegance and innovative in their silhouette and cut. His clothes, once the preserve of the radical avant-garde, have been appropriated by a glossier, more mainstream kind of woman – Nicole Kidman, French starlets and the late Carolyn Bessette Kennedy, who always looked both dramatic and dignified wearing Yohji Yamamoto. His clothes are sensual and ageless, they drape, twist, wrap or caress, they amuse, never abuse and, in these more recent collections, they have a certain refined glamour. Yohji still borrows extensively from the man's wardrobe with soft wide trousers or a jacket reminiscent of a morning coat, and he admits, 'The basic of my design is the concept: the more women wear mannish clothes, the more they look sexy and beautiful.' But there are resolutely feminine shapes as well, such as sheath dresses, a dramatic cowl-back dress with bracelet sleeves and draped satin skirts in creamy gold. This is the womenswear store for Paris, though there's also a slice of menswear. Staff are laid back and helpful and the store has an oversized feel, with huge mirrors propped against the wall and room for a small boutique in those changing rooms.

YOHJI YAMAMOTO, 3 rue de Grenelle, 75006
Tel: 01 42 84 28 87
Métro: St-Sulpice or Sèvres-Babylone
Opening Hours: Mon: 11.30–19.00, Tue–Sat: 10.30–19.00
August: open
Credit Cards: Visa, Amex, Diners, MC
Price Range: socks 230FF, women's suit from 6,000FF, overcoat from 18,000FF

ATSURO TAYAMA: JAPANESE DESIGNER

Former first assistant to Yohji Yamamoto, Atsuro Tayama is one of the younger generation of Japanese designers and he is influenced by the generation before in that he does that whole Japanese thing of exploring new cuts, wrapping fabric, distorting shapes – although he tends to do it in a more commercial way. Also on sale here is Indivi, his younger – read less expensive – line, which has nice-looking leather biker jackets, nylon sporty trousers and interesting knits.

ATSURO TAYAMA, 81 rue des Saints-Pères, 75006
Tel: 01 49 54 74 20
also at:
40 rue de Sévigné, 75003. Tel: 01 40 29 15 07
Opening Hours: Mon–Sat: 11.00–19.00
August: closed second week of the month
Credit Cards: Visa, Amex, MC, JCB
Price Range: top from 650FF, coat from 4,000FF, Indivi T-shirt 200FF, Indivi trousers 650FF

SPORTMAX: MAXMARA'S YOUNGER LINE

The trend for sportswear in fashion means MaxMara's younger sister line Sportmax is raising its profile by opening its own boutique here. The clothes have all the polished tailoring you expect from this Italian house but with edgier details and fabrics for a younger clientele. There are thick knit coats with rabbit-skin lining in sherbet orange, college scarves, stripy turtlenecks with sequin detail. Also worth checking out is the new line Sportmax Code which is pitched at a young, casual customer with jeans, T-shirts, parkas, sweatshirts and is priced around 30% less than Sportmax.

SPORTMAX, 72 rue des Saints-Pères, 75007
Tel: 01 45 49 22 03
Métro: Sèvres-Babylone
Opening Hours: Mon–Sat: 10.30–19.00
August: open
Credit Cards: Visa, Amex, Diners, MC, JCB
Price Range: trousers from 900FF, winter coats 3,000–10,000FF, trouser suit from 3,000FF, T-shirt from 200FF

ALAIN MIKLI: TREND EYEWEAR

French eyewear designer Alain Mikli has opened a store selling his own designs, including his bug-eyed yellow-lens shades designed for U2's Bono, as well as slick sunglasses by Jil Sander and Philippe Starck. The store is itself is cool, contemporary and designed by Mikli's friend Starck with acres of dark *wenge* wood and undulating 'walls' of white cotton curtains. Downstairs are the new Mikli clothes collection and his latest invention, a spectacle camera – a tiny video camera mounted on a pair of glasses.

ALAIN MIKLI, 74 rue des Saints-Pères, 75007
Tel: 01 45 49 40 00
Métro: Sèvres-Babylone
Opening Hours: Mon:11.00–19.00, Tue-Thu:10.00–19.00, Fri/Sat: 9.30–19.30
August: closed for five days around 15 Aug
Credit Cards: Visa, Amex, Diners, MC, JCB
Price Range: glasses 750–2,800FF

ANTEPRIMA: ITALIAN DESIGNER WEAR

The name is Italian, the look is Italian, but it's a Japanese designer Izumi Ogino behind the Anteprima label. Ogino has lived in Milan for years and says she's searching for a 'cosmopolitan simplicity' which, translated into clothes, means lots of glossy knitwear which is clean and lean in luxury colours to be worn day and night. She recently added a lot of suiting which is trouser-based, sharp, androgynous and elongated. It's a clever example of discreet dressing which speaks style. Bags are slick, made in Italy and come in brown moc-croc or burnished leathers with copper strip handles.

ANTEPRIMA, 81 rue des Saints-Pères, 75006
Tel: 01 45 44 44 41
Métro: Sèvres-Babylone
Opening Hours: Mon–Sat: 11.00–19.00
August: closed middle two weeks
Credit Cards: Visa, Amex, Diners, MC, JCB
Price Range: V-neck viscose dress 1,330FF, tunic top 1,260FF, trousers 1,140FF, leather bags 1,800–3,800FF

M.A.C.: COSMETICS

What started as an independent make-up brand invented by Canadian make-up artist Frank Toscan in his kitchen back in 1985 has since been bought out completely by cosmetics giant Estée Lauder – and in the process has lost some of its individualist magic. Gone are the free make-over lessons, now you pay 560FF for the pleasure. What remains is an army of sales assistants who manage to convey absolute fascination at your every foundation desire and lip-liner angst, as well as 150 great colours of lipstick, six types of foundation and a comprehensive range of skin-care and hair products. Other M.A.C. principles include a policy of donating annually around $1.5 million to AIDS-related charities and a recycling pledge for all products in plastic containers (return six empty containers and they give you a free lipstick).

M.A.C., 76 bis rue des Saints-Pères, 75006
Tel: 01 45 48 60 24
Métro: Sèvres-Babylone
also at:
62 rue de Passy, 75016. Tel: 01 53 92 08 60
Opening Hours: Mon–Sat: 10.30–19.00
Credit Cards: Visa, Amex, Diners, MC, JCB
Price Range: lipstick 90FF, nail varnish 60FF, foundation 115FF

RUE DU CHERCHE-MIDI

CAMPER: CULT AND CASUAL SHOES

Camper make cult shoes. Don't let that put you off; they also happen to make loads of comfortable, modern styles built for reality at reasonable prices. Based in Majorca, Camper do everything from simple stitched moccasins – as worn by the King of Spain – to their 'casual techno shoe', which is made from Gore-Tex on cushioned rubber soles. They are famous for their Camaleón rural shoes, a Camper take on the traditional Majorcan rustic shoe made from stitched canvas and recycled tyre soles. They are also cult for the 'twins' – two shoes which are complementary but never the same. The difference can be in the motif, the position of the laces, the direction of the stripes – whatever – the idea is asymmetrical footwear for those free thinkers who 'believe your left and right foot each has a mind of its own'.

CAMPER, 1 rue du Cherche-Midi, 75006
Tel: 01 45 48 22 00
Métro: St-Sulpice
also at:
9 rue des Francs Bourgeois, 75004. Tel: 01 48 87 09 09
Opening Hours: Mon–Sat: 10.00–19.00
August: open
Credit Cards: Visa, Amex, MC
Price Range: women's shoes 500–700FF, men's shoes 600–1,000FF

ROBERT CLERGERIE: DESIGNER SHOES

There are two other Robert Clergerie stores in Paris and a stand at Printemps, but in terms of range and fashion this store is the most important. The national shoe hero is now in his sixties and keeps turning out his grown-up, good-looking shoes which appeal to both the bourgeois and the fashion set. Looking less trendy over the last few seasons, there are the classic soft moccasins with or without a heel or masculine-feel brogues and lace-ups which come in serious shiny leather or fake crocodile in scarlet or chestnut brown. His signature design is an elongated toe.

ROBERT CLERGERIE, 5 rue du Cherche-Midi, 75006
Tel: 01 45 48 75 47
Métro: St-Sulpice
also at:
46 rue Croix des Petits Champs, 75001. Tel: 01 42 61 49 24
18 avenue Victor Hugo, 75016. Tel: 01 45 01 81 30
Opening Hours: Mon–Sat: 9.30–19.00
August: open
Credit Cards: Visa, Amex, MC, JCB
Price Range: about 1,200FF on average

MARE: FASHION SHOES AND BOOTS

Unashamedly non-classic with heaps of trend, this Italian label is doing well in Paris. There is no such thing as a Mare basic and whatever the season's look is, they've got it for men and women. There are lots of shoes and boots in polished leather with desert camel and beige colours, and that above-the-ankle boot with slightly chunky high heels is everywhere. A good place to get boots – I bought some last year in the sale and they've really kept their calf shape. Lenny Kravitz and Vanessa Paradis have been in to buy his and hers.

MARE, 4 rue du Cherche-Midi, 75006
Tel: 01 45 44 55 33
Métro: St-Sulpice
Opening Hours: Mon–Sat: 10.00–19.30
August: open
Credit Cards: Visa, Amex, Diners, MC, JCB
Price Range: women's 845–1,500FF, ankle boots 1,200FF, men's shoes 800–1,200FF

ERÈS: GREAT SWIMWEAR
See 9th arrondissement for details.
4 bis rue du Cherche-Midi, 75006. Tel: 01 45 44 95 54

GINKGO: QUILTED NYLON BAGS
Ginkgo make voluptuous quilted nylon bags which come in colours such as amber, plum, almond green and ice blue with a satin sheen finish. Shapes are purely practical, like a backpack, vanity case or shopper with popper fastener, while the optional finish of brown leather handles and flap adds flair. Designers Laurence Lagarde and Sabine Proux create the bags and Sabine's husband manufactures them in his factory. They do other lines in leather or satin but it's the quilting which is most in demand. Prices are nice at around 400FF.

GINKGO, 4 ter rue du Cherche-Midi, 75006
Tel: 01 45 44 90 87
Métro: St-Sulpice
Opening Hours: Mon: 11.30–18.00, Tue–Sat: 10.30–19.00
August: closed for one week, call for dates
Credit Cards: Visa, Amex, MC, JCB
Price Range: backpack with leather trim 480FF, all-nylon shopper 330FF

FAUSTO SANTINI: ITALIAN DESIGNER FOOTWEAR
Santini is an Italian shoe designer who makes luxury shoes for the footwear cognoscenti. Male or female, they come for his comfort, minimalist, original designs and, although they may never admit it, the warm sensation of brand kudos. Santini shoes are understated with hand-finished detail and all made in the softest, often glove, leather, lined in lamb leather and made with brown soles. Not a follower of trend, he designs shoes that are about width for maximum comfort and natural dyes: mainly in putty, navy, black and browns. Men's

shoes have a round-toed Japanese-slipper influence. The clientele is suitably discerning, Denzel Washington is a multi-purchase customer here and apparently all the staff from Miyake, Comme des Garçons and Yohji come for their shoes. No one said they were cheap – prices start at 1,000FF. And then there are the bags – superbly minimal and modern.

FAUSTO SANTINI, 4 ter rue du Cherche-Midi, 75006
Tel: 01 45 44 39 40
Métro: St-Sulpice
Opening Hours: Mon: 11.00–19.00, Tue–Sat: 10.00–19.00
August: closed middle two weeks
Credit Cards: Visa, Amex, MC
Price Range: men's shoes from 1,300FF, women's from 1,000FF, bags 2,000–3,500FF

YVES SAINT LAURENT SHOES: DESIGNER SHOES
Wildly glamorous shoes are the order of the day here: think purple satin espradrilles with a wedge heel and satin ribbons or sexy suede boots with killer heels. There are some everyday styles, but mostly these are shoes for the dry-martini-for-breakfast kind of girl.

YVES SAINT LAURENT SHOES, 13 rue du Cherche-Midi, 75006
Tel: 01 42 22 49 91
Métro: Sèvres-Babylone
Opening Hours: Mon: 11.00–19.00, Tue–Sat: 10.30–19.00
August: call for details
Credit Cards: Visa, Amex, Diners, MC, JCB
Price Range: sandals from 1,300FF, mules 1,300FF, boots from 2,800FF

GROOM: LIGHTWEIGHT NYLON AND LEATHER BAGS
See 16th arrondissement for details.
13 rue du Cherche-Midi, 75006. Tel: 01 45 48 49 36

REGINA RUBENS: FRENCH CLASSIC WOMENSWEAR
See 1st arrondissement for details.
13 rue du Cherche-Midi, 75006. Tel: 01 45 44 96 95

CUISINE DE BAR: LUNCH AND COFFEE STOP
Location-wise, this café picked the perfect spot – right next door to Paris's most famous bakery, Poilâne, and in the middle of a boutique-laden road. Not surprisingly the clientele here is predominantly sleek shopping females. Pick your way between heavyweight carrier bags and sit down to a tartine of crunchy brown Poilâne bread, toasted and then topped with something good – roast chicken, anchovies, capers and tomato with a smudge of garlic is nice, or there's a skinnier cottage cheese, celery and basil. All the tartines are served with a salad and home-made dressing. If you you want a quick and casual lunch or snack it's ideal and the price is right.

CUISINE DE BAR, 8 rue du Cherche-Midi, 75006
Tel: 01 45 48 45 69
Métro: Sèvres-Babylone or St-Sulpice
Opening Hours: Mon–Sat: 8.00–21.30
August: closed for two weeks mid-month, call for exact dates
Credit Cards: Visa, Amex, MC
Price Range: tartines 33–52FF, breakfast 40FF

MIU MIU: PRADA DIFFUSION LINE

The Italians call it 'screech chic'. A mix of man-made fabrics, quirky taste, urban cool, trashy tweed and witty details: for best results just add protruding cheek-bones. For the new model army, Miu Miu dressing spells real credibility and if you've got the body of a 16-year-old it'll look great on you too. It's the second Prada line and named after Miuccia's nickname. Prices are around 35% to 40% cheaper than Prada, so even if the clothes leave you cold, come for the bags and shoes which still look thoroughly Prada. A large Miu Miu store is scheduled to open on rue de Grenelle at the end of 2000.

miu miu · Rue du Cherche Midi

MIU MIU, 10 rue du Cherche-Midi, 75006
Tel: 01 45 48 63 33
Métro: St-Sulpice
Opening Hours: Mon–Sat: 10.30–19.00
August: closed for two weeks, call for dates
Credit Cards: Visa, Amex, Diners, MC, JCB
Price Range: shoes 1,200FF, boots 1,700FF, skirt from 800FF, knitwear 1,000FF

MYMA: WELL-PRICED, TREND SHOES

Price is the big draw here. They do the season's trends in shoes and boots with prices weighing in from 500 to 600FF for shoes. The clientele is teenage to 30-something searching for high fashion.

MYMA, 12 rue du Cherche-Midi, 75006
Tel: 01 45 48 02 08
Métro: Sèvres-Babylone or St-Sulpice
Opening Hours: Mon: 12.00–19.00, Tue–Sat: 11.00–19.00
August: open
Credit Cards: Visa, Amex, MC, JCB
Price Range: shoes 500–600FF, above-the-ankle boots 600–750FF, boots 995FF

CLIO BLUE: PRETTY SILVER JEWELLERY

In a city which still rates gob-stopping costume jewellery, Clio Blue offers mostly low-key designs for every day. Designer Annie Busson makes lots of plain silver link necklaces, bracelets and watches, but she also works with semi-precious stones like amethyst, grenadine and tourmaline as well as lapis lazuli. There is a pretty line of pale pink and baby-blue enamel in chokers, bracelets and rings. Everything is in silver and prices vary according to the weight of the silver, but are generally reasonable.

CLIO BLUE, 16 rue du Cherche-Midi, 75006
Tel: 01 42 22 37 36
Métro: Sèvres-Babylone or St-Sulpice
Opening Hours: Mon: 11.00–19.00, Tue–Sat: 10.00–19.00
August: closed 5–23 Aug
Credit Cards: Visa, Amex, MC
Price Range: silver motif to hang on a necklace 65FF, earrings from 280FF, rings from 250FF, bracelets from 350FF

LUNDI BLEU: FASHIONABLE BOOTS AND SHOES

Lundi Bleu makes fashionable shoes which are in the mid-range price bracket. It is the second line to Accessoire Diffusion which has a boutique in the same road at No. 6. Basically it's the same designer, Jean-Paul Barriol, but the shoes are made up in Spain and around 40% cheaper than the main line. Once past the gliding electric doors, you'll find the classic shapes and styles in the left-hand room as you go in, the trend styles to the right. For a classic look, they have flat moccasins in navy which French women live in, a low-heeled sort of jazz shoe, leather ballet pumps and lots of stretch suede.

LUNDI BLEU, 23–25 rue du Cherche-Midi, 75006
Tel: 01 42 22 47 94
Métro: St-Sulpice
Opening Hours: Mon–Sat: 10.00–19.00
August: closed 11–26 Aug
Credit Cards: Visa, Amex, JCB
Price Range: shoes from 550FF, most expensive boots 1,150FF

J FENESTRIER: MEN'S DESIGNER SHOES

This is the men's division of Robert Clergerie shoes, although the actual Fenestrier brand is over 100 years old and was founded by shoe-maker Joseph Fenestrier. These are luxury, hand-sewn shoes meant for urban life with a modern, rather than traditional, feel. Great quality and understated styling, as with their wallets and weekend bags.

J FENESTRIER, 23 rue du Cherche-Midi, 75006
Tel: 01 42 22 66 02
Métro: St-Sulpice
Opening Hours: Mon–Sat: 10.00–19.00
August: open
Credit Cards: Visa, Amex, MC, JCB
Price Range: ankle boots 1,900–2,200FF, loafer, lace-up or moccasin 1,600–1,800FF

CHERCHE-MIDI: ITALIAN RESTAURANT

A small traditional Italian restaurant with red gingham tablecloths which attracts a cool crowd, mixing Italians plus fashion and film people, plus locals (MC Solaar and Juliette Binoche). Open lunchtime and night it is always buzzing (you need to book in advance) and the menu includes Italian meats, tasty antipasti and a choice of three fresh pastas which change every day. Great coffee.

CHERCHE-MIDI, 22 rue du Cherche-Midi, 75006
Tel: 01 45 48 27 44
Métro: Sèvres-Babylone
Opening Hours: every day: 12.00–15.00, 20.00–23.45
August: open
Credit Cards: Visa, MC
Price Range: Italian meats 50–70FF, plate of pasta 78FF, meat or fish-based dish 90FF, around 200–250FF per head

JOYCE AND CO: BAGS, JEWELLERY, BELTS, HATS

Joyce and Co specialises in handbags and everything you can put in them. A former fashion editor, Joyce opened her shop in 1995 with the idea of making it a fun fashion store for mother and daughter to shop, so she gets her own daughter to help with some of the buying. Bag-wise the choice is fairly BCBG with Renaud Pellegrino satin bags for evening and Just Campagne sensible bags for day, while Peggy Huynh Kinh's bags in softest tan leathers add a fashion dimension.

JOYCE AND CO, 1 place Alphonse Deville, 75006
Tel: 01 42 22 05 69
Métro: Sèvres-Babylone
Opening Hours: Mon: 14.00–19.30, Tue–Sat: 10.30–19.30
August: closed, reopens from 25 Aug
Credit Cards: Visa, Amex, MC
Price Range: bags 300–4,000FF

PEGGY HUYNH KINH: CHIC ACCESSORIES

A former architect, Peggy Huynh Kinh takes the concept of utilitarian packaging and translates that into desirable bags. She borrows shapes from everyday – the paper grocery bag or the plastic supermarket bag – which she then transforms into a chic accessory in glazed calfskin, suede or dimple pigskin with steel handles. Her designs are pared down and sophisticated as well as that old cliché of modern yet time-less. They come in classic shades of tan, black, beige as well as more daring purple. Basically these are bags set for the executive woman who lives her life on Palm Pilot and does not (unlike others of us) drag around a small paper mountain with her day-to-day. Just as well, as the Peggy Huynh Kinh sleek lines do not cater for this kind of clutter. As well as bags, there are leather desk accessories such as beautiful notebooks and agendas and a range of jewellery which includes chunky silver rings with blobs of crystal.

PEGGY HUYNH KINH, 11 rue Coëtlogon, 75006
Tel: 01 45 63 48 17
Métro: Sèvres-Babylone or St-Sulpice
Opening Hours: Mon–Sat: 10.00–19.00
August: closed
Credit Cards: Visa, Amex, Diners, MC, JCB
Price Range: bags from 1,500FF, rings from 1,200FF, wallets from 1,000FF

RUE DU VIEUX COLOMBIER

CLAUDIE PIERLOT: FASHIONABLE WOMENSWEAR
See 2nd arrondissement for details.
23 rue du Vieux Colombier, 75006. Tel: 01 45 48 11 96

MARCEL LASSANCE: RELAXED, CHIC MENSWEAR
Marcel Lassance looks a bit like Alan Rickman (at least he does in the PR shot) and Alan Rickman is just the sort of man you could imagine being kitted out in his clothes. Lassance started out by designing fab-rics before moving into designing his own menswear, but he's still known for his quirky fabrics like a marijuana hemp summer jacket. The look is relaxed, artsy and very approachable. Gérard Depardieu and Jeff Goldblum both buy here. Jackets are cut wide, with slightly exaggerated but softly rounded shoulders meant to feel as if 'you're wearing a cardigan'. Less young-fogey are the combat trousers,

pea-coats and glazed cotton shirts which come in copper or deep lime. Lassance does the whole wardrobe from socks to blazers via polo sweaters and alterations can be done in a day if you are leaving town.

MARCEL LASSANCE, 17 rue du Vieux Colombier, 75006
Tel: 01 45 48 29 28
Métro: St-Sulpice
Opening Hours: Mon–Sat: 10.00–19.00
August: open
Credit Cards: Visa, Amex, Diners, MC, JCB
Price Range: winter suit around 4,500FF, shirt 695FF, tie 225FF, casual military-style trousers 645FF

VICTOIRE HOMME: SMART AND CHIC MENSWEAR

This is the brother to Victoire womenswear stores, but whereas the women's shops stock a choice of different designers, Victoire sticks predominantly to its own label, Hartford. Shirts are their strength and they offer five or so different collar styles and always come up with new and interesting textured cottons and weaves. Shirt style simmers between office and weekend – it's not as formal as Jermyn Street and never as casual as Gap. If you want to add some continental styling to your wardrobe, pick from shirts in hot pink or white linen gauze, tiny grey caviar or small dog's-tooth in royal blue and white. In winter Victoire gets into cashmere sweaters, suiting and velvet shirts, while for summer there are lots of shorts, Lycra swimmers and polo shirts.

VICTOIRE HOMME, 15 rue du Vieux Colombier, 75006
Tel: 01 45 44 28 02
Métro: St-Sulpice
also at:
10–12 rue du Colonel Driant, 75001. Tel: 01 42 97 44 87
Opening Hours: Mon–Sat: 10.00–19.00
August: open
Credit Cards: Visa, Amex, Diners
Price Range: shirts 450–550FF

VICTOIRE: CHIC, SMART WOMENSWEAR

This is less fashion-conscious than the flagship Victoire boutique over in place des Victoires (see 2nd arrondissement). There tends to be a lot of navy and neutrals dressing, sporty separates, DKNY and then quite a bit of fairly unexceptional Italian tailoring. It's a good place to find smart shirts, twinsets and suits which follow the French dress code of no-shock chic.

VICTOIRE, 1 rue Madame, 75006
Tel: 01 45 44 28 14
Métro: St-Sulpice
also at:

10–12 place des Victoires, 75002. Tel: 01 42 61 09 02
16 rue de Passy, 75016. Tel: 01 42 88 20 84
Opening Hours: Mon–Sat: 10.00–19.00
August: open
Credit Cards: Visa, Amex, Diners, MC, JCB
Price Range: hats 300–1,200FF, knitwear 800–3,000FF, suits 2,500–5,500FF,
summer dress 1,000–2,500FF

JEAN-CHARLES DE CASTELBAJAC:
LIFESTYLE/FASHION

French designer Jean-Charles de Castelbajac had fallen off the face of
fashion. Aged 50, he decided the time was ripe for a comeback. He
hired a hot PR and opened a new vast white space and called it a concept store. He took his signature blanket coats, bright colours and
graphic shapes and rejigged the lot for the new millennium. The result
is an upbeat store selling de Castelbajac's designs and plastic fluorescent wrist-bands boasting 'Place Vendôme', jewels by Erik Halley,
boiled-felt furniture plus the obligatory underground fashion mags.
And the clothes – felt coats the colour of boiled sweets with holes cut
out, nylon dresses, mohair hairy trousers and printed T-shirts. His signature primary colours and red cross graphics are everywhere.

JEAN-CHARLES DE CASTELBAJAC, 26 rue Madame, 75006
Tel: 01 45 48 40 55
Métro: St-Sulpice
Opening Hours: Mon–Sat: 10.00–19.00
August: closed for one week
Credit Cards: Visa, Amex, Diners, MC, JCB
Price Range: plastic fluorescent wrist-bands 70FF, nylon bag from 600FF, coat
from 3,000FF

FORMES: PREGNANCY WEAR
See 2nd arrondissement for details.
5 rue du Vieux Colombier, 75006. Tel: 01 45 49 09 80

AGNÈS B.:   FRENCH STYLE AND FASHION
See 2nd arrondissement for details.
6 rue du Vieux Colombier, 75006. Tel: 01 44 39 02 60

HERVÉ CHAPELIER: SMART NYLON BAGS
Despite what is possibly the dullest of shop fronts in Paris (i.e. bottle
green with a stiff little window display), don't be put off, get in there
and check out the bags. They are made of lightweight nylon, come in
duo colour combinations and just about every shape and size you
need from washbag to the perfect weekend bag. The colours change
every season and always stretch the style octave from urban fashion
(chocolate brown with ice pink) to rural Volvo estate (racing green and

bordeaux). The French use them a lot for the gym and for college, but it's the weekend sizes and vanity cases which are really great value. They look smart, are machine washable and easily stowable and one of those items you cannot get cheaper in England.

HERVÉ CHAPELIER, 1 rue du Vieux Colombier, 75006
Tel: 01 44 07 06 50
Métro: St-Sulpice
also at:
13 rue Gustave Courbet, 75016. Tel: 01 47 27 83 66
390 rue St-Honoré, 75001. Tel: 01 42 96 38 04
Opening Hours: Mon–Fri: 10.15–19.00, Sat: 10.00–19.15
August: open
Credit Cards: Visa, Amex, JCB
Price Range: toilet bag 135FF, weekend bag 300FF, vanity case 190FF, shopper 200FF

RUE ST-SULPICE

YVES SAINT LAURENT RIVE GAUCHE HOMME:
DESIGNER MENSWEAR

Not since the 1970s has Yves Saint Laurent Rive Gauche menswear looked so sexy. The designer responsible is Hedi Slimane, a hot young talent who has succeeded in making the brand modern and desirable again. 'My intention is to harness the spirit of Yves Saint Laurent's early collections,' says Slimane, and he has done it, reviving the Rive Gauche spirit with suits which are cut sharp and waisted, see-through chiffon shirts sprinkled with sequins, crêpe djellabas and lean leather trench-coats. The days of bland office suits are over; these are clothes cut for a fashion-aware man.

YVES SAINT LAURENT RIVE GAUCHE HOMME, 12 place St-Sulpice, 75006
Tel: 01 43 26 84 40
Métro: St-Sulpice
Opening Hours: Mon: 11.00–19.00, Tue–Sat: 10.30–19.00
August: open
Credit Cards: Visa, Amex, Diners, MC, JCB
Price Range: ties 640FF, suits from 6,900FF, leather jacket from 8,000FF, trousers from 1,200FF

ANNICK GOUTAL: PERFUMERY
See 1st arrondissement for details.
12 place St-Sulpice, 75006. Tel: 01 46 33 03 15

CAFÉ DE LA MAIRIE: LOCAL CAFÉ
Great stop for lunch as you can look and listen to the St-Sulpice fountains. What's more during spring and summer there's a bank of seats

around six deep out front where the clientele – student, glam-girl, artsy etc. – jostle for position. Food is good value for lunch: the house special is the Assiette Mairie of green salad, tomato, grated carrot, toasted Poilâne bread with roast beef and mayonnaise, or try two great big dollops of creamy goat's cheese on toast, price 42FF. The gossip bar for the neighbourhood; come here for a kick-start espresso or evening apéritif.

CAFÉ DE LA MAIRIE, 8 place St-Sulpice, 75006
Tel: 01 43 26 67 82
Métro: St-Sulpice
Opening Hours: Mon–Sat: 7.00–2.00am
August: open
Credit Cards: none
Price Range: Assiette Mairie 50FF, glass of kir 21FF

YVES SAINT LAURENT RIVE GAUCHE:
FRENCH DESIGNER

Yves Saint Laurent – perhaps the most wanted fashion brand in the business – was bought at the end of 1999 by the Gucci Group, who paid a significant $1 billion for it, but as Gucci chairman Domenico de Sole put it on the day of the sale, 'One billion dollars is a good price for the greatest brand in the world.'

Appointed creative director Tom Ford is working the same fashion alchemy that he used to turn Gucci around. While Tom designs the ready-to-wear, Monsieur Saint Laurent now concentrates on designing the haute couture, which remains an independent company. And what an incredible heritage Saint Laurent has left to ready-to-wear. From the icons of his career – le smoking, le saharien, the chubby fox furs, the trench-coats – to the very essence of his style–androgyny, the strength of silhouette, the exotic colour palette, the sexually charged Saint Laurent chic – it is a profound legacy and one that means the Saint Laurent influence can be felt throughout the fashion world.

YVES SAINT LAURENT RIVE GAUCHE, 6 place St-Sulpice, 75006
Tel: 01 43 29 43 00
Métro: St-Sulpice
also at:
38 rue du Faubourg St-Honoré, 75008. Tel: 01 42 65 74 59
19 avenue Victor Hugo, 75016. Tel: 01 45 00 64 64
Opening Hours: Mon–Sat: 10.00–19.00
August: open
Credit Cards: Visa, Amex, Diners, MC, JCB
Price Range: tunic dress 4,300FF, blazer 6,300FF

CHRISTIAN LACROIX: FRENCH COUTURIER

For full details, see the rue du Faubourg St-Honoré store in the 8th arrondissement. The store here sells the ready-to-wear, Bazar line, jeans and bed-linen.
2–4 place St-Sulpice, 75006. Tel: 01 46 33 48 95

SÉVERINE PERRAUDIN: STYLISH DRESSING

Séverine Perraudin's clothes are so simply stylish they make you want to buy the whole lot and take them home to make some sense of your wardrobe. She's had her own label since 1988 and a store over on the Right Bank, but this is her new venture on the quiet side of St-Sulpice overlooking the church. She started out as assistant to Michel Klein and has since worked as a designer with MaxMara and for four years for Missoni. She made her reputation with her cache-coeur but has since moved on, cutting elegant floor-length winter coats from boiled grey wool or fragile shirts from crumpled silk chiffon. Séverine says she like clothes 'which flow and touch the body rather than stick to it', so she works a lot on the bias and in 'authentic' fabrics such as tweeds, cashmere mixes, crêpes and jersey.

SÉVERINE PERRAUDIN, 5 place St-Sulpice, 75006
Tel: 01 43 54 10 63
Métro: St-Sulpice
Opening Hours: Mon–Sat: 11.00–19.00
August: open
Credit Cards: Visa, Amex
Price Range: trousers 700FF, jacket 2,400FF

SANDRA SERRAF: CLASSIC WOMENSWEAR

Sandra Serraf is the sort of designer who believes you should look elegant when you're out doing the Sainsbury's shop. Scary? Not really, at least she comes up with an affordable and wearable collection with which to do it. She focuses on the woman aged 30 and above with feminine, easy to wear, easy to put together separates in plain and subtle colours. All her suiting is sold separately, so for instance you can buy two different bottoms to work with one jacket. For summer she has pretty knits like a cotton halter-neck worn under a cardigan in pistachio green, while her cigarette and wide-legged trousers have become all-year shop staples. You'll never get caught out in the aisles again.

SANDRA SERRAF, 18 rue Mabillon, 75006
Tel: 01 43 25 21 24
Métro: Mabillon
Opening Hours: Mon–Sat: 11.00–19.00
August: closed for first three weeks
Credit Cards: Visa, Amex, MC, JCB
Price Range: cigarette trousers 640FF, skirts 400–600FF, jacket 1,200–1,500FF, knitwear 300–700FF

MUJI: JAPANESE ESSENTIALS

Japanese store Muji pulls the crowds with its well-designed essentials, fair prices, nice quality and because it manages to inject the concept of basic with a certain sex appeal. The store at No. 30 rue St-Sulpice sells household essentials, beige china, linen, cooking utensils and furniture, while diagonally opposite are the clothes collection and stationery. Great Muji buys include small snap-top plastic bottles (perfect for decanting cleanser and toner when travelling), concertina see-through wallets (handy for storing receipts), lightweight travel bags and fabric storage boxes. They have started expanding their furniture range to include sofa beds, wooden coffee tables and shelving. When it comes to clothing Muji is good for socks and vests, but when things get too radically pared down the clothes verge on the anaemic.

MUJI, 27 & 30 rue St-Sulpice, 75006
Tel: 01 46 34 01 10
Métro: Odéon or St-Sulpice
also at: 19 rue Auber, 75009. Tel: 01 43 12 54 00
Opening Hours: Mon–Sat: 10.00–20.00
August: open
Credit Cards: Visa, Amex, Diners, MC, JCB
Price Range: acrylic cosmetics box 60FF, lavender shampoo 50FF, beige porcelain teapot 95FF

MAISON DE FAMILLE: INTERIORS/LIFESTYLE
See 8th arrondissement for details.
29 rue St-Sulpice, 75006. Tel: 01 40 46 97 47

SISSO'S: ACCESSORIES
The idea here is to present a whole range of accessories – bags, shoes, sunglasses, scarves and jewellery – from a selection of designers and brands. The result is a mixed bag, the best of which includes Pierre Hardy's shoes, Fendissimo (Fendi's second line of bags), Cutler and Gross sunglasses and Sequoia bags (for which Pierre Hardy is creative consultant so worth checking out for less expensive trend pieces).

SISSO'S, 27 rue St-Sulpice, 75006
Tel: 01 44 07 11 40
Métro: Odéon
also at:
20 rue Mahler, 75004. Tel: 01 44 61 99 50
Opening Hours: Mon–Fri: 10.00–19.00, Sat: 10.30–19.30
August: call for details
Credit Cards: Visa, Amex, MC
Price Range: bags from 450FF, shoes from 1,100FF, sunglasses from 760FF

VANESSA BRUNO TREND WOMENSWEAR
A French young designer who does realism dressing. Her clothes used to be pretty classic-looking but have got progressively more hip. She cuts a great trouser which elongates the leg and sits low on the hip with a crisp front crease. Other staples include a cute knitted poncho, skinny knit polo-necks and three-quarter-length trousers. A second line, Athé, is sold alongside with more basic pieces such as T-shirts.

VANESSA BRUNO, 25 rue St-Sulpice, 75006
Tel: 01 43 54 41 04
Métro: Odéon or St-Sulpice
Opening Hours: Mon–Sat: 10.30–19.00
August: closed three weeks, call for dates
Credit Cards: Visa, Amex, Diners, JCB
Price Range: trousers from 795FF, coat from 1,900FF, skinny knit sweaters
from 295FF

MARIE MERCIÉ: FLAMBOYANT HATS

When she's creating hats Marie Mercié says she imagines 'a beautiful woman with panache, who would have fought in the Resistance'. The result is hats that are sometimes flamboyant, always stylish, and make, rather than sabotage, an outfit.

Former editor of the socialist magazine *Latitude*, Marie is self-taught and wanders around with a bulldog on a satin ribbon lead. Her hats in winter range from casual chenille styles which can be stuffed away in a handbag to strong and graphic shapes – a felt pod or crenellated brim. For more dressed-up hats the trend is for small perched cocktail styles in fruity colours like tangerine, lime, apricot and strawberry. During summer this is the place to go if you are looking for a smart hat which shouts Paris to wear to a wedding. She also creates some amazing bridal hats.

All hats are hand-made, beautifully finished and can be bought off the peg or made to measure, and the staff here are helpful with choosing the right shape. If you are in Paris just for the weekend they can be shipped to you. Eurostocracy, Catherine Deneuve, Shirley MacLaine and Faye Dunaway are all customers. These are hats to be worn by women of every age with attitude.

MARIE MERCIÉ, 23 rue St-Sulpice, 75006
Tel: 01 43 26 45 83
Métro: Odéon
also at:
(men's hats) Anthony Peto, 56 rue Tiquetonne, 75002. Tel: 01 40 26 60 68
Opening Hours: Mon–Sat: 11.00–19.00
August: closed on and off, call for exact dates
Credit Cards: Visa, Amex, Diners, MC, JCB
Price Range: everyday felt hat 800FF, smart wedding hat 2,000FF

LA CHAMBRE CLAIRE: PHOTOGRAPHY BOOKSHOP

A bookshop specialising in international photography with 3,500 titles including monographs of past and present photographers, exhibition catalogues, anthologies of work. There is a good section on fashion photography with all those books on, or of, photography by fashion stars, like Kelly Klein's book on underwear, Karl Lagerfeld's *Off the Record* and Donna Karan's every ad campaign. Downstairs is for exhibitions and sale stock. Fashion photographers like Patrick Demarchelier, Paolo Roversi, Peter Lindbergh, Helmut Newton and Ellen von Unworth come to browse and check out the competition.

LA CHAMBRE CLAIRE, 14 rue St-Sulpice, 75006
Tel: 01 46 34 04 31
Métro: Odéon
Opening Hours: Mon–Sat: 10.00–19.00
August: open
Credit Cards: Visa, MC

LIWAN: FASHION AND HOMEWEAR

A Lebanese boutique which sells the ultimate lounging kit for body and home designed by Lina Audi. The feel is Mediterranean Arabian with gorgeous coloured satin eiderdowns, embroidered slippers, hand-blown glassware and tiny beaded charm bracelets. Clothes-wise this is the ideal kit for floating around by the side of the pool or at home: there are silk and linen djellabas in soothing neutrals or sultry shades, easy cotton trousers and cool abayas, which are a kind of open buttonless jacket. Perfect cadeaux include satin mobile-phone holders, gold satin sausage cushions and anything for the bath such as vast chunks of Aleppo soap, embroidered towels and loofah slippers. Azzedine Alaïa, Paloma Picasso and Inès de la Fressange are all Liwan devotees and Rupert Everett buys his every hostess gift here.

LIWAN, 8 rue St-Sulpice 75006
Tel: 01 43 26 07 40
Métro: Odéon
Opening Hours: Mon: 14.00–19.00, Tue–Sat: 10.30–19.00
August: open
Credit Cards: Visa, Amex, Diners, JCB
Price Range: mobile-phone holder 80FF, djellabas 950–2,980FF, satin quilt from 1,980FF

RUE DES QUATRE VENTS

CHRISTIAN TORTU: FLORAL BOUTIQUE

Not content to be one of Paris's most fashionable florists, Christian Tortu has branched out into interiors, opening a boutique around the corner from his florist selling all things arts-de-la-table and flower-connected. There is a body line with shower gel and soaps as well as sprays for the house that include a delicious 'tomato leaves' scent. His china and glass have a stylish maison à la campagne feel, while vases are more urban with a collection in stone and glass designed by James Scott for Christian Tortu, plus his own dramatic design of zinc box vases. The perfect shop for buying gifts.

CHRISTIAN TORTU, 17 rue des Quatre Vents, 75006
Tél: 01 56 81 00 24
Métro: Odéon
Opening Hours: Mon–Sat: 10.00–19.00
August: closed for two weeks
Credit Cards: Visa, MC
Price Range: soaps from 32FF, zinc vases from 370FF, stone vases from 480FF

OCTÉE: COLOUR-CODED SCENT

Octée sells colour-coded perfume. It's a bright idea that was launched by Josiane Daudon in 1991. There are twelve different fragrances divided into three colour groups. You walk into the shop and the sales assistant asks a couple of really probing questions like: 'What perfume do you normally wear?' She then points you to your identification group which is one of Sensuous, Fresh, Floral and Gourmet. You're then supposed to choose your scent from a choice of four. Before doing this Daudon was a marketing director with L'Oréal and it shows. The whole concept has been meticulously planned from the colour coding, testing via little squares of satin, scents (the fashionable vanilla and 'clean' green are there), down to the packaging – tissue paper of the same colour as your bottle. So zealous is the marketing approach, it can leave you feeling a little underwhelmed by the scents themselves.

OCTÉE, 18 rue des Quatre Vents, 75006
Tel: 01 45 81 00 24
Métro: Odéon
Opening Hours: Mon–Sat: 11.00–19.00
August: open
Credit Cards: Visa, Amex, Diners, MC, JCB
Price Range: all eau de parfum 30ml sprays 185FF, 75ml specially designed bottle 325FF, body lotion 180FF, soap 60FF, shower gel 140FF

PIERRE SAMARY: RELAXED LUXURY MENSWEAR

Pierre Samary has found his style for menswear and is sticking to it. He describes it as 'the Kennedy feel of relaxed elegance'. His jackets are always shrug-on two-button single-breasted with softly moulded shoulders. Trousers are always with one front pleat and a button fly, even when the trousers are made from cashmere. A production perfectionist, he has his trousers made up in France, but the jackets are manufactured in Italy by the same factories that handle Dior, Lanvin and Hermès. Winter suits are in cashmere, Irish tweeds or silk wool mix, in summer it's a silk/linen mix which stops creasing. His pet palette is made up of greys, black and white. Jackets and trousers are sold separately so you can mix on sizes.

PIERRE SAMARY, 9 rue des Quatre Vents, 75006
Tel: 01 46 33 59 99
Métro: Odéon
Opening Hours: Mon–Sat: 10.30–19.30
August: closed 25 July–25 Aug
Credit Cards: Visa, Amex, Diners, MC, JCB
Price Range: trousers from 1,000FF, jackets from 3,000FF, linen shirt 500–700FF

AU NOM DE LA ROSE: ROSE FLORIST

See 7th arrondissement for details.
4 rue de Tournon, 75006. Tel: 01 46 34 10 64

SOUTH

A.P.C.: ULTIMATE FASHION BASICS

A.P.C. is fashion with a utilitarian edge. The initials stand for Atelier de Production et Création, and designer Jean Touitou makes consciously simple, precision-cut clothes for men and women. They do some of the best fashion industry basics around like little V-neck Shetland sweaters, leather pea-coats, straight-leg cotton gabardine trousers, needlecord jeans and cotton tank tops. He and the A.P.C. groupie both share the same obsession for cut and fabric: the hem on those gabardine trousers has got to be exactly 20cm wide, that shirt dress can only be in the super-stiff indigo chambray and jeans look right in heavy waxed cotton or the house special, ramie, which is like a painted canvas. Touitou is a bit of a fabrics snob – he's only interested in fabrics the rest of the fashion industry hasn't yet discovered.

You can dress head-to-toe in A.P.C. and still come out looking effortlessly hip, which is what all fashion girls/boys are striving for.

A.P.C.: womenswear: 3 rue de Fleurus, 75006
Tel: 01 42 22 12 77
menswear: 4 rue de Fleurus, 75006
Tel: 01 45 49 19 15
Métro: St-Placide
also at:
25 bis rue Benjamin Franklin, 75016. Tel: 01 45 53 28 28
Opening Hours: Mon–Sat: 10.30–19.00
August: closed for the week around 15 Aug, call for exact dates
Credit Cards: Visa, Amex, MC
Price Range: men's suit 3,000FF, work trousers 500FF, T-shirts 250FF, jeans 480FF; womenswear: Shetland V-neck 550FF, shirt dress 650FF, chino trousers 500FF, cotton tank top 160FF

A.P.C. GENERAL: BASICS

The general store sells life's essentials A.P.C.-style, that means extra virgin olive oil from Tunisia, specially selected CDs, the jeans, the bags, the perfect basics.

A.P.C. GENERAL, 4 rue de Fleurus, 75006
Tel: 01 45 48 72 42
Métro: St-Placide
Opening Hours: Mon–Sat: 10.30–19.00
August: call for exact dates
Credit Cards: Visa, Amex
Price Range: olive oil 40FF, CDs 100FF, jeans 480FF

A.P.C. SURPLUS: A.P.C. PERMANENT SALE SHOP

This is the A.P.C. sale shop and a well-kept secret even among Parisians. As sales shops go this is superior; it sells mostly clothes from the collection before the current one, i.e., just a season old, as opposed to most sale shops which sell year-old styles. It is not about clearing lipstick-stained damaged kit and the prices are at least 50% off and are often reduced by 60% to 70%. The basics like the perfect-cut jeans and T-shirts are usually thin on the ground and it's more about seasonal pieces. There are some brilliant finds like a pewter leather mini-dress with long sleeves, a stiff cotton shirt dress for 300FF or a saffron leather lace-up shirt for 1,200FF. But because it's the leftover stock it may be available only in one size. In the back room there is a selection of men's stock which seems to have more of the basics plus suiting and military pants (250FF). You can also pick up great accessories like wood and plastic mules or a pearly leather purse pouch for 50FF. Stock changes every ten days.

A.P.C. SURPLUS, 45 rue Madame, 75006
Tel: 01 45 48 43 71
Métro: Rennes or St-Sulpice
Opening Hours: Mon–Sat: 13.00–19.00
August: closed for one week, call for dates
Credit Cards: Visa, MC
Price Range: reduced by 70% or more, T-shirts 100–150FF, leather skirt 600FF, cotton jacket 700FF, men's jacket 700FF, linen sailor's jacket 750FF

PÔLES: CHIC KNITWEAR

Unfortunately French women do not turn off the chic at the weekend – it's full on seven days a week. For weekend knitwear they come to Pôles, which has got the 'relaxed chic' sweater sussed. For winter there are merino wool sweaters in rust or sea-green to wear with your khakis and your J.P. Tods or mohair tops which button up the back, while for summer there are cream chunky cotton silk sweaters or more fashion halter-neck tops. There's a slightly artisan feel to their knitwear, in that it's all finished by hand, but it is never too 'arts and crafts'. The shop is just in front of the Jardins du Luxembourg.

PÔLES, 8 place de l'Odéon, 75006
Tel: 01 46 33 33 32
Métro: Odéon
also at:
17 rue du Jour, 75001. Tel: 01 45 08 93 67
Opening Hours: Mon–Sat: 11.00–13.00, 14.00–19.00
August: closed first two weeks
Credit Cards: Visa, Amex
Price Range: cotton Lycra halter-neck 525FF, zip-up cardigan 925FF, sweaters from 725FF

JARDINS DU LUXEMBOURG: PARK

A wonderful slab of green to the south of the 6th arrondissement. Grab a picnic lunch and the papers (there's a newsagent nearby in rue de Médicis which sells foreign newspapers) and take a break in here.

Residents of the 6th all use it as their back garden so it's full of kids and families sailing toy boats (to hire) in the pond, tennis players, old men playing pétanque, chess champions and people practising kick-boxing. UV skin-baking takes place against the red-hot brick wall of the Orangerie. The best place to read the newspapers is in the shade of the rococo Fontaine Médicis which is deliciously green, calm and a French poets' corner. The gardens were built for Marie de Médici in 1613 and the former palace now houses the Senate, but they won't let you into the Palais without an appointment.

JARDINS DU LUXEMBOURG
Opening Hours: approx. dawn to dusk
Métro: Rennes, St-Placide or RER Luxembourg

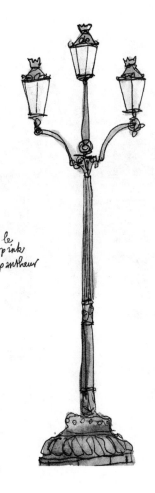

le
p'ink
panthew

7TH ARRONDISSEMENT

In the Paris address system your postcode says a lot about who you are. Never more so than when your address ends in 75007. Deeply establishment and very residential, the 7th arrondissement is beautiful, grand and utterly self-assured. The aristocracy moved in to the area in the 18th century and, despite the hiccough of the Revolution and the absence of royalty, they're still going strong. Of the 200 or so mansions they built, only 50 still exist and they are now divided between embassies, government ministeries, grandes familles and the prime minister, who has a peach of a residence, Hôtel Matignon, in rue de Varenne. The streets here reek of old money: nannies and cord knickerbockers, Labradors and Alice bands, with a spectacular florist on every corner. Très chic, très cher, it's Chelsea without the rock stars.

Although the arrondissement is large, fashion-wise shopping is mostly concentrated in a walkable area on the eastern edge between rue des Saints-Pères to the right and rue du Bac to the left. Rue de Grenelle, which starts near the St-Sulpice métro and actually dips into the 6th, is like some sort of luxury shoe bazaar, while boulevard St-Germain, rue du Bac and boulevard Raspail are also hot to shop. Clothes take their lead from the residents and the emphasis here is on discreet good taste. Confidential, in-the-know boutique addresses count for maximum snob-appeal. At the bottom of rue du Bac is Paris's oldest department store, Le Bon Marché, with metal structure designed by Gustave Eiffel. Take a walk round Le Bon Marché food hall, La Grande Épicerie, to observe the 7th residents in their preferred cornershop.

When it comes to monuments and cultural time out, the 7th is well-serviced, with the Eiffel Tower, Assemblée Nationale and the Hôtel des Invalides where Napoleon's body lies. The Musée d'Orsay is the converted railway station now filled with a bevy of Impressionist paintings. Up on the fifth floor, past people weeping over the water lilies, you will find the museum's lively café in the shadow of an enormous station clock. There's a fabulous view from the balcony over the city and Sacré Coeur.

RUE DE GRENELLE

Rue de Grenelle starts in the 6th with Prada but once you've crossed the rue des Saints-Pères, you're officially in the 7th. It's a long street cutting right across the arrondissement, but for fashion the section up to rue du Bac is the most important. The Oxbridge of Paris, Science Po, is along here, down rue St-Guillaume, so all the students use Le Basile café on the corner as a sort of college bar. It's a good stop for coffee or a salad if you're into cord jackets, cigarette smoke and intellectual angst.

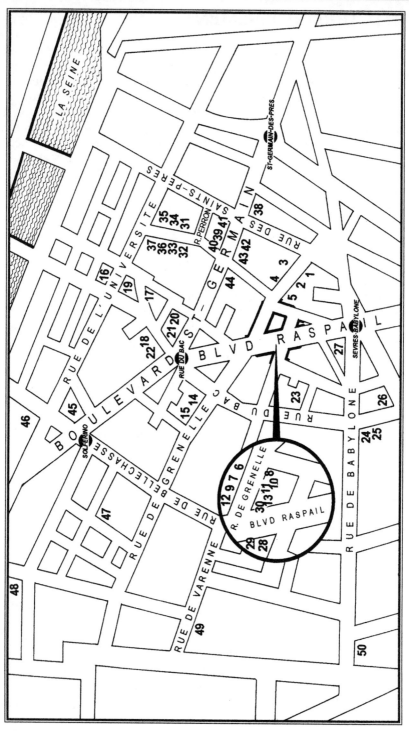

1 MARTINE SITBON
2 STÉPHANE KÉLIAN
3 SERGIO ROSSI
4 FREE LANCE POUR HOMMES
5 PATRICK COX
6 CORINNE ZAQUINE
7 CHRISTIAN LOUBOUTIN
8 AUX FILS DU TEMPS
9 CERRUTI
10 BARBARA BUI
11 MERCERIE D'UN SOIR
12 STEPHEN
13 MAUD PERL
14 BONPOINT FIN DE SÉRIES
15 MAÎTRE PARFUMEUR
16 LES NUITS DES THÉS
17 LUCIEN PELLAT-FINET
18 CHRISTIAN LIAIGRE
19 MISSONI
20 JEANETTE
21 THIERRY MUGLER
22 AU NOM DE LA ROSE
23 LEE YOUNG-HEE
24 ORDNING & REDA
25 LE PETIT TIBERIO

26 LE BON MARCHÉ
27 FLOWER
28 PAUL SMITH
29 KENZO
30 KENZO HOMME
31 MARION LESAGE
32 VICE VERSA
33 IRIÉ
34 ACCESSOIRE DÉTENTE
35 LAURENCE TAVERNIER
36 LES PRAIRIES DE PARIS
37 CORINNE SARRUT
38 SONIA RYKIEL FEMME
39 PAULE KA
40 SONIA RYKIEL HOMME
41 APOSTROPHE
42 ETRO
43 LA PERLA
44 PLEATS PLEASE
45 BONPOINT
46 1 ET 1 FONT 3
47 IMH
48 GALERIE NAILA DE MONTBRISON
49 MUSÉE RODIN
50 LA PAGODE

MARTINE SITBON: DESIGNER WOMENSWEAR

French designer Martine Sitbon has a cult following among fashion insiders. This is her only store, a slick and stark space – harsh orange, purple and cherry tungsten lighting softened by the original stone-tiled floor and chocolate velvet sofas – echoing the sort of contrasts found in Sitbon's own collections. Her designs veer between the sharp and the romantic: she can cut a lean, angular suit with just a 1970s retro tinge, or dream up a slip of a geometric dévoré dress or a chiffon ruffle top with tendril sleeves. Her style is modern femininity with edge. The store stocks her menswear and cool shoe collection plus eyewear.

MARTINE SITBON, 13 rue de Grenelle, 75007
Tel: 01 44 39 84 44
Métro: Sèvres-Babylone or Rue du Bac
Opening Hours: Mon–Sat: 10.30–19.00
August: closed some of the time
Credit Cards: Visa, Amex, MC
Price Range: sweaters from 1,350FF, shoes from 1,300FF, PVC coat 4,960FF

STÉPHANE KÉLIAN: DESIGNER SHOES

As a brand Stéphane Kélian has an enviable image of trend, without intimidation. You can come here for a pair of knee-high stretch-skin vinyl kinky boots or alternatively for a pair of navy and cream flat lace-ups in leather woven trellis. It's this hand-woven leather tressé which first made Kélian and his two elder brothers their cash. They used to make woven leather shoes for men with sensitive/problem feet, before Kélian fell for fashion and swapped to women's footwear in 1977. The range of tressé shoes and accessories is still woven by hand down in their factory in Romans, which is why the shoe is so soft and moulds to the foot. There are five stores in Paris; this branch has the widest selection and also stocks the Claude Montana, Martine Sitbon and Jean Paul Gaultier ranges of shoes which are all manufactured by Kélian. There is also a Stéphane Kélian men's range here.

STÉPHANE KÉLIAN, 13 bis rue de Grenelle, 75007
Tel: 01 42 22 93 03
Métro: Sèvres-Babylone or Rue du Bac
also at:
6 place des Victoires, 75002. Tel: 01 42 61 60 74
26 avenue des Champs-Élysées, 75008. Tel: 01 42 56 42 26
5 rue du Faubourg St-Honoré, 75008
20 avenue Victor Hugo, 75016. Tel: 01 45 00 44 41
Opening Hours: Mon–Sat: 10.00–19.00
August: open
Credit Cards: Visa, Amex, MC
Price Range: women's shoes 800–2,000FF, boots 1,600–3,000FF, navy and cream woven lace-ups 1,300FF, men's shoes 1,300–1,900FF, woven leather from 2,000FF

SERGIO ROSSI: DESIGNER SHOES

This is still the hottest shoe shop in Paris. Come the collections, there is a stampede of fashion editors, models and buyers on the comparative shop and models Naomi, Helena, Claudia tripping in to get their fix. Why so hot? For a start, Gucci recently bought a major chunk of the brand. The shoes are classic but hip, comfortable but cool. Sergio Rossi has been going for 30-odd years, but only opened his store in Paris about two years ago and has been kick-started back into fashion with the retro revival. Shoes are dressy, feminine and there are always 3cm, 5cm, 7cm and 9cm heels to choose from. Boots come calf-high in colours ranging from glorious camel to deep glazed brown leather, with round metal buckles on the side and narrow heel, at 2,000FF. It's a smooth store with bordeaux velvet chaise longue, massive gilt wood carved mirrors, Chinese rugs and harpsichord music piping out.

SERGIO ROSSI, 22 rue de Grenelle, 75007
Tel: 01 42 84 07 24
Métro: Sèvres-Babylone
also at:
11 rue du Faubourg St-Honoré, 75008. Tel: 01 40 07 10 89
Opening Hours: Mon–Sat: 10.30–19.00
August: closed middle two weeks
Credit Cards: Visa, Amex, MC, JCB
Price Range: shoes 1,000–1,500FF, boots from 2,000FF

FREE LANCE POUR HOMMES: DESIGNER SHOES
See 6th arrondissement for details.
24 rue de Grenelle, 75007. Tel: 01 45 49 95 83

PATRICK COX: DESIGNER LOAFERS AND SHOES
See 2nd arrondissement for details.
21 rue de Grenelle, 75007. Tel: 01 45 49 24 28

CORINNE ZAQUINE: SMART HATS

If you want a hat that looks like you've spent loads of cash on it, head this way. Corinne Zaquine's hats tend to be fairly classic shapes draped in lengths of silk satin tied in a voluptuous bow or knot and hand-stitched into place. Painstakingly good finish and not a skinny ribbon in sight. For summer there are sugar-almond swathes of satin on palest sisal fibres while for winter there are lots of hairy felts. Clients are 7th arrondissement aristo ladies and daughters, brides and wedding guests and racegoers. Corinne says she thinks of a hat as a traditional beautiful accessory rather than a statement on your head. There are no everyday basics and not a hint of eccentricity – the mad hatter's tea party is probably her idea of a very bad dream. You can buy off the shelf or made-to-measure which takes two weeks; the prices are the same. Hats can be sent on to you at home.

CORINNE ZAQUINE, 38 rue de Grenelle, 75007
Tel: 01 45 48 93 03
Métro: Rue du Bac or Sèvres-Babylone
Opening Hours: Tue–Sat: 11.00–19.00
August: closed
Credit Cards: Visa, MC
Price Range: 1,200–2,000FF

CHRISTIAN LOUBOUTIN: DESIGNER SHOES
See 1st arrondissement for details.
38 rue de Grenelle, 75007. Tel. 01 42 22 33 07

AUX FILS DU TEMPS: TEXTILES
A favourite address among decorators, collectors and textile designers, this boutique specialises in textiles dating from the 16th century up until the 1930s. Owner Marie-Noëlle Sudre has a great eye and sells mostly French fabrics and textiles which are from both clothing and furnishings. At the back of the boutique is a huge armoire filled with prints, velvets, brocades. Last time I went by there were several metres of glorious apricot and gold silk velvet from the 1930s. There are both 18th-century original fabrics which are vegetable dyed, plus the more affordable 19th-century copies of 18th-century designs, and there is also a sort of bargain basket stacked high with pieces of fabric. There is always some terribly important decorator in here snooping around looking for a 'fabulous throw' for a house he's working on down in the South of France.

AUX FILS DU TEMPS, 33 rue de Grenelle, 75007
Tel: 01 45 48 14 68
Métro: Rue du Bac
Opening Hours: Mon–Fri: 14.00–19.00, closed Sat/Sun
August: closed
Credit Cards: Visa, Amex

CERRUTI: SMART, CLASSIC WOMENSWEAR
See 8th arrondissement for details.
42 rue de Grenelle, 75007. Tel: 01 42 22 92 28

BARBARA BUI: FASHIONABLE WOMENSWEAR
See 8th arrondissement for details.
35 rue de Grenelle, 75007. Tel: 01 45 44 85 14

MERCERIE D'UN SOIR: WEDDING WEAR
This is the evening and wedding dress parlour to the Étienne Brunel store just down the road in rue des Saints-Pères. Mireille Brunel, the designer, offers two services. The first is made-to-measure design, so you go along to discuss your wish and your budget, and she'll come up with a whimsical, exotic, or simple dress for a ball, cocktail or your

wedding. Right now she's big into paper wedding dresses, light and layered in a silk voile with a bit of feathering, but you can just as easily get a more extravagant embroidered lace look. The second service is to transform what you've already got, which is why the front of the shop is what Mireille describes as a 'buffet' of beads, paste, sequins, feathers, braids, metallic netting and plastic daisy chains. She'll titivate a pair of trousers or lop a lot off a jacket. She sits out back with the windows open on to a courtyard sewing and dreaming up frocks. Made-to-measure dresses usually take at least a week and can be sent on to you.

MERCERIE D'UN SOIR, 37 rue de Grenelle, 75007
Tel: 01 45 48 26 13
Métro: Sèvres-Babylone
Opening Hours: Mon–Sat: 8.30–20.00
August: closed
Credit Cards: Visa, Amex
Price Range: ball dress from 2,000FF to suit your budget, wedding dress according to your budget

STEPHEN: SHOE SALE SHOP

A great new address is the Stephen boutique which has turned into the sale shop for both Michel Perry shoes and his diffusion line Stephen. That means you can find last year, same season's boots, shoes, mules at around half price. Seeing as Michel Perry is seriously talented, this counts as a real fashion find. For this season's boots, shoes etc. see his boutique in the 2nd arrondissement.

STEPHEN, 42 rue de Grenelle, 75007
Tel: 01 42 84 12 45
Métro: Rue du Bac or Sèvres-Babylone
Opening Hours: Mon–Fri: 11.00–14.00, 15.00–19.00, Sat: 11.00–12.30, 13.30–19.00
August: closed for week of 15 Aug
Credit Cards: Visa, Amex
Price Range: shoes from 600FF, boots from 1,200FF, ankle boots from 900FF

MAUD PERL: SILK WOMENSWEAR

Maud Perl designs in an artsy style which is sophisticated, never lentil-bake. She uses only silk but, within that, explores around fifteen different kinds of silk like dupion, gauze, waffle, jersey and Razimir. Every season there are 50 colours to choose from and silks are dyed at her atelier in the Marais in shades such as mother-of-pearl pink, conker brown, citrus shot with gold and coral. Each colour is made up of at least five other pigments which, combined with the quality of silk, give a wonderful depth and luminosity.

The collection is made up of 'basics', like silk dupion jeans, waffle jacket or jersey T-shirts, plus new pieces each season. Either you can

159

buy off the peg or you can pick out any style and have it made in a colour of your choice, which takes ten days but does not cost extra. Perl fans are women artists, writers, film producers and publishers but there is also a younger clientele who go for, say, a slip of a silk jersey dress on tiny satin straps. Silk jersey shapes work well if you are pregnant as you can wear them with or without a bump. Most of the clothes are hand-washable. Good news is that the sizes at Maud Perl go up to 16.

MAUD PERL, 39 rue de Grenelle, 75007
Tel: 01 45 44 26 27
Métro: Rue du Bac
Opening Hours: Mon: 14.00–19.00, Tues–Sat: 11.00–19.00
August: closed for two weeks
Credit Cards: Visa, Amex, MC
Price Range: silk dupion jeans 1,850FF, heavy silk jersey T-shirt 1,250FF, scarves from 450FF, slip dress in silk jersey 1,400FF

BONPOINT FIN DE SÉRIES:
CHILDREN'S SALE SHOP

A closely guarded secret among Paris protective mums, this is the sale shop for Bonpoint, makers of darling childrenswear (see main entry). All the clothes are from the previous year, but the same season, and prices are reduced from 30% to 50%. Clothes go from new-born to aged 12 for boys and aged 16 for girls. This is not a place to come looking for basics, it's a shop for party dresses, smocking and cashmere all done in quintessentially French good taste. I found a gorgeous white matinée coat in here for Lily reduced from 750FF to 250FF.

BONPOINT FIN DE SÉRIES, 82 rue de Grenelle, 75007
Tel: 01 45 48 05 45
Métro: Rue du Bac
Opening Hours: Mon–Sat: 10.30–18.30
August: closed
Credit Cards: Visa, MC
Price Range: 30–50% reductions

MAÎTRE PARFUMEUR: PERFUME HOUSE

Perfumeries are a Parisian habit worth exploring. It's not as extreme as having a perfume made exclusively for you (although you can do that too in Paris if you've got the cash), it's about finding a small perfume house with delicious scents that haven't been subject to a Liz Hurley ad campaign. Exclusivity is joy.

The house of nose Jean François Laporte, maître parfumeur, is where to go for heady florals. There are twenty-one scents for women, thirteen for men, all sold only in eau de toilette. For women the jasmine is exquisite and smells as if you are in Rajasthan and garlanded in the flowers, while for men Eau des Îles is coffee-bean exotica. The shop setting and fragrances are 18th-century-inspired and there's a Fragonard-look trompe-l'oeil ceiling with balconies swathed in flowers. Price varies according to the scent you pick – jasmine is 600FF and tuberose, the most expensive, is 850FF. Great service includes salespeople who are prepared to talk you through every note of a scent or leave you free to test. There is an international mail order service for restocking.

MAÎTRE PARFUMEUR, 84 bis rue de Grenelle, 75007
Tel: 01 45 44 61 57
Métro: Rue du Bac
Opening Hours: Mon–Sat: 10.30–18.30
also at:
5 rue des Capucines, 75001. Tel: 01 42 96 35 13
August: open
Credit Cards: Visa, Diners, Amex, MC, JCB
Price Range: men's fragrances (90ml) 350–380FF, women's fragrances (100ml) 340–850FF

ON AND OFF RUE DU BAC

LES NUITS DES THÉS: TEAROOM

Limoges porcelain cups and saucers arranged in a dresser in the window set the genteel tone. Ladies chat over Lapsang Souchong and pick over slices of sticky tarte Tatin. The interior is plain good taste with pinkish toile de Jouy tablecloths and white wooden chairs, while the clientele is a mix of gallery owners, publishing queens from Gallimard, interior decorators, fashion journalists and Isabelle Adjani. It is run by Jacqueline Cédelle, daughter Florence and her fox terrier. Their big specialities are chicken pie with a hint of curry and a caramelised fromage blanc tart which, like all the food, is made in the kitchen upstairs. They've now started a take-away service so you can order a whole tart and from October to May they do a brunch on Sunday with scones, muffins, eggs and crumble for 148FF.

LES NUITS DES THÉS, 22 rue de Beaune 75007
Tel: 01 47 03 92 07
Métro: Rue du Bac
Opening Hours: every day: 12.00–19.00
August: closed
Credit Cards: none
Price Range: tarte Tatin 47FF, pot of tea 25FF, chicken pie with green salad 75FF

LUCIEN PELLAT-FINET: DESIGNER CASHMERE

Cashmere was once all about sugary twinsets and pearls, until Lucien Pellat-Finet came along and made it count. The French designer has given it fashion credibility with abbreviated sweaters, sorbet colours and of course a stellar clientele including Tom Cruise and Nicole Kidman (both serial Pellat-Finet wearers), Stella Tennant and Juliette Binoche. He opened his first boutique recently in Paris; designed by Christian Biecher in Pellat-Finet's signature pop/techno colours, it has quirky furnishings such as a squashy 'boudin' sofa in putty-coloured stretch nylon. Not content with just baby-soft cashmere, he has added animal stripes and tattoos and knitted it up into chunky sweaters or baseball sweatshirt complete with number and city name. This store sells both women's and men's cashmere, a home line of throws and cushions plus a collection of sweet mini cashmere for kids.

LUCIEN PELLAT-FINET, 1 rue Montalembert, 75007
Tel: 01 42 22 22 77
Métro: Rue du Bac
Opening Hours: Mon–Fri: 10.00–19.00, Sat: 11.00–19.00
August: closed for two weeks
Credit Cards: Visa, Amex, MC
Price Range: women's from 2,730FF, men's from 3,300FF, children's from 1,430FF

CHRISTIAN LIAIGRE: INTERIOR DESIGNER

Christian Liaigre is fashion's interior designer of choice: any self-respecting space these days is designed by him, from Calvin Klein's Tribeca apartment to Valentino's new offices on place Vendôme, from the utterly cool Mercer Hotel in New York to Marc Jacobs's Soho boutique. French and in his early 50s, Liaigre has developed a signature style of restrained minimalism, dark exotic woods, sensual textures and monumental volume – now imitated the world over. For the real thing, shop here at Liaigre's new spacious boutique and showroom where you can find his Brancusi-inspired stools and luxuriously large sofas. Some of the smaller pieces can be bought and taken away there and then, but most furniture is made to order which takes 10 to 12 weeks. And be warned: Liaigre doesn't pander to every client-with-cash whim: overheard at the boutique recently was an assistant telling one bourgeois Madame, 'Monsieur Liaigre doesn't do round tables.'

CHRISTIAN LIAIGRE, 42 rue du Bac, 75007
Tel: 01 53 63 33 66
Métro: Rue du Bac
Opening Hours: Mon–Sat: 10.00–19.00
August: closed for two weeks mid-month
Credit Cards: Visa, Amex, MC, JCB
Price Range: Brancusi-style stools from 3,500FF, lamps from 1,200FF, sofas from 20,000FF, low table from 15,000FF

MISSONI: ITALIAN DESIGNER

Another Italian family fashion house determined to keep it in the family, Missoni has passed the design baton to the next generation. Angela Missoni has taken over from her parents Ottavio and Rosita who founded the house in 1953 with their distinctive and highly original graphic knitwear. Whereas they combined optical patterns with smashing, often clashing, colour (up to 12 colours in one piece), Angela has so far opted for a softer approach. She has kept the signature space dye technique but introduced faded pastels and new textures as well as more relaxed shapes such as wrap skirts and asymmetric dresses.

In essence, the brand is still all about jet-set luxurious knitwear from tiny triangular bikinis to knit sweaters divided by tufts of fur. And the Missoni faithful still swear by the originality of design, comfort factor and perfect fluidity of the clothes. Upstairs are menswear and the slightly less expensive Missoni Sport collection.

MISSONI, 42 rue du Bac, 75007
Tel: 01 45 48 38 02
Métro: Rue du Bac
also at:
1 rue du Faubourg St-Honoré, 75008
Opening Hours: Mon–Sat: 10.00–19.00
August: closed for part of month, call for exact dates
Credit Cards: Visa, Amex, Diners, MC
Price Range: jacket 3,740FF, skirt 2,230FF, summer-weight sweater 1,920FF

JEANETTE: CLASSIC MATURE DESIGNER DRESSING

Jeanette is not so much into selling an item of designer clothing as into conjuring up her own look for a customer. She started in fashion by opening the Lagerfeld Chloé shop in Paris in 1969, then opened her own boutique here in 1972. She is still a faithful Lagerfeld lover, selling his own line as well as Rochas, Christian Lacroix and Jean Paul Gaultier. She also has quite a few less expensive diffusion lines from some of the heavyweights like Miss V from Valentino, Ungaro's Sola Donna and State of Claude Montana. A boutique for moneyed, mature women (say, aged 50 upwards) in search of a bit of direction in dress. As soon as you walk through that door, she says, she's already imagining your outfit: 'I take a client, I personalise her, I harmonise her. If it's a Lacroix all-over lady, I calm her right down.' She has a smart selection of evening and cocktail dresses and can dress sizes from 6 to 20.

JEANETTE, 2 bis–3 rue de Gribeauval, 75007
Tel: 01 45 44 02 04
Métro: Rue du Bac
Opening Hours: Mon–Sat: 9.30–19.00
August: open
Credit Cards: Visa, Amex, Diners, JCB
Price Range: suiting 4,000–9,000FF, cocktail dress 6,000FF

THIERRY MUGLER: FRENCH DESIGNER WEAR

Mugler's muse Jerry Hall just about sums up his design aesthetic – rock chick with attitude. His silhouette is super-curvaceous, with built-in room for bosom and hips. This means, according to store director Liza Wanklyn, 'If you've got hips and bosom you're going to come out looking sexy whether you're size 8 or 18.'

His shows may be packed with models trussed up in vinyl bodysuits and brandishing whips, but in reality the store sells siren silk dresses, while for winter accentuating suiting comes in cashmere or velvet in camels, beige or lipstick-red and grey flannel. The store here is the new flagship and stocks the widest range of Mugler in Paris, with Mugler Couture – the luxury ready-to-wear line – Thierry Mugler and Mugler Trade Mark, a newish lower-priced line based around jeans and space-cadet sportswear. There is also menswear, accessories and both the women's perfume Angel and the men's fragrance A Men. Mugler spends half his life in New York (working out in a gym by the looks of his body) and half in Paris. What's interesting about his business is that he is one of the few French designers to produce vertically: he has his own factory in the middle of France where practically all the women's range and most of the menswear is manufactured. He tends to get carried away with over-the-top fashion shows, getting all his mates like Verushka, Jerry and Marie Helvin to model for him.

THIERRY MUGLER, 45 rue du Bac, 75007
Tel: 01 45 44 44 44
Métro: Rue du Bac
also at:
49 avenue Montaigne, 75008. Tel: 01 47 23 37 62
10 place des Victoires, 75002. Tel: 01 42 60 06 37
10 rue Boissy d'Anglas, 75008. Tel: 01 43 12 57 57
Opening Hours: Mon–Sat: 10.00–19.00
August: open
Credit Cards: Visa, Amex, Diners, MC, JCB
Price Range: couture suiting 8,000–12,000FF, Thierry Mugler suiting
3,000–5,000FF, Mugler Trade Mark range 500–2,000FF

AU NOM DE LA ROSE: ROSE FLORIST

It's hard to resist this shamelessly romantic florist where all they sell is roses. Not the bland anaemic kind, but scented garden roses and old strains from as far back as the 17th century. This is where fashionable Paris – Joseph, Inès de la Fressange, Christian Lacroix – comes to buy bouquets. Every day there is a choice of 60 different types of roses, from teeny buds to full-blown blooms in shades that go from velvety claret to clotted cream. Manager Francis Brumel is a former drag queen who sees himself as a chevalier de la rose reviving old favourites like 'Alaska' or 'Jardins de Bagatelle'. They package it all up in thick white paper, adding a stroke of marketing genius by tying a real rose to the outside of the packet – this is given free and whether you've bought the cheapest single rose or a big bouquet. If you're in Paris on a trip and want to take the romance home they will wrap the stems in a special no-leak packet which will keep damp for up to ten hours.

Adjoining this branch of Au Nom de la Rose is a little shop selling rosy knick-knacks including pots of jam made from rose petals, 45FF, and boxed rose petals of soap, 80FF – good if you're stuck for last-minute gifts to take home. Frankly, though, she'd prefer the bouquet.

AU NOM DE LA ROSE, 46 rue du Bac, 75007
Tel: 01 42 22 08 09
Métro: Rue du Bac
also at:
4 rue de Tournon, 75006. Tel: 01 46 34 10 64
Opening Hours: florist: Mon–Sat: 9.00–21.00, Sun: 9.00–14.00; shop: Mon–Sat: 10.00–19.30
August: closed (but store in the 6th stays open)
Credit Cards: Visa, Diners, MC
Price Range: seasonal – 8–50FF per stem in summer, 12–50FF in winter

LEE YOUNG-HEE: KOREAN FASHION

This feels more like a cultural embassy than a boutique selling clothes. Lee Young-Hee designs the traditional South Korean hanbok as well as contemporary clothes and sells them in a setting of Korean artefacts and furniture – enamel hairgrips, jade rings, linen chests – some of which aren't for sale but come from her own private collection. She

opened in Paris in 1995 and is based in Korea where she has seven stores. In summer the feel is ethereal with gossamer-light silk, cotton voile or linen dresses which tie around the body. Her daughter has just started showing her designs in the store; they have the same traditions of Korean technique, but are aimed at a younger woman. Avant-garde French women fall for her embossed silk hanboks as the perfect wedding dress.

LEE YOUNG-HEE, 109 rue du Bac, 75007
Tel: 01 42 84 24 84
Métro: Sèvres-Babylone
Opening Hours: Mon–Sat: 10.00–19.00
August: closed for three weeks, call for exact dates
Credit Cards: Visa, Amex, Diners, MC, JCB
Price Range: jacket from 4,000FF, silk dress from 3,400FF

ORDNING & REDA: STATIONERY
See Le Marais for details.
130 rue du Bac, 75007. Tel: 01 42 22 73 66

LE PETIT TIBERIO: ITALIAN LOCAL BISTRO
If you're shopping at Le Bon Marché and need to break for a bowl of pasta, come here. Le Petit Tiberio serves up geographically mixed Italian cooking in a friendly atmosphere and for a reasonable price. Try a delicious penne alla tiberio with fat tubes of pasta tossed in tuna, olives and raisins, or a house favourite: a gratin of aubergines with fresh mozzarella melted on top. Paul Smith has his shop up the road and is always in here and at night it's a real lively local restaurant. Lots of dashing Italian waiters and chrysanthemum oil paintings on the walls.

LE PETIT TIBERIO, 132 rue du Bac, 75007
Tel: 01 45 48 76 25
Métro: Sèvres-Babylone
Opening Hours: Mon–Sat: 12.00–14.30, 19.00–22.30
August: open
Credit Cards: Visa
Price Range: bowl of pasta 54FF, carpaccio 42FF, dinner with pasta, meat course and wine around 150FF

LE BON MARCHÉ: DEPARTMENT STORE
Le Bon Marché is a sort of glammed-up version of Peter Jones. It prides itself on being a Rive gauche neighbourhood store and it's true, customers are usually the local type – Courchevel tans, tennis racquets and husky jackets. Compared to the Right Bank department stores, the clothing here for men and women is more about an elegant well-bred Parisian style than cutting-edge, although they are becoming more fashion-aware. For women they stock Joseph, Dries Van Noten, Y's,

Helmut Lang Jeans, Balenciaga, Galliano and Gaultier. On the first floor you will find a nice and inoffensive selection of knitwear, suiting and dresses made under their own label, St-Germain-des-Prés.

Another possession in Bernard Arnault's LVMH empire, Le Bon Marché is in the process of an overhaul. They now boast a slick perfumery selling brands such as Bobbi Brown, Shu Uemura and skincare by cult New York brand Bliss. Up on the first floor is an enormous lingerie department, also part of the redesign, where you can choose from brands such as Erès, Prada, Dior and Dolce & Gabbana. The French take their lingerie seriously (no surprise), and there is a bra here for every occasion: seduction, daywear, designer or Diva. They have very thoughtfully put phones in the changing rooms so you can ring out to an assistant who will go and find you another size or colour, so you're not obliged to get dressed again to go and hunt around.

On the ground floor is a massive menswear department called Balthazar. They've got the classic urban man sussed, with ties, shirts and city suiting by designers like Yves Saint Laurent, Christian Dior, Kenzo and Céline. There are also whole sections of Le Bon Marché's own less expensive label, Balthazar. The city shirts and suits are worth checking out for the competitive price and nice styling. Weekend sportswear is strong, with casual cotton or linen shirts like a coloured short-sleeved check at 299FF and acres of jeans, chinos, cords, T-shirts and sweatshirts. There are men-friendly shopping devices like the section devoted to navy blue blazers with a range of different prices, styles and brands – that way you get to see the shop's choice in one glance. In October and March there are 'très bon marché' days, with discounts and special offers for ten days. There is also a hotel delivery service for packages.

LE BON MARCHÉ, 22 rue de Sèvres, 75007
Tel: 01 44 39 80 00
Métro: Sèvres-Babylone
Opening Hours: Mon–Fri: 9.30–19.00, Sat: 9.30–20.00
August: open
Credit Cards: Visa, Amex, Diners, JCB

FLOWER: DESIGNER MENSWEAR
Temporarily closed; due to reopen September 2000.
7 rue Chomel, 75007. Tel: 01 42 22 11 78

BOULEVARD RASPAIL

PAUL SMITH: BRITISH DESIGNER WEAR
Paul Smith's alternative window-dressing has caused hot flushes among the 7th residents. First he has a female dummy who has just laid out a skittle-load of male dummies with a well-aimed bowling ball (complaints from the neighbours). A couple of months later, up pops another vengeful female throwing darts, one of which is embedded in the target T-shirt of a male dummy (more complaints). His British sense of irony seems to go down better here when it's expressed in clothes. On the ground floor you'll find everything for the sharp-dressed man from knickers to towelling suits with a lot of classic three-button single-breasted suits in between. The shop manager calls it 'the Paul Smith mix of branché, banal and classic'. Downstairs is the womenswear, which is looking much stronger nowadays and seems to be relying far less on the male silhouette for inspiration. Paul Smith Paris boys include Lionel Richie, Jean Michel Jarre and Gilles Dufour.

PAUL SMITH, 22 boulevard Raspail, 75007
Tel: 01 42 84 15 30
Métro: Rue du Bac
Opening Hours: Mon: 11.30–19.30, Tue–Sat: 10.30–19.30
August: open
Credit Cards: Visa, Amex, Diners, MC, JCB
Price Range: men's suits 3,500–5,000FF, shirts 500–800FF, tie 200–500FF, jeans 500FF, women's suiting 2,800–5,000FF

KENZO: FRENCH DESIGNER
Since Kenzo retired in 1999, French designer Gilles Rosier has taken charge of womenswear design. Keeping Kenzo's signature exotic, ethnic and floral mix, Rosier is charged with taking the house hipper than before. There are four stores in Paris and this one stocks the whole Kenzo universe from sunglasses and handbags to swimming costumes and home furnishings. There are still some loud fauna prints hanging around, but now you are just as likely to find a well-tailored pin-striped suit or a diaphanous layered dress.

KENZO, 16 boulevard Raspail, 75007
Tel: 01 42 22 09 38
Métro: Rue du Bac
also at:
2 place des Victoires, 75001. Tel: 01 40 39 72 03
18 avenue George V, 75008. Tel: 01 47 23 33 49
22 boulevard de la Madeleine, 75001. Tel: 01 42 61 04 14
99 rue de Passy, 75016. Tel: 01 42 24 92 92
Opening Hours: Mon: 11.00–19.00, Tue–Sat: 10.00–19.00
August: open
Credit Cards: Visa, Amex, Diners, MC
Price Range: cotton swimming costume 430FF, jeans around 800FF, Kenzo
Jungle suiting around 3,500FF, Kenzo couture suiting 5,500FF

KENZO HOMME: DESIGNER MENSWEAR

Directly opposite is Kenzo menswear which is also undergoing a
design transformation. The Kenzo Homme is holding on to the sport
chic with colour but adding a more urban feel to some of the suiting.
Previously, the Kenzo cut was always wide and relaxed; now it's a far
neater fit.

KENZO HOMME, 17 boulevard Raspail, 75007
Tel: 01 45 49 33 75
Métro: Rue du Bac
also at:
2 place des Victoires, 75001. Tel: 01 40 39 72 03
18 avenue George V, 75008. Tel: 01 47 23 33 49
22 boulevard de la Madeleine, 75001. Tel: 01 42 61 04 51
99 rue de Passy, 75016. Tel: 01 42 24 92 92
Opening Hours: Mon–Sat: 10.00–19.00
August: open
Credit Cards: Visa, Amex, Diners, MC
Price Range: suits 4,000–6,000FF, jackets 2,000–3,000FF, tie 490FF, shirt
500–600FF, waistcoat 1,000–1,500FF

RUE DU PRÉ AUX CLERCS

As a quiet road off the shopping highway, rue du Pré aux Clercs makes
for perfect discreet VIP shopping. Regulars are the Queen of Spain,
Jerry Hall, Catherine Deneuve and Princess Caroline, who tend to nip
into Irié while keeping the armoured car running outside.

MARION LESAGE: EXOTIC LIFESTYLE STORE

Artist Marion Lesage has opened a space selling her own paintings
and sketches of people and places observed on her travels around
Morocco, Africa and Asia. She also sells a range of simple-cut clothing
in linens and silky cottons, plus pieces picked up on her travels – a
bamboo stool from Thailand, embroidered slips from Madras and
Chinese silk cushions.

MARION LESAGE, 15 rue du Pré aux Clercs, 75007
Tel: 01 45 48 32 06
Métro: St-Germain-des-Prés
Opening Hours: Mon–Sat: 12.00–19.00
August: closed
Credit Cards: Visa, Amex, MC
Price Range: crocheted silk ankle socks 150FF, trousers from 1,000FF, sketch-books with hand-painted front cover from 200FF

VICE VERSA: CLASSIC DESIGNER WOMENSWEAR

A small boutique selling an edited selection of collections by British designer Sara Sturgeon and Belgian Rue Blanche plus knitwear by Tiki Tirawa and Liviana Conti. Buyer Nathalie Brunel's colour choice is strictly neutral with lots of beige, camel, cream, navy, sometimes warmed up with a palest rose or ice-blue. She's strong on well-cut suiting for mature women who want to look immaculately groomed without drawing attention to their clothes.

VICE VERSA, 16 rue du Pré aux Clercs, 75007
Tel: 01 42 22 10 78
Métro: St-Germain-des-Prés
Opening Hours: Mon–Sat: 10.30–13.30, 14.30–19.00
August: closed
Credit Cards: Visa, MC
Price Range: knitwear 900–1,800FF, suiting around 3,200FF

IRIÉ: CLASSIC CHIC

The Irié label has serious but low-key cachet on the Paris scene. Seduced by the Paris of Jean-Luc Godard movies, Japanese Irié moved from Tokyo in 1970 and worked for Kenzo for ten years, starting as salesman and leaving as first assistant. He launched his own label in 1983 and now has three stores in this street all done up in camper-than-Christmas style with lashings of marble, Corinthian columns, a stuffed tiger in one shop and a stuffed zebra in another. He's big on stretch and the shop at No. 6 is just full of it – cigarette-cut trousers, jodhpurs, short skirts, and the perfect-cut Irié jeans in stretch Lycra. Next door at No. 8 is more of a contemporary tailored look, where working women opt for his polyester crêpe suiting as it doesn't crease and you can fling it in the washing machine. There is always some breed of animal-skin print in an Irié collection, which goes down well with the Parisians for whom big cat spells big glamour.

Opposite is the marble shop selling veiny marble fragments, objets, vases and benches which Irié has picked up over the years at the puces (flea market).

IRIÉ, 8 rue du Pré aux Clercs, 75007
Tel: 01 42 61 18 28
Métro: St-Germain-des-Prés
Opening Hours: Mon–Sat: 10.00–19.00
August: closed
Credit Cards: Visa, MC
Price Range: jackets 2,200–2,800FF, stretch trousers 800–990FF, print T-shirt
from 350FF

ACCESSOIRE DÉTENTE: CASUAL SHOES

A box of a shop selling the new weekend sporty line of shoes from
Accessoire Diffusion, it is here to provide summer essentials for
French bourgeois time off – espadrilles, beach shoes, docksiders and
tennis shoes – while for winter it's more about pavement-pounding
rubber soles.

ACCESSOIRE DÉTENTE, 11 rue du Pré aux Clercs, 75007
Tel: 01 42 84 26 85
Métro: St-Germain-des-Prés
Opening Hours: Mon–Sat: 11.00–19.00
August: closed
Credit Cards: Visa, Amex, MC
Price Range: tennis shoes 250FF, espadrilles 350FF, shoes 550–660FF

LAURENCE TAVERNIER: NIGHTWEAR

French women do not climb into track pants when they get back from
the office, nor do they wear baggy T-shirts in bed. Therefore Laurence
Tavernier makes them suitable kit to wear around the home, in bed or,
as the shop assistant puts it, 'for breakfast on the terrace'. This is bon
goût bourgeois style: crisp cotton piqué or white satinised cotton pyjamas with écru edging, cashmere dressing gowns, embroidered slippers. Fabrics are cotton for summer, wool, angora and cashmere for
winter, while the colours are predominantly white, pale blue, pale rose
and écru. There is also a men's collection.

LAURENCE TAVERNIER, 7 rue du Pré aux Clercs, 75007
Tel: 01 49 27 03 95
Métro: St-Germain-des-Prés or Rue du Bac
also at:
3 rue Benjamin Franklin, 75016. Tel: 01 46 47 89 39
Opening Hours: Mon–Sat: 10.00–19.00
August: closed first three weeks
Credit Cards: Visa, MC
Price Range: from 750–1,250FF

LES PRAIRIES DE PARIS: FRENCH HIP FASHION

Designer Laeticia Ivanez does a pert, quintessentially Parisian fashion
look. Her pretty summer dresses in glazed cotton with tiny spaghetti
straps or crisp waisted shirts are snapped up by the Rive gauche well-

heeled hipster. This is easy chic and fashion that is soothing, not scary. Les Prairies de Paris clothes come slim-cut and simple with an emphasis on gorgeous detail: shirts with pretty cap sleeves and one visible button in mother-of-pearl, tulle layered skirts scattered with crystals and sharp leather jackets in lilac or duck-egg blue.

LES PRAIRIES DE PARIS, 6 rue du Pré aux Clercs, 75007
Tel: 01 40 20 44 12
Métro: St-Germain-des-Prés or Rue du Bac
Opening Hours: Mon–Sat: 10.30–13.30, 14.30–19.00
August: closed first two weeks
Credit Cards: Visa, Amex, MC
Price Range: skirt 600–800FF, trousers 600–900FF, coat 1,300–1,600FF

CORINNE SARRUT: PRETTY FASHION

Corinne Sarrut clothes have a definite girly look. It's not that she designs for young girls – middle-aged women are big Sarrut fans – but it's a pretty style. Her collections are full of mignon little dresses with flounce, slightly '40s teeny floral prints and faded colours with ribbons underlining the bust. If you're petite, slim and into wearing schoolgirl blue knit cardigans teamed with sensible shoes and ankle straps, this store's for you. Other signature Sarrut signs are the belted jacket, perched black beret, mother-of-pearl buttons and Peter Pan collars. The Sarrut style seems to work best for spring and summer when all those fresh prints and dresses really come into their own.

CORINNE SARRUT, 4 rue du Pré aux Clercs, 75007
Tel: 01 42 61 71 60
Métro: St-Germain-des-Prés
Opening Hours: Mon–Sat: 10.00–19.00
August: closed for ten days, call for exact dates
Credit Cards: Visa, Amex, MC
Price Range: knitwear from 790FF, jackets 1,700–2,500FF, silk dress 1,500FF

BOULEVARD ST-GERMAIN

SONIA RYKIEL: DESIGNER FASHION

Sonia Rykiel is the grande dame of Rive gauche fashion. Her customer is generally 40 or over and, according to Madame Rykiel, 'an intellectual, sophisticated woman, very Parisienne, who loves life, literature, dining out and going to the theatre at night'. Rykiel designs to match the Left Bank lifestyle with a relaxed but chic style. There is always jersey and knitwear for which she is famous, in twinsets, sweaters, separates and suiting. She also has more businesslike, structured but supple suiting in wool crêpe – a favourite with French politicians.

Recently, Rykiel has hotted things up considerably with a younger, flirtier collection which knocks a good 20 years off her usual customer profile. There are sexy little knits in a rainbow of sorbet colours or shrunken black tops jangling with big black sequins. She's also got a new jeans line with pure '80s rhinestone trim. But one thing she won't let die is the jogging suit – those velour lounge suits up on the first floor still look very Florida rest home. Also new is a great range of accessories with bags, wallets and purses in nylon leopard-skin print.

SONIA RYKIEL FEMME, 175 boulevard St-Germain, 75006
Tel: 01 49 54 60 60
Métro: St-Germain-des-Prés
also at:
70 rue du Faubourg St-Honoré, 75008. Tel: 01 42 65 20 81
Opening Hours: Mon–Sat: 10.00–19.00
August: open
Credit Cards: Visa, Amex, Diners, MC, JCB, as well as dollars, yen
Price Range: sweaters 1,250–1,800FF, suiting jackets 4,500FF, skirt or trousers 2,500FF

PAULE KA: SMART CHIC WOMENSWEAR
See Le Marais for details.
192 boulevard St-Germain, 75007. Tel: 01 45 44 92 60

SONIA RYKIEL HOMME: DESIGNER MENSWEAR
By contrast for menswear, Rykiel takes velour and makes it decent by ladding it up in citrus stripes. Customers are divided between the fashion man who likes to strut in the James Bond polo-neck and leather fitted pea-coat, and the fogey gallery and publishing crew of

St-Germain, who opt for classic sportswear. Then there's media-man –
Madame Rykiel must dress every self-respecting male TV presenter in
this town. She makes some of the handsomest men's leather around,
whether classic caramel suede safari jacket or racing zipped-up
bomber. Her signature seams on the outside appear with grey seams
on navy jackets. Towards the back of the store is all the work-wear,
neat suits, blazers, work shirts and ties.

SONIA RYKIEL HOMME, 194 boulevard St-Germain, 75007
Tel: 01 45 44 83 19
Métro: St-Germain-des-Prés
Opening Hours: Mon–Sat: 10.00–19.00
August: open
Credit Cards: Visa, Amex, Diners, MC, JCB, as well as dollars, yen
Price Range: knitwear 900–1,500FF, shirts 500–800FF, suits 3,700–5,200,
zipped leather bomber 7,000FF

APOSTROPHE: FRENCH CHIC WOMENSWEAR
See 8th arrondissement for details.
190 boulevard St-Germain, 75007

ETRO: DESIGNER WOMEN'S & MEN'S WEAR
A family Italian firm that has recently regained fashion credibility, Etro
mixes up a well-bred eccentric, bohemian but always luxurious look.
The emphasis for both menswear and womenswear is on textiles as
well as a certain artisan sensibility seen in embroidered bags and
dreamy tweeds. Veronica Kean, one of the sisters of the family, has
recently taken over design control. For winter there are cashmere
cardigans edged with fur or knitted ponchos to wrap up in, while
come summertime the Etro woman wafts around in djellabas made
from Indian sari fabrics, peasant shirts in paisley silk and caftans
teamed with fringed bags and low-slung Tibetan belts. On the ground
floor of this store are Etro's famous scarves and shawls in fabulously
soft paisley wools and cashmere.

ETRO, 177 boulevard St-Germain, 75007
Tel: 01 45 48 18 17
Métro: St-Germain-des-Prés
also at:
66 rue du Faubourg St-Honoré, 75008. Tel: 01 40 07 09 40
Opening Hours: Mon–Sat: 10.00–13.00, 14.00–19.00
August: closed first 15 days
Credit Cards: Visa, Amex, Diners, MC, JCB
Price Range: scarves from 1,000FF, trousers from 1,500FF, cashmere cardigan
from 2,000FF, evening dress 6,000–10,000FF

LA PERLA: ITALIAN LINGERIE
See 8th arrondissement for details.
179 boulevard St-Germain, 75007. Tel: 01 45 44 45 76

PLEATS PLEASE: ISSEY MIYAKE'S SECOND LINE

The Pleats Please woman demands deep pigment, sculptural form and an easy wash cycle – for her only Issey Miyake can deliver. Pleats Please is his second line, made up of thirteen basic shapes in lightweight polyester which have been permanently pleated and dipped in dye. Shapes are long and lean and include full-length sleeveless dress and coat, several versions of trousers and a polo-neck shell. They look striking on the hanger, even better on a body where they take shape without clinging. There are nine basic colours with a couple more added for each season and the palette goes from écru, steel or black to guava and lime. Miyake has recently started doing duo-colour pleats (half and half colours) as well as adding zips in a couple of pieces like a jacket and a waistcoat, available in black only.

Women who work in the fashion industry swear by Pleats Please as you can travel in them, wash them in your hotel bathroom and they'll be dry by the morning. The dresses look great on pregnant women.

PLEATS PLEASE, 201 boulevard St-Germain, 75007
Tel: 01 45 48 10 44
Métro: Rue du Bac
also at:
3 bis rue des Rosiers, 75004. Tel: 01 40 29 99 66
Opening Hours: Mon–Sat: 10.00–19.00
August: closed for two weeks, call for exact dates
Credit Cards: Visa, Amex, Diners, JCB
Price Range: vest top 800FF, coat 2,400FF

BONPOINT: CHILDREN'S WEAR

This is how you wished your mother had dressed you. Bonpoint clothes are deliciously French, strictly good taste with a retro sensibility such as blossom-pink Viyella dresses and velvet-collared wool coats. The clothes go up to age 16 for boys and girls, but it's the clothes for little people which are truly irresistible such as sugar-pink sun dresses embroidered with tiny rose-buds at the waist and with matching knickers or bridesmaid dresses in layers of stiff organza. They have recently introduced a line of cashmere as well as pashmina shawls for wrapping up your new-born. As you may have gathered this is a store to indulge at, rather than stock up on Babygros.

Along the road at 7 rue de Solférino is the furniture and furnishings store for kitting out the nursery, and see earlier in this chapter for the Bonpoint sale shop, definitely worth going to for reduced-price clothes.

BONPOINT, 67 rue de l'Université, 75007
Tel: 01 45 55 63 70
Métro: Solférino
also at:

15 rue Royale, 75008. Tel: 01 47 42 52 63
12 Avenue Montaigne, 75008. Tel: 01 47 42 52 63
50 rue Étienne Marcel, 75002. Tel: 01 40 26 20 90
Opening Hours: Mon–Sat: 10.00–19.00
August: open
Credit Cards: Visa, Diners, Amex, MC, JCB
Price Range: sweater from 280FF, dress from 650FF, pashmina shawl for baby
2,700FF

1 ET 1 FONT 3   PREGNANCY WEAR

Just as soon as the Parisian girl gets the pregnancy test positive, she
whips round to 1 et 1 font 3 to invest in the pregnancy wardrobe. What
is best here are the weekend, casual clothes, as well as the evening and
occasion (wedding, party etc.) kit. Designer Juliette Swildens is not
into dressing you up as Mummy. Instead she cuts a reasonably fashionable silhouette – we're talking black wrap-around sexy jersey
dresses and well-cut stretch cotton trousers. Their basics include a
great stretch trouser which has an almost jean-cut leg (as in it is not a
pair of leggings), crisp cotton shirts, straight, cigarette and boot-legged
trousers, plus sophisticated swimming costumes and nice knitwear.
Two tips: you need to get here early in the season otherwise everything
black has gone; also this is a good store if you happen to be full-on
pregnant during those hot summer months and despairing of what to
wear, as they do pretty and, most importantly, flattering summer
dresses.

1 ET 1 FONT 3, 3 rue de Solférino, 75007
Tel: 01 40 62 92 15
Métro: Solférino
Opening Hours: Mon–Fri: 10.30–13.00, 13.30–19.00, Sat: 10.30–19.00
August: closed first three weeks
Credit Cards: Visa, Amex, MC
Price Range: stretch jersey plain dress 640FF, long stretch skirt 445FF, jeans
490FF, two-shade swimming costume 380FF

IMH: INTERIOR DESIGNER

'There are so many fabrics I enjoy wearing which I would like to use
in my interiors,' says India Mahdavi Hudson, plucking at a pair of Etro
tweed pants as an example. 'Fashion fabrics are so much more funky
and modern than furnishing fabrics which still tend to be dated and
chi-chi.' Interior designer Mahdavi Hudson has a design style which
splices sober form with sensuous and unexpected fabrics, such as a
slinky curtain in fine stainless-steel chain mail, a beige flannel armchair or a day bed in white terry cloth destined for a Chelsea bathroom. She spent seven years working for Christian Liaigre before
going it alone and already she has built an impressive clientele
(including retailer Joseph Ettegdui) who are attracted by her cool sensibility and subtle use of colour. Mahdavi Hudson's signature pieces

so far include day beds in stretch nylon, a standard lamp with chrome metal link stand and a dusty lilac lacquered dressing table. Her showroom is open for viewing by appointment; all pieces are made to order and take six to eight weeks for delivery.

IMH, 3 rue Las Cases, 75007
Tel: 01 45 51 63 89
Métro: Solférino
Opening Hours: Mon–Sat: 9.00–19.00
August: closed
Credit Cards: none
Price Range: small lamps from 1,900FF, sofas 25,000–35,000FF, desk 12,000–15,000FF, chair 4,000–6,300FF

GALERIE NAILA DE MONTBRISON:

JEWELLERY

Naila de Montbrison's jewellery gallery has left behind its ethnic image and is heading increasingly contemporary with work by designers Christiane Billet, Taher Chemirik, Giampaolo Babetto and others. There is still some ancient jewellery, striking pieces from Africa and Indonesia, huge collar chokers from Uzbekistan, but alongside are contemporary pieces such as a hunk of a silver bangle stoppered at either end with a rough cut amethyst or a stunning gold ring studded with fire opal and opal. The gallery pulls a chic, cultivated, Rive gauche woman who, like Naila, believes that it doesn't matter what jewellery is made of, it's the level of creativity that counts.

GALERIE NAILA DE MONTBRISON, 6 rue de Bourgogne, 75007
Tel: 01 47 05 11 15
Métro: Invalides or Assemblée Nationale
Opening Hours: Tue–Sat: 11.30–13.30, 14.30–19.00
August: closed
Credit Cards: Visa, Amex, MC
Price Range: 800–120,000FF

MUSÉE RODIN: MUSEUM AND GARDENS

A delightful museum of Auguste Rodin's sculptures and sketches is situated in the gardens and mansion where he once lived. It's an intensely sensory trip round from the langorous love clinches to the frenetic 'Gates of Hell'. Add to that a beautiful setting of an 18th-century mansion with gardens lined in lime trees, and it must be the most romantic of Paris's museums. There's a café outside which is open from March to September; shame about the pigeons.

MUSÉE RODIN, 77 rue de Varenne, 75007
Tel: 01 47 05 01 34
Métro: Varenne
Opening Hours: Tue–Sun: 9.30–17.15 (16.15 winter months)
Entry Fee: 28FF (reduced rate 18FF), garden only 5FF

LA PAGODE: CINEMA AND TEA ROOM

This magical Chinese-style pagoda has been turned into a cinema and tea rooms. Situated a little incongruously in a smart 7th residential street, it was built in 1895 by a Monsieur Morin, director of Le Bon Marché department store, as a love token to his wife. They had exotic soirées and got dressed up as the emperor and empress, but the party ended a year later when she ran off with his partner's son. It is now a cinema with two auditoriums. One room is decorated in flamboyant Japanese style with carved ceiling and leaping dragons, the other is standard brylon cinema seating. It's the most divine place in Paris to watch a film, and savvy Parisians – regardless of the choice of film – always opt for the Japanese room.

There is also a tea room, which in winter is inside with low cane tables. In summer, you can sit out in the front garden among bamboo plants and lion statues. Fruity-flavour teas or lemon-grass infusions are served in heavy iron teapots.

LA PAGODE, 57 bis rue de Babylone, 75007
Tel: 08 36 68 75 07
Métro: St-François Xavier
Opening Hours of tea room: Mon–Sat: 16.00–22.00, Sun: 14.00–20.00
August: open
Credit Cards: none (nor cheques)
Price Range: cinema tickets 50FF, pot of tea or infusion 22FF

Champs
Elysées

8TH ARRONDISSEMENT

What counts in the 8th arrondissement is luxury designer fashion. There are women in Paris who will shop for clothes only here, in the avenue Montaigne and the rue du Faubourg St-Honoré. They are mostly loaded. Formerly a ladies-who-lunch kind of street, in recent years the avenue Montaigne has headed positively hip with Italians Prada and Dolce & Gabbana having opened stores; Calvin Klein has moved in with both a menswear and a womenswear store, while Céline now designed by Michael Kors has a huge new store. These two streets plus rue Royale and the avenue George V make up the full-flavour Rive droite shopping trip and are a credit-card-battering experience.

The 8th is where practically all the couture houses have their offices and ateliers. It's where Christian Dior opened in avenue Montaigne at the end of 1946 and where Christian Lacroix, the newest of French couture houses, opened in rue du Faubourg St-Honoré in 1987.

No matter that many of today's couturiers at the illustrious old French houses are foreign – John Galliano, Alexander McQueen and Karl Lagerfeld – or that only 2,000 or so women worldwide can still afford to dress in the stuff, or that a cocktail dress costs at least 150,000FF (£20,000). This is the dream-like world of haute couture, with its defiant élitism and dedication to beauty, which still set Paris apart in an increasingly international fashion arena. However, in reality what sells around here are the ready-to-wear and the diffusion collections. The stores in the 8th stock the prêt-à-porter collections from every big international designer across the style spectrum, from Jil Sander to Valentino. Then there are the diffusion lines, which are less expensive and mostly intended for a younger customer. Often these lines are not designed by the designer him- or herself, rather inspired by their style. These collections can cost as much as 60% less than the main line.

The rue du Faubourg St-Honoré and the avenue Montaigne, while selling basically the same kind of product – global brands, luxury fashion – are totally different in character. The avenue Montaigne is wide and grand with monumental stores. It is lined with chestnut trees and 45-year-old women with the body parts of a 20-year-old. Somehow the street always looks empty, but know that behind every glass store door, the platinum credit cards are pounding. This is where Yorkshire terriers get to run wild on marble floors while Mummy tries on a little something in the changing rooms.

Over in the Faubourg St-Honoré the street is crowded and bumper to bumper with orange Hermès carrier bags. The President lives down here at the Élysée Palace. It's very Parisian as a road, yet full of tourists. Partly because it's a narrow road and partly because the shops are fairly small, it makes for perfect window shopping and buying is

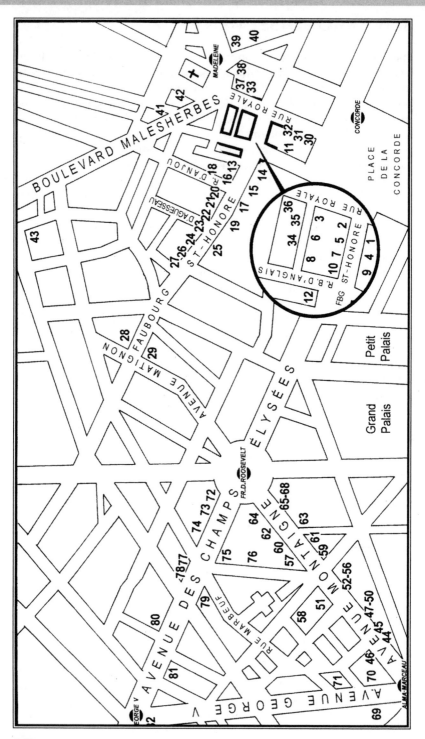

1 MISSONI
2 GUCCI
3 PRADA
4 STÉPHANE KÉLIAN
5 LOFT
6 LOLITA LEMPICKA
7 RENAUD PELLEGRINO
8 LA PERLA
9 SERGIO ROSSI
10 LANVIN
11 BUDDHA BAR
12 HERMÈS
13 GIVENCHY
14 OSCAR DE LA RENTA
15 VALENTINO
16 YVES SAINT LAURENT INSTITUT
17 INSTITUT LANCÔME
18 YVES SAINT LAURENT
19 HERVÉ LÉGER
20 CHRISTIAN DIOR
21 DELLA VALLE
22 CHLOÉ
23 GUERLAIN
24 VERSACE
25 APOSTROPHE
26 ETRO
27 SONIA RYKIEL
28 ANNA LOWE
29 CHRISTIAN LACROIX
30 DANIEL SWAROVSKI
31 SALON DE THÉ BERNARDAUD
32 BONPOINT
33 LADURÉE
34 VILLAGE ROYAL (shopping arcade)
35 CHANEL
36 ET VOUS
37 RALPH LAUREN
38 MAISON DE FAMILLE
39 KENZO HOMME
40 KENZO
41 BURBERRY

42 CERRUTI 1881
43 MAKE UP FOR EVER
44 DOLCE & GABBANA
45 EMANUEL UNGARO
46 VALENTINO
47 BAR DES THÉÂTRES
48 PRADA
49 MALO
50 BONPOINT
51 MAXMARA
52 JOSEPH
53 CHRISTIAN LACROIX
54 BABY DIOR
55 CHRISTIAN DIOR JOAILLERIE
56 CHRISTIAN DIOR
57 L'AVENUE
58 PIERRE BALMAIN
59 CÉLINE
60 CALVIN KLEIN
61 CHANEL
62 THIERRY MUGLER
63 LOEWE
64 51 MONTAIGNE
65 BARBARA BUI
66 JIL SANDER
67 LOUIS VUITTON
68 CALVIN KLEIN
69 GIVENCHY
70 BALENCIAGA
71 KENZO
72 L'ÉCLAIREUR
73 STÉPHANE KÉLIAN
74 ZARA
75 SPOON FOOD & WINE
76 ZENTA
77 GUERLAIN
78 SEPHORA
79 TARA JARMON
80 FREE
81 LADURÉE
82 LOUIS VUITTON

not compulsory – although always preferable.

For less financially challenging purchases check out Et Vous just near the Madeleine church or Zara on the Champs-Élysées, while Anna Lowe on the Faubourg St-Honoré is a great source for discount designer wear. Prisunic, also on the Champs-Élysées, is a brilliant place to buy kids' clothes, while mega-store Sephora is a retail temple to cosmetics and fragrance. For a break from shopping there are always blockbusting art shows at the Grand Palais and awesome eight-lane traffic jams in the Champs-Élysées.

RUE DU FAUBOURG ST-HONORÉ

MISSONI: ITALIAN DESIGNER
See 7th arrondissement for details.
1 rue du Faubourg St-Honoré, 75008

GUCCI: ITALIAN DESIGNER
God bless Tom Ford. He's pulled Gucci off the rack of navy loafers and made it hip again. He's taken every Gucci trademark from bamboo handles and snaffles to the G logo and made them new, contemporary and must-have. Nowadays every Gucci fashion show prompts a sluice of fash-pack tears and multi-national waiting lists, while another container load of fake snaffle bits hits the high street.

Ford's campaign project since he became creative director in 1993 has been to make Gucci as white hot as it was in the 1960s when Grace

Kelly, Audrey Hepburn and Brigitte Bardot all shopped here. And he's done it. In 1992 Gucci losses ran at $32 million; in 1999 Gucci sales hit $1 billion. No wonder LVMH's Bernard Arnault became so obsessed with buying the company. Amid bitter fighting, François Pinault (owner of among other things Printemps department store, Yves Saint Laurent and French mail order giant La Redoute) came along and bought a 40% stake in the company for $3 billion.

What Ford does best is inject every aspect of Gucci, from beaded jeans to logoed bags, from slick ad campaigns to store window display, with full-on sex appeal. He designs sleek, modern sensual clothes keeping an eye on the 1970s, but at the same time mixing it up and cutting the silhouette for now. (He cuts the perfect trouser – hip-hugging and flared at the calf.) And he has all the marketing and merchandising savvy of a true American designer. It means Gucci is now worn by Madonna, Uma Thurman, Gwyneth Paltrow, rapper Foxy Brown and the rest of Hollywood.

This store has been transformed into a huge Gucci mega-store selling the womenswear, menswear, luggage, bags, shoes and home collection.

GUCCI, 2 rue du Faubourg St-Honoré, 75008
Tel: 01 53 05 11 11
Métro: Concorde or Madeleine
also at:
(menswear) 350 rue St-Honoré, 75001. Tel: 01 42 96 83 27
Opening Hours: Mon–Sat: 9.30–19.00
August: open
Credit Cards: Visa, Amex, Diners, MC, JCB
Price Range: trousers from 2,000FF, jackets from 2,800FF, shoes from 1,400FF, coat from 4,000FF, bags from 2,300FF

PRADA: ITALIAN DESIGNER
See later in this chapter for details.
6 rue du Faubourg St-Honoré, 75008.

STÉPHANE KÉLIAN: DESIGNER SHOES
See 7th arrondissement for details.
5 rue du Faubourg St-Honoré, 75008.

LOFT: BASICS
Loft is a late-1980s concept of basics for work and play, but what still works for men has lost its way for women. It's definitely worth having a look at the menswear as they have good-quality shirts which are reasonably priced. Rough linen pants and thick-ribbed V-necks work too. But for women suiting is drab, building-site grey and not a great cut. The little cotton cropped twinsets are sweet, but you've got to be wary of a shop that tries to sell you a suit with flared shorts. Service? Let's just hope the manageress is nothing to go by.

LOFT, 12 rue du Faubourg St-Honoré, 75008
Tel: 01 42 65 59 65
Métro: Concorde
also at:
56 rue de Rennes, 75006. Tel: 01 45 44 88 99
Opening Hours: Mon–Sat: 10.00–19.00
August: open
Credit Cards: Visa, Amex, Diners, JCB
Price Range: thick-ribbed V-necks 695FF, linen pants 395FF, shirts 310FF

LOLITA LEMPICKA: COQUETTE DESIGNER WEAR

Break out the lace, Lolita Lempicka is intended as a coquette look. About three-quarters of the women who shop here come for the evening dresses. Full-length dresses are backless or strapless and cut to the thigh, built for lithe limbs and party entrances. The cocktail party wear is more frou-frou and nostalgia. The second floor here is devoted to evening wear: it's beautifully done out with Empire furniture of piano, chaise longue and cream and caramel raw silk curtains. Downstairs are the day dresses like a floaty number in black and cream polka dots with red roses. They're sunny, but not stupendous and at the sort of price you'd be more inclined to spend on something for the evening. French actress and face of Lancôme Cristiana Réali loves Lolita clothes.

LOLITA LEMPICKA, 14 rue du Faubourg St-Honoré, 75008
Tel: 01 49 24 94 01
Métro: Concorde
also at:
46 avenue Victor Hugo, 75016. Tel: 01 45 02 14 46
Opening Hours: Mon–Sat: 10.30–19.00
August: open
Credit Cards: Visa, Amex, Diners, MC, JCB
Price Range: evening dresses from 3,000 up to 10,995FF for a structured corset and masses of tulle

RENAUD PELLEGRINO: DRESSED-UP HANDBAGS

This is a story about Renaud Pellegrino. A client came in looking for a shopping bag, and picked out a wide criss-cross straw shopper – not really what you'd take down the supermarket, more somewhere to put your foie gras from Fauchon. Her only reservation was that she had friends with the same bag; she wanted hers to be different. Pellegrino told her to go home and bring him back all the old Hermès scarves she no longer wore. She returned and he stitched them into a glorious bag within a bag. That is what Paris style is all about and doesn't it make you want to weep into your half-pint of lager shandy.

When he's not performing miracles, Pellegrino is designing lady-like bags: little rigid satin party bags, clutch bags, peardrop-shaped leather bags and bags with a twist of glass beads as a handle. There are 32 colours to choose from as for him 'life without colour doesn't exist'.

RENAUD PELLEGRINO, courtyard of 14 rue du Faubourg St-Honoré, 75008
Tel: 01 42 65 35 52
Métro: Concorde
Opening Hours: Mon–Sat: 10.00–19.00
August: closed for part of month, call for exact dates
Credit Cards: Visa, Amex, MC
Price Range: satin bags from 1,500FF, leather 2,500FF and up

LA PERLA: ITALIAN LINGERIE

France is positively nationalistic when it comes to lingerie – except where Italian brand La Perla is concerned. The French – men and women – love it. They love the sophisticated colours (plum, caffè latte, platinum grey etc.), the fabrics, the detail (Leavers lace, embroidery, stretch tulle insets), but most of all they love the Italian sex appeal. There are several different lines in here including La Perla (the classic lacy, luxurious collection), Malizia (more fashion-led), La Perla Studio (a more minimal, everyday feel) and Marvel (sexier, racier than the rest). There are also wildly glamorous swimming costumes and boudoir-wear. Expect to find high prices, sculptural results and great quality. Do not expect to find whispering, blushing male customers side-stepping round the satin g-strings; French men are totally at ease with their lingerie-buying habits. Sizing goes from 32B to 38D.

LA PERLA, 20 rue Faubourg St-Honoré, 75008
Tel: 01 43 12 33 60
Métro: Concorde or Madeleine
also at:
179 boulevard St-Germain, 75007. Tel: 01 45 44 45 76
Opening Hours: Mon–Sat: 10.00–19.00
August: open
Credit Cards: Visa, Amex, Diners, MC, JCB
Price Range: bra from 400FF, body from 850FF, swimwear from 850FF

SERGIO ROSSI: DESIGNER SHOES

See 7th arrondissement for details.
11 rue du Faubourg St-Honoré, 75008. Tel: 01 40 07 10 89

LANVIN: FRENCH DESIGNER

'I'm trying to bring a freshness to the house, a sense of comfort and a feeling of Jeanne Lanvin,' explains Cristina Ortiz, Lanvin's womenswear designer, 'at the same time bringing a femininity that I feel is missing from fashion.' After three years spent in Milan as Miuccia Prada's right-hand designer, Spanish Ortiz took on the task of guiding the house of Lanvin out of the fashion wilderness.

So far she has fused a feminine but spare silhouette with sportswear looks, geometric beading and cutting. She makes coats which shrug on like a cardigan but are tailored to perfection in unlined double-faced cashmere; she cuts a skinny jacket zipped up the front, while trousers are extended to elongate the leg.

LANVIN, 22 rue du Faubourg St-Honoré, 75008
Tel: 01 44 71 31 83
Métro: Concorde or Madeleine
Opening Hours: Mon–Sat: 10.00–18.45
August: call for exact dates
Credit Cards: Visa, Amex, Diners, MC, JCB
Price Range: trousers from 1,950FF, knitwear from 1,835FF, coat from 8,500FF, skirt from 2,000FF

BUDDHA BAR: FASHIONABLE BAR AND RESTAURANT

This is a flash, fashionable bar and restaurant lined with hipless girls and fat expense accounts. It's downstairs, dark and exotic with an enormous and serene Buddha, low-slung Indonesian wooden chairs and a jungle of floral and fauna arrangements. It's a totally 'm'as-tu vu' scene (French equivalent of posing), with Robert de Niro, Leonardo DiCaprio, Janet Jackson and Madonna dropping by when in town.

BUDDHA BAR, 8 rue Boissy d'Anglas, 75008
Tel: 01 53 05 90 00
Métro: Concorde or Madeleine
Opening Hours: every day except Sat/Sun lunch: lunch 12.00–15.00, bar 18.00–2.00am, dinner from 19.30
August: open
Credit Cards: Visa, Amex, MC
Price Range: cocktails from 69FF, starter from 86FF, main course from 95FF

HERMÈS: FRENCH LUXURY LEATHER

Hermès has become fashionable quite by stealth. It has turned from bourgeois brand to discreet cool, while keeping sacrosanct its image of the noble artisan and ultimate quality. Jean Louis Dumas is the man responsible. A fifth-generation Hermès, he speaks in mystical riddles, but know beneath that gentlemanly eccentric exterior ticks a visionary brain for business. He has taken on Martin Margiela to design womenswear, a brilliant avant-garde talent who has built an identifiable Hermès look which is a hit with a certain chic woman with cash/class, aged 40 or so. She adores his long tunics in cashmere, short trenchcoats, fluid trousers and luxury sporty sweaters. Alongside the clothes are shoes designed by Pierre Hardy who has brought us Quick trainers in chestnut-brown leather and divine summer sandals with overstitched H.

And then there are the bags. The Kelly bag, size 32cm, is forever the best seller, but fashionable right now is the Herbag which is made from leather and toile and comes with two different-size bag parts so you can swap to make it backpack or handbag. Many bags involve a waiting list of around six months; all are expensive – you're looking at from 17,000FF for a Birkin and from 15,100FF for the darling Constance bag (shoulder strap, wide metal H snapper, as worn by Jackie O).

Thierry Hermès started the business as a saddler and harness-maker in 1837 and it's in leather that the heart of the house still belongs. For a slice of Parisian life come here – it's the best people-watching store in town.

HERMÈS, 24 rue du Faubourg St-Honoré, 75008
Tel: 01 40 17 47 17
Métro: Concorde or Madeleine
Opening Hours: Mon: 10.00–13.00, 14.15–18.30, Tue–Sat: 10.00–18.30
August: open
Credit Cards: Visa, Amex, Diners, MC, JCB
Price Range: silk square scarf 1,475FF, Kelly bag in box leather from 19,400FF, Herbag from 5,500FF, Quick trainers from 2,600FF

GIVENCHY: FRENCH COUTURIER
See later in this chapter for details.
28 rue du Faubourg St-Honoré, 750008. Tel: 01 42 65 54 54

OSCAR DE LA RENTA: AMERICAN DESIGNER
Dominican-born, American-bred, Oscar de la Renta has got the New York society scene sewn up (at least among the grandes dames). Here in Paris he has his own boutique and he also jets in to design the haute couture for the house of Balmain. Come here for lunching suits and glamorous gala dresses with lashings of embroidery, opulent brocades and pretty sorbet colours.

OSCAR DE LA RENTA, 25 rue du Faubourg St-Honoré, 75008
Tel: 01 42 66 05 64
Métro: Concorde or Madeleine
Opening Hours: Tue–Fri: 10.30–19.00, Sat/Mon: 11.30–19.00

August: open
Credit Cards: Visa, Amex, MC
Price Range: suit from 15,000FF, cocktail dress from 9,500FF, long evening
dress from 15,000FF

VALENTINO: ITALIAN COUTURIER
See later in this chapter for details.
27 rue du Faubourg St-Honoré, 75008. Tel: 01 42 66 95 94

YVES SAINT LAURENT INSTITUT:
BEAUTY SALON
The Yves Saint Laurent Institut's speciality is the pedicure. It's a reve-
lation. Make sure you ask for Monsieur Ho (he does Catherine
Deneuve's feet too); he will massage, pare, file, primp your feet to
make them look good enough for a pair of Manolo mules and – best of
all – he is not shocked by serial high-heel addiction. The Institut ambience is exotic Saint Laurent style, with lots of gilt and hot fuchsia decor
and the smell of Opium in the air.

YVES SAINT LAURENT INSTITUT, 32 rue du Faubourg St-Honoré, 75008
Tel: 01 49 24 99 66
Métro: Madeleine or Concorde
Opening Hours: Mon–Fri: 9.00–19.30, Sat: 9.00–19.00
August: open
Credit Cards: Visa, Amex, Diners, MC, JCB
Price Range: pedicure from 420FF, Soin Éclat facial 380FF, manicure from 255FF

INSTITUT LANCÔME: BEAUTY SALON
In Paris each beauty salon has a reputation for being great at something. I reckon Lancôme is the best in town for waxing, in terms of both thoroughness and being relatively pain-free. As well as their waxing, they do a pretty dreamy facial, service is great and they serve you custom-made herbal tea. And if you've ever wondered how all those Paris girls on the terrasses are already enviably bronzed come the first week of May, then ask at Lancôme for the 'bronze flash application' (for body or face) and you'll understand how.

INSTITUT LANCÔME, 29 rue du Faubourg St-Honoré, 75008
Tel: 01 42 65 30 74
Métro: Madeleine or Concorde
Opening Hours: Mon–Fri: 10.00–20.00, Sat: 10.00–19.00
August: open
Credit Cards: Visa, Amex, Diners, MC, JCB
Price Range: flash bronzer face 100FF/body 250FF, facial 400FF, waxing 170–370FF

YVES SAINT LAURENT: FRENCH COUTURIER
See 6th arrondissement for details.
38 rue du Faubourg St-Honoré, 75008. Tel: 01 42 65 74 59

HERVÉ LÉGER: SEXY BANDAGE DRESSING
The house of Hervé Léger is undergoing a radical rethink after being bought out by French fashion company BCBG, who then threw out founding designer Hervé Léger (and you can't get much more radical than that).

HERVÉ LÉGER, 29 rue du Faubourg St-Honoré, 75008
Tel: 01 44 51 62 36
Métro: Concorde
Opening Hours: Mon–Sat: 10.00–19.00
August: open
Credit Cards: Visa, Diners, Amex, MC, JCB
Price Range: swimming costumes 1,200–1,300FF, ready-to-wear top 3,000FF, dress 7,000FF, skirt 3,500FF, jacket 9,500FF

CHRISTIAN DIOR: FRENCH COUTURIER
See later in this chapter for details.
46 rue du Faubourg St-Honoré, 75008. Tel: 01 44 51 55 51

DELLA VALLE: CULT ITALIAN SHOES

Every time you go by this store it is relentlessly busy. On the big easy sofas lounge handsome older men with full heads of hair who look like they left the 80ft yacht parked outside, while around the shop pace chillingly well-dressed women who no doubt wake up looking like that. They are all in search of the J.P. Tod shoe, which manages to be both classic élitist symbol and fashion item. What we're talking about here is in fact a hand-made, unisex flat moccasin shoe with weeny little rubber stoppers all over the sole, modelled on the American car shoe. There are several styles, including a block heel, and colours change every season with pastels and bright patents, but it's those suntan neutrals that are most in demand. People can get a little precious about their J.P. Tods. They swear by their comfort, say they couldn't fly without them and pull a tantrum if the store doesn't have their size. Claudia Schiffer was in recently and bought thirteen pairs, Uma Thurman wears them, so do Fergie and her daughters.

Despite the name it's an Italian brand; owner Diego Della Valle discovered the no-slip car shoes on a trip to the States in the 1970s. He brought the shoes back, redesigned them with Italian flair, gave a pair to Mr Agnelli who wore them everywhere and Italian society copied. That was 1979, and it has now become such a marketing coup that Della Valle is featured in the Harvard Business School case-book. While you're in the store check out another style icon, the eau de Cologne Acqua di Parma which was created in the '30s, smells delicious and was worn by Cary Grant and Audrey Hepburn.

DELLA VALLE, 52 rue du Faubourg St-Honoré, 75008
Tel: 01 42 66 66 65
Métro: Concorde
Opening Hours: Mon–Sat: 10.30–19.00
August: open
Credit Cards: Visa, Amex, Diners, MC, JCB
Price Range: basic J.P. Tod 1,300–1,800FF, crocodile 5,600FF, most are around 1,280FF; 50ml Acqua di Parma 210FF

CHLOÉ: FRENCH DESIGNER

Stella McCartney has slashed the average Chloé client age by half with her steamy, provocative rock-chick clothes which she toughens up with a little London tailoring. Trained at Central Saint Martin's, daughter of, she's no fashion revolutionary, but nor does she claim to be. Instead she's a Portobello savvy kind of girl who hangs out with Kate Moss and Tom Ford and can make a pretty 1930s-feel dress in faded floral, a great pair of sexy jeans or a wicked trouser suit with 1970s one-buttoned waisted jacket and wide-legged hipster pants. She fuses hip-hop with hippie, Paris luxury with London credibility, hot sex with sweet femininity. She makes exactly what girls like her want to wear.

CHLOÉ, 56 rue du Faubourg St-Honoré, 75008
Tel: 01 44 94 33 00
Métro: Concorde or Madeleine
Opening Hours: Mon–Sat: 10.00–19.00
August: open
Credit Cards: Visa, Amex, Diners, MC, JCB
Price Range: skirt from 2,000FF, bag 1,500–3,000FF, trouser suit from 9,000FF, evening dress from 10,000FF

GUERLAIN: SCENT
See later in this chapter for details.
56 rue du Faubourg St-Honoré, 75008

VERSACE: ITALIAN DESIGNER
Since Gianni Versace's murder in Miami in 1997, his younger sister Donatella has taken over design of the house and held true to her brother's vision. Blonde and sassy, she has gone from muse and confidante to designer. She has continued the Versace legacy of sexual thrust and extravagant colour, adding to it a woman's sense of femininity. 'I know sexy,' she has famously declared, 'I'm a Versace.' That means she does diving décolletage, jeans studded with Swarovski crystals, chainmail lamé dresses and vivacious prints – all inspired by her late brother's oeuvre. And most importantly she understands the Versace fusion of rock, Hollywood, flesh. She is great mates with Madonna, Kate Moss and Courtney Love and the show front row is always a gridlock of stars: Puff Daddy, Robbie Williams, Matt Dillon, Rupert Everett, Melanie Griffith and Jennifer Lopez have all been in the front-row hot-seat.

The Faubourg store is an enormous Versace emporium stocking on the ground floor menswear, cosmetics and luggage, while upstairs there is womenswear and the home collection. Someone must have shouted 'hold' on the taste factor when they built this store: it's a brief history in time with baroque, neo-classicism, mythology, stainless-steel columns, frescos, Versacology and a whole lot of product thrown in. But it's fun, ostentatious and great for people-watching.

VERSACE, 62 rue du Faubourg St-Honoré, 75008
Tel: 01 47 42 88 02
Métro: Concorde or Madeleine
also at:
41 rue François Premier, 75008. Tel: 01 47 23 88 30
Opening Hours: Mon: 11.00–19.00, Tue–Sat: 10.00–19.00
August: open
Credit Cards: Visa, Amex, Diners, JCB
Price Range: trouser suit 15,600FF, coat dress 13,000FF, long evening dress 16,000–22,000FF, corset cocktail dress 14,350FF; menswear: suit from 7,900FF, print shirt 3,600FF, knitwear 2,700–3,500FF, leather trousers from 8,880FF; interiors: small cushion 800FF

APOSTROPHE: FRENCH CHIC WOMENSWEAR

Apostrophe is for you if you are what the French describe as a 'femme active'. That means aged 35 or so, maybe with a couple of kids, job, home life, supermarket shop to do, meeting to chair, deadline to meet, run off your feet, dinner to go to and you want to look reasonably fashionable, but most of all smart and elegant. Put it this way, Apostrophe is where Hillary Clinton comes to stock up when she's in town.

They do classic but fashion-aware clothes, both work-wear and more recently a weekend collection, which are cut both realistically and to flatter (for instance they will do a version of the zip-up leather blouson, but they will makes theirs longer to cover the hips). The Apostrophe classic pieces include bottom-friendly trousers, single-breasted three-button leather jackets and nice cashmere sweaters. Colours are neutrals, navy, black, cream, beige, with every season something a little more daring thrown in. Sizes go up to 46.

APOSTROPHE, 43 rue du Faubourg St-Honoré, 75008
Tel: 01 40 06 91 60
Métro: Concorde, Madeleine or Miromesnil
also at:
190 boulevard St-Germain, 75007
54 rue Bonaparte, 75006. Tel: 01 43 54 91 73
1 place des Victoires, 75001. Tel: 01 40 41 91 00
11 avenue Victor Hugo, 75016. Tel: 01 45 01 66 91
Opening Hours: Mon–Sat: 10.00–19.00
August: open
Credit Cards: Visa, Amex, Diners, MC, JCB
Price Range: cashmere tops from 800FF, trousers from 1,200FF, leather jacket from 6,500FF

ETRO: ITALIAN DESIGNER

See 7th arrondissement for details.
66 rue du Faubourg St-Honoré, 75008. Tel: 01 40 07 09 40

SONIA RYKIEL: FRENCH DESIGNER

See 7th arrondissement for details.
70 rue du Faubourg St-Honoré, 75008. Tel: 01 42 65 20 81

ANNA LOWE: DESIGNER SALE SHOP

This is a designer sale shop selling ready-to-wear from couturiers like Valentino, Ungaro, Chanel, Yves Saint Laurent, Christian Dior and Lacroix as well as clothes from designers such as Mugler, Montana, Sonia Rykiel and Hermès. Prices are reduced by 50% and clothes are all new but often a year old, factory overruns or more recent sale stock which provincial boutiques can't budge. From time to time owner Suzy gets samples from the shows, particularly Valentino and Dior, which is great if you weigh in at a slim-fast size 8. When I was looking last, there was a great cashmere coat from Margiela at Hermès, a beautiful full-length ribboned cape from a recent Galliano-for-Dior couture show, plus winter coats from Céline. There is also a special Chanel rail where two Texans were busy screaming at the prices and fighting over a lilac glittery tweed Chanel suit. The week before, there'd been a delivery of a whole load of Lacroix suits from the current season, which were all gone in three days. Service is English-speaking and friendly.

ANNA LOWE, 104 rue du Faubourg St-Honoré, 75008
Tel: 01 42 66 11 32
Métro: Miromesnil or Franklin D. Roosevelt
Opening Hours: Mon–Sat: 10.00–19.00
August: open
Credit Cards: Visa, Amex, Diners, JCB
Price Range: Lacroix suit 2,900–4,500FF, Chanel suit around 8,500FF, Dior black and white trouser suit 4,950FF

CHRISTIAN LACROIX: FRENCH COUTURIER

This store is the jewel in the corset of Christian Lacroix's empire. Upstairs are his offices and at the back of the courtyard are the couture salons where you can come to be fitted in zephyrs of black Chantilly lace or corsets choked in pearls. In the shop you'll find the ready-to-wear collection, the much-improved second line, Bazar, and the accessories laden in gilt. French women love the dashing romance of Lacroix. Born in Arles in Provence and a die-hard dandy, he can mix up the 18th century, the smashing clashing colour of the South, the myths, the gypsies and the fairy-tale dresses and make it all his own. More than any of the other couturiers, when a woman buys Lacroix, even if it's just a pair of jeans, it is the haute-couture spectacle of billowing taffetas, tall black mantillas and acres of guipure into which she is buying.

Lacroix worked for a bit as a couturier at Jean Patou, but says he didn't want to be condemned to a life of cream and navy sporty chic, so left to start up his own couture house with the backing of LVMH in 1987. He's been brought on fast in the LVMH hot-house and under pressure to make a success.

On the first floor of the store are the evening dresses, where anything that shouts Lacroix – big gilt buttons, period drama satins, Chantilly lace over satin – quickly sells out. On the ground floor is the daywear from the main collection, as well as Bazar which these days is looking sexier and younger than ever. There are gorgeous hippie knit skirts and tops, bohemian embroidered dresses in jewel colours and crocheted ponchos.

CHRISTIAN LACROIX, 73 rue du Faubourg St-Honoré, 75008
Tel: 01 42 68 79 00
Métro: Miromesnil
also at:
26 avenue Montaigne, 75008. Tel: 01 47 20 68 95
2 place St-Sulpice, 75006. Tel: 01 46 33 48 95
Opening Hours: Mon–Sat: 10.00–19.00
August: open
Credit Cards: Visa, Amex, Diners, JCB
Price Range: brooches 500–1,500FF, Bazar line suit 3,500FF, ready-to-wear suit
10,000–15,000FF, evening dress with corseting 25,000FF

RUE ROYALE

DANIEL SWAROVSKI: CRYSTAL ACCESSORIES

Daniel Swarovksi broke into fashion by making the scintillating crystals with which couturiers like Saint Laurent and Lacroix encrust their couture outfits. Then in 1992 this 100-year-old Austrian firm opened a store here to sell its own crystal accessories range, based around bags and jewellery. All the crystals are man-made and reflect light fabulously against the skin. There are twirly bracelets inset with champagne-coloured crystals, or a ring and necklace made up of hundreds of quivering lilac crystals on stalks, like sea anemones. Bags are best when the crystal is kept light and delicate, like a satin evening bag with a bronze lurex and crystal knitted handle. Some of the bags are pretty serious gala-night affairs, but there are younger looks and particularly in the jewellery you can find affordable glamour to transform a little black dress.

DANIEL SWAROVSKI, 7 rue Royale, 75008
Tel: 01 40 17 07 40
Métro: Concorde
Opening Hours: Mon–Sat: 10.00–18.30
August: open
Credit Cards: Visa, Amex, Diners, MC, JCB
Price Range: sea anemone ring 720FF, bags 2,200–15,820FF, bracelets 690–6,760FF, earrings 530–2,385FF

SALON DE THÉ BERNARDAUD:
LUNCH, TEA STOP

For a discreet and chic tea stop, the Salon de Thé Bernardaud is ideal and located in a gallery of luxury porcelain and silverware stores. Against a deep aubergine velvet backdrop designed by Olivier Gagnère, Parisians snack on dainty teatime pastries, sandwiches and tarte citron. Just down the street from the rue du Faubourg St-Honoré, it is, not surprisingly, a knot of Hermès scarves in here. As Bernardaud is one of France's major luxury porcelain-makers, they've designed several different ranges of porcelain especially for use in the tea room, so when you order your food or drink, you also get the chance to choose exactly which plate or cup design you would like to eat or drink from.

SALON DE THÉ BERNARDAUD, 9 rue Royale, 75008
Tel: 01 42 66 22 55
Métro: Concorde or Madeleine
Opening Hours: Mon–Sat: 8.00–19.00
August: open
Credit Cards: Visa, Amex, JCB
Price Range: coffee 22FF, pot of tea 34FF, tarte citron 32FF, starter from 55FF, main course from 90FF

BONPOINT:
CHILDREN'S WEAR

See 7th arrondissement for details.
15 rue Royale, 75008. Tel: 01 47 42 52 63

LADURÉE:
SALON DE THÉ

Ladurée is the ultimate Paris tea room. It was founded in 1862 as a bakery and pâtisserie, and in 1890 the salon de thé was added. A sugar-almond green exterior, frescos of fat little cherubs dressed in chef's hats putting brioches in to bake on a rising sun, and cupid arrows through lampshades, all lend this place un charme fou. It's worth waiting for a seat on the ground floor, as the first floor is a little insipid by comparison. The ambience is intimate and most of the customers are regulars who come at least once a week, as much for the scene as for the food. Gilles Dufour and Gaultier are regulars and there are always queues of macaroon junkies (including Tom Ford) as Ladurée do the best, whether in pistachio, chocolate or coffee (in summer try them with ice cream). Two serious Ladurée advantages: all the seats are arranged so that you sit tête-à-tête alongside your companion and look on to the room and the people. The second is that everything – macaroons, pastries, sandwiches etc. – is made in the kitchens (not always the case with a lot of these 'traditonal' salons de thé), so they are fresh and delicious. Prices are realistic, service is friendly. And quelle location – bang opposite Gucci.

LADURÉE, 16 rue Royale, 75008
Tel: 01 42 60 21 79
Métro: Concorde or Madeleine
also at:
75 avenue des Champs-Élysées, 75008. Tel: 01 40 75 08 75
Opening Hours: Mon–Sat: 8.30–19.00, Sun: 10.00–19.00; breakfast served 8.30–12.00, lunch 11.30–15.00
August: open
Credit Cards: Visa, Amex, MC, JCB
Price Range: large macaroon 18FF, club sandwich 26FF, bacon salad 52FF, giant éclair 21FF, bowl of strawberries 47FF, glass of kir 20FF

VILLAGE ROYAL:
SHOPPING ARCADE

This smart shopping arcade is located right opposite the Ralph Lauren store in rue Royale. It is done out to look a bit like a 17th-century French village, give or take a couple of espresso bars. At its height of fame the arcade housed the army barracks for the King's troops in 1745. Now it's lined with bijou boutiques.

CHANEL:
DESIGNER SHOES

This store sells the Chanel shoe collection only, which is looking considerably younger and more fashionable than before. See 1st arrondissement for main Chanel entry.
25 rue Royale, 75008. Tel: 01 44 51 92 93

ET VOUS: CONTEMPORARY WOMENSWEAR

Et Vous makes trend-inspired collections for a fashion-conscious girl. That means that whatever the trends on other catwalks that season – artsy wool effect on skirts, motor-bike leather cropped jackets, knit ponchos, fur tops etc. – you will find them at Et Vous served up in a sort of palatable, mainstream way. There are also good basic pieces – a well-cut trouser, nice coats and sexy knits. What's odd about Et Vous is that Koji Tatsuno, who designs the collection, is a talented designer in his own right, so it seems a waste to have him churning out collections inspired by the catwalks of others. Koji does also have his own collection which is sold at a shared Et Vous, Koji Tatsuno boutique in the Palais Royal.

ET VOUS, 25 rue Royale, 75008
Tel: 01 47 42 31 00
Métro: Madeleine
also at:
6 rue des Francs Bourgeois, 75003. Tel: 01 42 71 75 11
72 rue de Passy, 75016. Tel: 01 45 20 47 15
(permanent sale shop) 15–17 rue de Turbigo, 75002. Tel: 01 40 13 04 12
Opening Hours: Mon–Sat: 10.30–19.30
August: open
Credit Cards: Visa, Amex, Diners, MC, JCB
Price Range: trousers 700–1,000FF, jackets from 2,000FF, dresses 1,500FF, coats from 2,500FF, little knits 500–600FF

RALPH LAUREN: AMERICAN DESIGNER

The dark wood panelling, the full-blown flower arrangements, the photographs of patricians at play, all go to conjure up the perfect WASP, Ivy League all-American way of life. That's because Ralph Lauren is all about style and lifestyle rather than fashion. On the ground floor is the menswear which is divided between the Purple label tailoring, the Polo shirts and ties and the casual weekend wear of tweedy sports jackets and conker-brown leather jackets (imagine how Ralph dresses at the weekend and you've more or less got the picture). Upstairs you will find womenswear: there are now four different labels, which go from the main ready-to-wear collection shown on the catwalk to the more casual Sports Woman, all mixed up and sold alongside. The clothes are far less formal than in the past; that's because there's been a push for a slightly younger, more relaxed kind of feel to Ralph Lauren's womenswear. There is less of the trouser suiting, more of thick knit cardigans with outsize stitching, sexy wrap skirts, low-slung cargo pants and cropped cashmere polo-necks. Lauren has always had a thing about a woman looking like a 'natural spirit' and that is still his ideal today with classic good-taste clothes for women wanting an elegant and timeless look. In the basement is the Polo Sport activewear which is cool kit for men and women for skiing, sailing, golf etc. This floor is the favourite haunt of the kind of Parisian girl who turns up with kilometres of legs looking for something matt and black to wear skiing on the slopes of Megève.

RALPH LAUREN, 2 place Madeleine, 75008. Tel: 01 44 77 53 50
Métro: Madeleine
Opening Hours: Mon–Sat: 10.00–19.00
August: open
Credit Cards: Visa, Amex, Diners, MC, JCB

MAISON DE FAMILLE: INTERIORS/LIFESTYLE

Imagine a sort of Frenchified Ralph Lauren lifestyle and interiors store and you've got the idea of Maison de Famille. Huge leather-bound photo albums, tasteful creamy bed-linen, sofa throws and waffle cotton bathrobes are what this store's about. The watchwords here are neutral colours, good taste, verging on the rustic and fairly bourgeois. It's a great place for finding typically French gifts as they do very nice arts de la table – place mats, ceramic plates and bowls or candlesticks. Upstairs you will find safe-looking womenswear, menswear, bed-linen and the bath collection.

MAISON DE FAMILLE, 10 place Madeleine, 75008
Tel: 01 53 45 82 00
also at:
29 rue St-Sulpice, 75006. Tel: 01 40 46 97 47
Métro: Madeleine
Opening Hours: Mon–Sat: 10.30–19.00
August: open
Credit Cards: Visa, Amex, MC
Price Range: from 45FF to 20,000FF

KENZO HOMME: DESIGNER MENSWEAR

See 7th arrondissement for details.
10 place de la Madeleine, 75008. Tel: 01 42 61 04 51

KENZO: JAPANESE/FRENCH DESIGNER WEAR

See 7th arrondissement for details.
22 boulevard de la Madeleine, 75008. Tel: 01 42 61 04 14

BURBERRY: BRITISH FASHION

A couple of years back think Burberry, think American tourist taking a break from the golf club to tour Europe dressed in Burberry's mac teamed with white polo-neck and trainers. Aspirational it was not. Then came the re-look. Human dynamo Rose-Marie Bravo was lured away from her job as president of Saks Fifth Avenue and charged with masterminding the overhaul. She hired Italian designer Roberto Menichetti, who has worked with Jil Sander and is a natural with textiles. Drawing on the house's pedigree (it was founded in 1856 by Thomas Burberry who invented, among other things, gabardine),

Menichetti has taken the Burberry icons and given them edge. He has enlarged the signature house check, cut the trench-coat lean and made sexy motorcycle leather trousers and biker jackets and fluttering bias-cut dresses with faded checks. Get Mario Testino to shoot the ads, Stella Tennant to model, throw in a Jack Russell and some funky accessories, rename the collection Prorsum (more to impress with your Latin learning) and you have the makings of a hot brand. There is still the original London collection (V-neck cashmeres, rain macs etc.) if you happen to be in town taking a break from the fairway.

BURBERRY, 8 boulevard Malesherbes, 75008
Tel: 01 40 07 77 77
also at:
55 rue de Rennes, 75006. Tel: 01 45 48 52 71
Métro: Madeleine
Opening Hours: Mon–Sat: 10.00–19.00
August: open
Credit Cards: Visa, Amex, Diners, MC, JCB
Price Range: Prorsum collection trousers from 2,395FF, trench-coat from 6,295FF, bag from 3,295FF

CERRUTI 1881: ITALIAN DESIGNER

Over the past few years Cerruti has undergone a considerable hike in fashion credibility, thanks in part to designer Peter Speliopoulos who designs the Arte womenswear line. Former assistant to Donna Karan, he has a natural inclination for designing for real life, as well as heeding Nino Cerruti's ethos of 'A person who likes the Cerruti aesthetic has personality and likes to have that framed rather than hidden.'

He has moved the house on from its serious suiting with modern, sportswear pieces which combine simple shapes and the signature luxe Cerruti fabrics with pretty but subtle decoration such as beading or a trace of sequins, ruching at the neckline or punched open-work leather. Speliopoulos is not into the idea of day and evening distinction, nor of clothing for a specific event; instead, he says, 'Modern dressing today is about a sportswear mix, an effortless pairing of clothes. Now everything has got to have many purposes.'

CERRUTI 1881, 15 place de la Madeleine, 75008
Tel: 01 47 42 10 78
Métro: Madeleine
also at:
42 rue de Grenelle, 75007. Tel: 01 42 22 92 28
17 avenue Victor Hugo, 75016. Tel: 01 45 01 66 12
(menswear) 27 rue Royale, 75008. Tel: 01 53 30 18 81
Opening Hours: Mon–Sat: 10.15–19.00
August: open
Credit Cards: Visa, Amex, Diners, MC, JCB
Price Range: Arte collection trousers from 3,000FF, dress from 6,400FF, knitwear from 2,300FF, coat 11,200FF

MAKE UP FOR EVER: PROFESSIONAL MAKE-UP

In a courtyard off rue La Boétie, Make Up For Ever is another of those confidential addresses you only find out about when a careless Parisienne lets slip her brand of foundation. It's a professional make-up brand for real life. Catherine Deneuve, Vanessa Paradis and Moulin Rouge showgirls come for the wide range of lipstick colours, matt foundations, powders and corrector bases.

Compared with other professional brands and designer brands, prices here are very reasonable, but packaging is not as slick. What's popular here are those products you can't find everywhere: waterproof body foundation if you don't want to expose yourself to the sun, and pre-make-up bases which enhance skin tone and cosmetics' staying power. There is also a good range for black skin with specifically formulated colours, pigments and finishes. Printemps department store also stocks a selection of Make Up For Ever.

MAKE UP FOR EVER, 5 rue La Boétie, 75008
Tel: 01 42 66 01 60
Métro: St-Augustin or Miromesnil
Opening Hours: Mon–Sat: 10.00–18.45
August: open
Credit Cards: Visa, Amex, JCB
Price Range: lipstick 50FF, foundation 80FF, lipstick pencil 27FF, loose powder 68FF

AVENUE MONTAIGNE

DOLCE & GABBANA: ITALIAN DESIGNER FASHION

Another Italian fashion house to stake their claim in Paris, Dolce & Gabbana opened up in a former bank at one end of the avenue. It's a lush and Latin store decor with the clothes for men and women downstairs. Theirs is a Mediterranean brand of sexy and dominant dressing and Sicilian-style menswear which generates a $200-million business. Gorgeous prints, body-sculpting corset dresses and sharp tailored

suits explain why Dolce & Gabbana are a hit with women with everything to flaunt. Domenico is the one who was born in Sicily and whose father was a tailor, so he brings the heritage of southern Italian passion-fashion to the partnership, while Stefano was born in Venice and studied graphic design. They design the collections totally in tandem. The newish diffusion line, D & G, has so far been a crazy success. It's a more affordable and younger trend line with logo overload which makes for de rigueur dressing for clubbers.

DOLCE & GABBANA, 2 avenue Montaigne, 75008
Tel: 01 47 20 42 43
Métro: Alma-Marceau
Opening Hours: Mon–Sat: 10.00–19.30
August: open
Credit Cards: Visa, Amex, Diners, MC, JCB
Price Range: dress from 7,000FF, suit from 7,000FF, men's suit from 8,500FF

EMANUEL UNGARO: FRENCH COUTURIER

Ever since Emanuel Ungaro was bought out by Italian shoe house Salvatore Ferragamo, there has been some radical dusting off of the house image. Ungaro is still there as designer but he has shelved his loud check suits and instead re-explored themes from his past with deluxe hippie looks, sweet femininity and disco sexy divas. He has kept the Ungaro rich decoration, profusion of colours, prints and drape but he has given the lot a lighter touch. There are still his famous diagonally draped mousseline dresses but they are cut shorter, flirtier and are built for fun in hot fuschia or daffodil-yellow.

The heating up of the label has also had a knock-on effect on his haute couture which is in demand from the 20-something daughters of the French grandes familles including Cordelia de Castellane and Angélique Hennessy. The store has also been overhauled, and inside as well as the main Parallèle collection you can find the less expensive U line, plus accessories such as long clutch bags and fringed paisley shawls.

EMANUEL UNGARO, 2 avenue Montaigne, 75008
Tel: 01 53 57 00 00
Métro: Alma-Marceau
Opening Hours: Mon–Fri: 10.00–19.00, Sat: 10.00–18.30
August: open
Credit Cards: Visa, Amex, Diners, MC, JCB
Price Range: Parallèle cocktail dress 12,000–30,000FF, suit from 9,000FF, U suit from 4,500FF, swimming costume from 660FF, bags from 3,000FF

VALENTINO: ITALIAN COUTURIER

He's a smooth operator and knows how to keep every generation sweet. In every collection Valentino's got the wardrobe staple for the Euro society lady: the glamorous but utterly elegant evening dresses and those little lunching suits with lacy blouses. But he's got the look right for her daughter too: slim-fitted cashmere flannel jumpsuits, cashmere dresses embellished with delicate embroideries and sugar-almond-coloured suits for Euro-Royal weddings. His front rows at the couture shows are always a stellar turnout and sum up the Valentino allure from Princess Firyal of Jordan and Jacqueline de Ribes to the Miller girls and Ashley Judd. Valentino's aesthetic is dedicated to luxe and he's got the lifestyle to match his clients, with houses in Rome, Capri, Gstaad and London, châteaux in France, yacht and private plane.

He started his own couture house in Rome back in 1960 with a loan from his parents and sold the company in 1998 for $300 million to industrial Italian giant HdP. He continues to design the collection. The store on avenue Montaigne has two entrances, right for Valentino Boutique (the main ready-to-wear line), left for the diffusion lines and upstairs for menswear.

VALENTINO, 19 avenue Montaigne, 75008
Tel: 01 47 23 64 61
Métro: Alma-Marceau
Opening Hours: Mon–Sat: 10.00–19.00
August: open
Credit Cards: Visa, Amex, Diners, JCB
Price Range: Valentino Boutique suit 5,000–8,000FF, evening dress 42,000–60,000FF, Miss V suit 4,300FF, O by Valentino suit from 6,000FF

BAR DES THÉÂTRES: BAR, CAFÉ, RESTAURANT
This is the meeting point for everyone who works along or around this street: shop girls, models, shoppers, actors from the theatre opposite, smooth-talking lawyers, stars staying at the Plaza Hotel, theatre-goers in the early evening – everyone comes here. It's a real local Parisian café, bar and restaurant which means you can snatch a coffee at the bar, sit and eat a sandwich or go next door for a restaurant lunch or dinner. The fearless can try their famous steak tartare and chips (lap up that raw egg and raw minced beef) or less of a challenge is a mushroom omelette. It's always packed at lunch and has a glam cosmopolitan atmosphere without being smug – the right place to come if you're feeling a little shaky after an avenue Montaigne shopping blow-out. Lauren Bacall and Jean Paul Belmondo are regulars.

BAR DES THÉÂTRES, 6 avenue Montaigne, 75008
Tel: 01 47 23 34 63
Métro: Alma-Marceau
Opening Hours: every day: 6.00–2.00am
August: closed for week of 15 Aug
Credit Cards: Visa, Amex
Price Range: mushroom omelette 45FF, steak tartare 90FF

PRADA: ITALIAN DESIGNER

Still one of the most influential fashion houses around (particularly now it owns a 51% stake in Helmut Lang and 75% of Jil Sander, and shares ownership of Fendi with LVMH), Prada sets the international fashion pace with a resolutely avant-garde, yet ruthlessly commercial approach. A feminist and former Communist campaigner (although with all these acquisitions that's long behind her now), Miuccia Prada is hailed as the ultimate woman's designer who delivers modern,

appealing, at times deliberately challenging, but always cool, clothes. Meanwhile her husband Patrizio Bertelli is Prada's CEO and a wily fashion strategist who is out there building himself a fashion empire.

Miuccia stayed clear of the Milanese family luxury leather-goods business, Fratelli Prada, until 1978 when she joined aged 31. The company had a heritage of steamer trunks, Viennese leather and ivory, to which Miuccia, with what was to become characteristic fashion-forward vision, introduced a nylon backpack. At first it failed to sell, then the low-key 1990s dawned and the Prada nylon bag became the only solution to discreet designer dressing. A fan of wearing old couture, Miuccia added womenswear to the company in 1985.

The store here tells the tale of expansion since: on the ground floor are the shoe, bag, luggage and small-leather-goods collections as well as the womenswear; upstairs are men's clothing and Prada Sport, a second line of urban activewear.

PRADA, 10 avenue Montaigne, 75008
Tel: 01 53 23 99 40
Métro: Alma-Marceau
also at:
6 rue du Faubourg St-Honoré, 75008
5 rue de Grenelle, 75006. Tel: 01 45 48 53 14
Opening Hours: Mon–Sat: 10.00–19.00
August: closed for four days around 15 Aug
Credit Cards: Visa, Amex, Diners, MC, JCB
Price Range: knitwear from 2,000FF, jacket from 4,000FF, coat from 7,000FF, shoes from 1,400FF, boots from 2,200FF, bags from 1,500FF

MALO: LUXURY ITALIAN CASHMERE

Like many of the jewellers along this street, Malo has a security guard outside. The difference is, Malo sells sweaters not diamonds. Sweaters, however, that are expensive and made in Tuscany from sumptuous cashmere. What Malo is good at is taking a traditional classic yarn and putting a sportswear or fashion spin on it. For winter there are superior 'sweatshirts' or zip-up ribbed cardigans and polo-necks for men and women, while for summer there are darling little cashmere twinsets in emerald green and close-fitting V-necks in ice-cream colours. All Malo knitwear is finished by hand and prices give pause for thought: womenswear goes from 2,000 to 6,000FF, while menswear is from 3,000 to 8,000FF. Apparently it is just snapped up by grand French families like the Rothschilds who, according to the assistant, regard cashmere as 'just another investment'.

MALO, 12 avenue Montaigne, 75008
Tel: 01 47 20 26 08
Métro: Alma-Marceau
Opening Hours: Mon–Sat: 10.00–19.00
August: open
Credit Cards: Visa, Amex, Diners, MC
Price Range: gloves from 630FF, twinset 4,500FF, short skirt 2,200FF, men's cashmere 'sweatshirt' from 3,300FF

BONPOINT: CHILDREN'S WEAR

See 7th arrondissement for details.
12 avenue Montaigne, 75008. Tel: 01 47 20 42 10

MAXMARA: SLEEK ITALIAN WOMENSWEAR

You can't identify the brand at 100 paces, but you know that the woman walking down the street with a smooth self-assurance is wearing MaxMara. The look is grown-up, well-groomed, effortlessly chic in wealthy colours: beige, camel, espresso, navy blue, cream and lots of white for winter and summer. And you've got to be committed to high maintenance to carry it off – that means French manicure, nude lipstick and no roots. They do perfect suits for the big interview, while in winter the main attactions are coats which are beautifully cut and in luxe fabrics like cashmere, baby alpaca, wool and angora at 6,000–7,000FF.

The store has been recently refurbished and stocks the main line as well as Sportmax, and the weekend and evening line Pianoforte.The Sportmax line is more into the trends: suits are cut closer to the body, skirts a little leaner, and they use edgier fabrics such as a wax-look-covered sweater. It's aimed at a younger woman, say around 30, and is less expensive.

Founded in 1951 by Achille Maramotti and now run by his three children, MaxMara is famously discreet. They use big-name designers to work on all their lines but they won't tell you who they are. They are Italy's third biggest company and produce twelve different lines. Their sheer volume of production means they can be competitive on prices, and they're envied within the industry for their quality, finish and fabrics.

MAXMARA, 31 avenue Montaigne, 75008
Tel: 01 47 20 61 13
Métro: Alma-Marceau
also at:
37 rue du Four, 75006. Tel: 01 43 29 91 10
265 rue St-Honoré, 75001. Tel: 01 40 20 04 58
100 avenue Paul Doumer, 75016. Tel: 01 40 50 34 05
Opening Hours: Mon–Sat: 10.30–19.00
August: open
Credit Cards: Visa, Amex, Diners, MC, JCB
Price Range: MaxMara suit 3,000–4,000FF, linen shirt from 900FF, dress from 1,600FF, Sportmax suit 2,500–2,800FF

JOSEPH: CONTEMPORARY WOMENSWEAR

Retailer Joseph Ettegdui has a deceptively simple and clever concept of sexy basics with seasonal fashion edge. He has four stores in Paris of which this is the largest and most glamorous. Although he started off selling masses of designers, he now sells less and less of them, keeping some evening pieces by Azzedine Alaïa – a Paris woman wardrobe staple – and shoes by Manolo Blahnik. Otherwise he's doing more and more of his own label, with signature knitwear, both chunky weekend sweaters and skinny lurex tops, suiting, soft suede pieces and the essential T-shirts. What's clever about Joseph is that, for example with the suiting, it's actually fairly classic but with enough of a fashion attitude to please the Joseph girl. What really sells here are the trousers; cut lean and hip-hugging they fly out of the shop. Situated just opposite the Plaza Hotel, the store is a favourite shop-stop for Tom and Nicole, Caroline de Monaco, Naomi and Lauren Bacall.

JOSEPH, 14 avenue Montaigne, 75008
Tel: 01 47 20 39 55
Métro: Alma-Marceau
also at:
68–70 rue Bonaparte, 75006. Tel: 01 46 33 45 75
27 rue de Passy, 75016. Tel: 01 45 24 24 32
44 rue Étienne Marcel, 75002. Tel: 01 42 36 87 83
Opening Hours: Mon–Sat: 10.00–19.00
August: open
Credit Cards: Visa, Amex, Diners
Price Range: basic trousers from 990FF, knitwear from 850FF, trouser suit
from 3,400FF, Manolo Blahnik shoes from 2,500FF

CHRISTIAN LACROIX: FRENCH COUTURIER
See earlier in this chapter for details.
26 avenue Montaigne, 75008. Tel: 01 47 20 68 95

BABY DIOR: DESIGNER BABY
Little did I think I would ever be advising people to take a retail trip
round Baby Dior, but that's what happens when the hormones kick in.
There are some inevitably gorgeous children's clothes in here with lily-
of-the-valley motifs, beautiful fabrics such as linens and dupion silks
(not machine-washable at 40°) and divine colours. Indulge your hormones while you can – this time next year she'll be wanting to dress
like Posh Spice.

BABY DIOR, 28 avenue Montaigne, 75008
Tel: 01 40 73 54 44
Métro: Franklin D. Roosevelt
also at:
252 Boulevard St-Germain, 75006. Tel: 01 42 22 90 90
Opening Hours: Mon–Sat: 10.00–19.00
August: open
Credit Cards: Visa, Amex, Diners, MC, JCB
Price Range: dresses from 400FF, coats from 1,000FF, new-born baby clothes
from 300FF

CHRISTIAN DIOR JOAILLERIE: FINE JEWELS
'There is not enough sensuality and sexuality on the place Vendôme,'
declares Victoire de Castellane waving her ringed fingers around in
the air. 'The jewellery there adds 20 years to your face. Instead what I
am doing for Dior is refined, sophisticated, modern, poetic, at the same
time sexy.' After 14 years at Chanel designing the costume jewellery,
Victoire de Castellane moved to Christian Dior to design its first ever
collection of fine jewellery. Seeking inspiration in Monsieur Dior and
his enchanted world of haute couture, she has transformed his ribbons, feathers, bows, lace and lily of the valley with her effervescent
imagination. She has designed feathered platinum chokers of diamonds and pink sapphires and a flaming necklace of 3,000 orange and

yellow sapphires and diamonds, while for the girl 'who doesn't want to wait for her man to buy her jewels', says Victoire, there are chunky gold rings embossed with the Dior hound's-tooth check.

CHRISTIAN DIOR JOAILLERIE, 28 avenue Montaigne, 75008
Tel: 01 47 23 52 39
Métro: Franklin D. Roosevelt
Opening Hours: Mon–Sat: 10.00–13.00, 14.00–18.30
August: open
Credit Cards: Visa, Amex, Diners, MC, JCB
Price Range: small-charm white gold ring 3,900FF, four-spice jewelled ring (diamond, amethyst, aquamarine, tourmaline etc.) 68,000FF, feathered diamond and platinum necklace from 3 million FF

CHRISTIAN DIOR: FRENCH COUTURIER

Since joining Dior in 1997, John Galliano has pulled the couture house from cold storage and made it gorgeous again. A prodigious talent, Galliano has that mix of breath-taking romanticism, careering imagination and bad-boy genius which guarantees LVMH president Bernard Arnault acres of media coverage. 'Monsieur Dior loved women,' says Galliano. 'That's why obviously at Dior today there is an emphasis on a beautiful bosom, waist and hips.' He has indeed made the house silhouette resolutely feminine with his bias-cut siren dress as well as changing the emphasis of the collection from daywear to dead of night (evening wear now represents 80% of ready-to-wear business as opposed to 20% before). And most importantly he has made the house hot: Dior clothes keep turning up on Nicole Kidman, Lauryn Hill, Cate Blanchett and Céline Dion.

As well as the clothes, the bags are obviously a big draw, not just the Lady Dior stitched cane effect, but more creative, funkier pieces in animal prints, while the shoe collection is brilliant. The store was transformed a couple of years ago by Peter Marino who fitted the place out in the house signature dove-grey and white but with witty boudoir touches such as black lace over silk in the lingerie changing rooms and Louis XVI-look chairs wrapped in silk striped bows. It is a beautiful store to look round; there is lingerie and nightwear, menswear, the home collection with jewel-coloured glass and embroidered napkins, cosmetics as well as the Dior ready-to-wear and at the front of the store the bags and silk scarves.

CHRISTIAN DIOR, 30 avenue Montaigne, 75008
Tel: 01 40 73 54 44
Métro: Franklin D. Roosevelt
Opening Hours: Mon–Sat: 10.00–19.00
August: open
Credit Cards: Visa, Amex, Diners, MC, JCB
Price Range: suit from 9,000FF, day dress from 5,000FF, evening dress from 9,000FF, shoes from 1,700FF, knitwear from 1,300FF, Malice bag from 2,800FF

L'AVENUE: FASHIONABLE RESTAURANT

Another of the Costes brothers' acquisitions, L'Avenue has been transformed by decorator Jacques Garcia into a fashionable aubergine velvet kind of restaurant. Food is the usual Costes contemporary brasserie fare (tuna steak and potato purée with olive oil slick in the middle), but as with all the Costes places, you don't go for the food, you go for the scene. It is packed at lunch and dinner and has a great terrasse – ideal for Rive droite posing as long as you can stand the competition: you're up against Catherine Deneuve, Juliette Binoche, Sting and Lenny Kravitz. You need to reserve; tables 19 and 21 are the best tables on the terrasse.

L'AVENUE, 41 avenue Montaigne, 75008
Tel: 01 40 70 14 91
Métro: Franklin D. Roosevelt
Opening Hours: every day: 8.00–2.00am
August: open
Credit Cards: Visa, Amex, Diners, MC, JCB
Price Range: around 250FF per head

BALMAIN: FRENCH COUTURIER

After many years as Karl Lagerfeld's right-hand man over at Chanel, Gilles Dufour joined Balmain in 1998 to shake up the ready-to-wear. (The couture collection is designed by Oscar de la Renta). Dufour has a great sense of colour and fun which is just as well because the Balmain clothes need both. What works best here are the spring wrap coats and pretty mousseline dresses, plus Dufour's sweetest of pastel cashmere twinsets.

PIERRE BALMAIN, 35 & 44 rue François Premier, 75008
Tel: 01 56 89 16 29
Métro: Franklin D. Roosevelt
Opening Hours: Mon–Sat: 10.00–19.00
August: closed
Credit Cards: Visa, Amex, MC
Price Range: 3,000–15,000FF

CÉLINE: FRENCH DESIGNER CHIC

American designer Michael Kors has breathed sexiness into this formerly frumpy French line. More than anything else Kors is a designer who understands his customer's every need and desire. She's a glossy kind of wealthy woman with an ever-ready tan and a gym-toned body who wants easily digestible glamour. Kors delivers with a smart take on American sportswear fused with some key French dictates of luxury and chic. Since his arrival at Céline in 1997, he has turned the house into one of LVMH's fastest-growing fashion labels.

He is not into designer-angst or avant-garde statements; instead Kors thinks in design terms of 'Jennifer Lopez meets Jackie O' and 'getaway glamour'. He's looking to come up with 'the perfect jean, T-shirt, tank, jacket' and so on. He makes a great cashmere turtleneck sweater, boot-cut leather or suede trouser, one-shoulder sexy silk jersey dress and a buttery leather trench. And he doesn't forget that the Céline woman wants the accessories to match – he has all the boots, bags and shoes she needs, logoed up and ready to party.

CÉLINE, 36 avenue Montaigne, 75008
Tel: 01 56 89 07 91
also at:
3 avenue Victor Hugo, 75016. Tel: 01 45 01 80 01
Métro: Franklin D. Roosevelt or Alma-Marceau
Opening Hours: Mon–Sat: 10.00–19.00
August: open
Credit Cards: Visa, Amex, Diners, MC, JCB
Price Range: trousers from 2,200FF, sweater from 2,500FF, skirt from 2,000FF, jacket from 4,500FF, coat from 9,000FF, bags from 2,000FF

CALVIN KLEIN: AMERICAN DESIGNER

Calvin Klein, known as 'le prince de la mode américaine' in France, has two major stores here on avenue Montaigne. This is the womenswear and home store. The ground floor has his signature pared down, clean and elegant clothes with strapless silk dresses, stretch silk trousers, tube tops and stovepipe-collar coats – it all amounts to what the Americans describe as 'no-brainer' dressing, meaning hassle-free, solution clothes. Also on this floor are the bags, eyewear, lingerie and shoes. Upstairs is the home collection which frankly is so neutrally restful it could send you off to sleep there and then. The focus is on colour or more precisely the lack of it, as the collection is a sea of beige, camel, cream, stone, anthracite (towels and bed-linen are fairly bachelor pad-ish) plus cool cut china and glass.

CALVIN KLEIN, 45 avenue Montaigne, 75008
Tel: 01 47 23 62 22
Métro: Franklin D. Roosevelt
Opening Hours: Mon–Sat: 10.00–19.30
August: open

Credit Cards: Visa, Diners, Amex, MC
Price Range: sweaters from 1,500FF, bags from 2,950FF, dresses from 3,500FF, trouser suits from 5,900FF

CHANEL: FRENCH COUTURIER
See 1st arrondissement for details.
42 avenue Montaigne, 75008. Tel: 01 47 23 74 12

THIERRY MUGLER: FRENCH DESIGNER
See 7th arrondissement for details.
49 avenue Montaigne, 75008. Tel: 01 47 23 37 62

LOEWE: SPANISH LEATHER HOUSE
Spanish house Loewe has always been revered for its leather rather than its fashion, but LVMH has brought in designer Narciso Rodriguez to change all that. Since he joined in 1998, Narciso has taken the house soft leather and sliced it into sleek clothes. Cuban/American, Narciso developed his pared down, modern aesthetic working for Calvin Klein in New York, then for two seasons at Cerruti. But he made his name with the beautiful slip of a wedding dress he designed for his great friend the late Carolyn Bessette Kennedy. At Loewe, unlike so many of the LVMH houses, there is no existing fashion heritage to play with, so he's making it up himself with sexy halter dresses, leather bodysuits, python jeans and crystal and leather body-hugging tops – all gorgeous if you and the word cellulite are not yet acquainted. An easier fit are the handbags which are beautiful quality, plus some of the chicest weekend bags around.

LOEWE, 46 avenue Montaigne, 75008
Tel: 01 53 57 92 50
Métro: Franklin D. Roosevelt
Opening Hours: Mon–Sat: 10.00–19.00
August: open
Credit Cards: Visa, Amex, Diners, MC, JCB
Price Range: small leather goods from 300FF, weekend bag from 5,460FF, leather trousers from 4,470FF, leather coat from 12,000FF

51 MONTAIGNE: ITALIAN DESIGNER FASHION
If you like wearing your labels on the outside rather than the inside of your clothes – this store is for you. It's mostly Italian designer labels like Moschino Couture, Iceberg, Byblos, Sui by Anna Sui (she works in the US but this, her diffusion line, is manufactured in Italy), masses of Dolce & Gabbana's second logoed line D & G, Laurence Steele and, a more recent addition, Vivienne Westwood. The D & G is phenomenally popular, with suiting, jackets, sneakers, plastic bags, jeans, bras, men's sweatshirting, gym kit, towelling tops – in fact anything that can fit the D & G logo initials on the front. The overall look, according to the store director, is 'sexy, young, fun', it's for going out at night and

wearing with a tan. They have a selection of shoes by Christian Louboutin and Sergio Rossi. Clientele ranges from teenager to a pair of cheekbones with bodyguard. Adjacent to the store and under the same ownership is a massive Genny boutique aimed at a slightly more classic customer, worth checking out for their dress and coat suits and glam evening wear.

51 MONTAIGNE, 51 avenue Montaigne, 75008
Tel: 01 43 59 05 32
Métro: Franklin D. Roosevelt
Opening Hours: Mon–Sat: 10.00–19.30
August: open
Credit Cards: Visa, Amex, Diners, JCB
Price Range: D & G T-shirt 490FF, little linen D & G summer suit 3,690FF, dress from Sui by Anna Sui 1,690FF

BARBARA BUI:
CONTEMPORARY WOMEN'S & MEN'S WEAR
Barbara Bui is inspired by the whole Helmut Lang, Jil Sander, Prada Sport school of dressing. She does a French take on it with a fairly anonymous, 'modern' kind of look which picks up on the trends of the season and seems to feature one detail per piece of clothing (as in could be a coat with train, a shiny techno fabric, a checked tulle overlay to a skirt) and that's it on the decorative-interest front. She cuts a mean pair of pants in leather or fabric with shapes ranging from what the French call a 'garçons de café' wide cut to an urban track pant. Colours are kind of predictable – nudes, écru, putty, khaki, black, white. There is menswear here as well, plus a slightly less expensive line called Barbara Bui Initials which sells your wardrobe basic needs vacuum-packed in clear plastic.

BARBARA BUI, 50 avenue Montaigne, 75008
Tel: 01 42 25 05 25
Métro: Franklin D. Roosevelt
also at:
23 rue Étienne Marcel, 75002. Tel: 01 40 26 43 65
35 rue de Grenelle, 75007. Tel: 01 45 44 85 14
Opening Hours: Mon–Sat: 10.30–19.00
August: open
Credit Cards: Visa, Amex, Diners, MC, JCB
Price Range: trousers from 800FF, T-shirt from 370FF, leather jacket from 4,500FF, coat from 3,500FF

JIL SANDER: GERMAN DESIGNER
So clean, so pure, so radically lacking in fuss. Once Jil Sander was the thinking woman's designer, now she is the darling of the fashion pack. It's not that she's changed, more that fashion has come round to her way of thinking, and that is modernism. On the rail in her four-floor statement of a store in avenue Montaigne the clothes look shockingly

simple (particularly next to what you normally find down this street). There are countless trouser-suit options, a white glove-leather shell top, a shrunken navy felt shirt with trousers or a cashmere dress. On the body they look elegant, precise and sensuous rather than sexy. She's a non-colourist working in the blackest of navy, black, white, steel grey and beige, but warms it up a degree with shell shades and camels. Her lean winter overcoats and anything in leather are to cry for.

Unmistakably expensive and reassuringly luxe, her clothes are now worn by Nicole Kidman, who describes them as 'fresh and fluid, so easy to wear', Sharon Stone, Charlotte Rampling, Carole Bouquet and Wynona Ryder. Sander still works in Hamburg but since 1985 has shown at Milan fashion week. She opened the store in Paris in 1993 on the site of Madeleine Vionnet's couture house. It is a cathedral of a shop, severely minimal and lined in stone – it doesn't exactly hum 'have a nice day'.

Jil Sander

JIL SANDER, 50 avenue Montaigne, 75008
Tel: 01 44 95 06 70
Métro: Franklin D. Roosevelt
Opening Hours: Mon–Sat: 10.00–18.30
August: open
Credit Cards: Visa, Amex, Diners, MC, JCB
Price Range: suit 10,000FF, trousers from 2,150FF, shirt jacket in felt 1,860FF

LOUIS VUITTON: LUXURY CLOTHES, LUGGAGE
See later in this chapter for details.
54 avenue Montaigne, 75008. Tel: 01 45 62 47 00

CALVIN KLEIN: MENSWEAR
A two-floor store designed by London architect John Pawson and selling the complete Calvin Klein men's range from ready-to-wear to the still-famous underwear.

CALVIN KLEIN, 56 avenue Montaigne, 75008
Tel: 01 43 59 10 10
Métro: Franklin D. Roosevelt
Opening Hours: Mon–Sat: 10.00–19.30
August: open
Credit Cards: Visa, Amex, Diners, MC, JCB
Price Range: ties from 600FF, shirts from 800FF, jackets from 3,500FF, trousers from 1,200FF, suits from 5,500FF

AVENUE GEORGE V

GIVENCHY: FRENCH COUTURIER
Alexander McQueen for Givenchy gives you hard-core glamour, sharp tough tailoring and clever construction. It's not exactly for the shy and retiring type of girl, but since McQueen joined in 1996, he has built a whole new clientele for the house – both couture and ready-to-wear. It didn't always look set to go that way. When he first arrived – a raw and swaggering hero of London fashion storming the gilded and genteel realms of haute couture – the French balked or more accurately wept and screamed. After a couple of shaky couture seasons, McQueen won their respect. He has imported his signature tailoring from London with sharp-shouldered trouser suits, has added graphic blocks of colour, jumpsuits and cowl low-necks, and has punched out softest leather and cut razor-edge wide pants. He conjures up theatre with haughty high collars, frock coats and corsets with exquisite embroideries. And, most significantly, he has opted to dump the house past and make his own future. 'I'm about progression and aesthetically moving tailoring into the 21st century,' says McQueen. Disappointingly, the boutique here never gives you the whole McQueen-for-Givenchy picture, the selection of his ready-to-wear is still limited and the bland shop interior hardly reflects his savage imagination.

GIVENCHY, 3 avenue George V, 75008
Tel: 01 44 31 50 23
Métro: Alma-Marceau
also at:
28 rue du Faubourg St-Honoré, 75008. Tel: 01 42 65 54 54
Opening Hours: Mon–Sat: 10.00–19.00
August: open
Credit Cards: Visa, Amex, Diners, MC, JCB
Price Range: trouser suit from 7,500FF, leather three-quarter jacket from
15,000FF, coat from 9,500FF

BALENCIAGA: FRENCH DESIGNER

Keeping a deliberately low profile, French designer Nicolas
Ghesquière is turning Balenciaga into an influential fashion house
once more. His clothes have a rigorous cut and a certain Parisian sexiness with bite. He makes sly references to Balenciaga's 1950s architectural form, teaming that with his own personal aesthetic, drawing on
the 1980s, Flemish paintings and Princess Leila for inspiration. He
plays with juxtapositions in silhouette (tailored against volume), fabric (structure versus floaty) and taste (bad versus chic). Unlike every
other designer charged with turning fashion houses around, Nicolas is
French (rather than British or American) and he never went to fashion
school. Instead he worked as an assistant for Jean Paul Gaultier and
then worked freelance for several years before turning up at
Balenciaga.

The boutique is on the site of Balenciaga's original couture house. It
has been refurbished recently to fuse the original house icons of the
black and white tiled floor and the Spanish studded leather chairs with
a more contemporary feel of slate wall and cement floor. The clothes
here attract a fashionable downtown shopper who comes in search of
Ghesquière's sexy-cut trouser, cross-your-heart silk jersey dresses and
signature culotte skirt.

BALENCIAGA, 10 avenue George V, 75008
Tel: 01 47 20 21 11
Métro: Alma-Marceau or George V
Opening Hours: Mon–Sat: 10.00–19.00
August: open
Credit Cards: Visa, Amex, Diners, MC, JCB
Price Range: trousers from 2,000FF, jacket from 3,500FF, skirt 2,000FF, top
from 1,500FF

KENZO: FRENCH DESIGNER

See 7th arrondissement for details.
18 avenue George V, 75008. Tel: 01 47 23 33 49

AVENUE DES CHAMPS-ÉLYSÉES

For so long a retail no-man's land, avenue des Champs-Élysées is experiencing an upgrade as new flagship stores – such as Louis Vuitton, Sephora and music mega-shop FNAC – move in.

L'ÉCLAIREUR: INTERNATIONAL DESIGNER STORE
See Le Marais for details.
26 avenue des Champs-Élysées, 75008. Tel: 01 45 62 12 32

STÉPHANE KÉLIAN: DESIGNER FOOTWEAR
See 7th arrondissement for details.
26 avenue des Champs-Élysées, 75008. Tel: 01 42 56 42 26

ZARA: FASHIONABLE CHAIN STORE
See 9th arrondissement for details.
44 avenue des Champs-Élysées, 75008. Tel: 01 45 61 52 80

SPOON: INTERNATIONAL RESTAURANT
In the city that prides itself on being the last bastion of nationalistic cooking, culinary global warming has arrived. French mega-chef Alain Ducasse – he of six Michelin stars – has opened Spoon, an international restaurant offering a hybrid of Chinese, Indian, American, Thai, Italian and British cuisine. The menu is free-style and quirky encouraging diners to mix and match their main courses, salads, dressing, vegetables and sauces (just get the waiter to explain how to order), while the scene is fashion – Michael Kors and Christian Lacroix plus business suits. Even the wine list is international, offering mainly New World wines – formerly unheard-of in a chic Parisian restaurant. Any blow to national pride is lessened by Ducasse's declaration that at Spoon the diner has the right to 'total menu liberty'– a rallying call that goes straight to the heart of every French citoyen. You need to reserve for lunch and dinner well in advance.

SPOON, 14 rue de Marignan, 75008
Tel: 01 40 76 34 44
Métro: Franklin D. Roosevelt
Opening Hours: Mon–Fri: 11.45–14.30, 18.30–23.30, closed Sat/Sun
August: closed for a couple of weeks, call for exact dates
Credit Cards: Visa, Amex, Diners, MC, JCB
Price Range: soups from 80FF, salads from 80FF, main course from 135FF, pudding from 60FF

ZENTA: INTERNATIONAL DESIGNER WEAR
Zenta is a large designer store selling, among others, Hussein Chalayan, Antonio Berardi, Alexander McQueen, Galliano, Gaultier, Olivier Theyskens and Missoni. They've got a vast buying budget, but they tend to spend it on the more classic pieces from each designer's

le
pink
panther

collection and their eye is very much on the main stream. They have so much stock and so many different designers it can be quite hard to shop here, but there are masses of staff on hand to sort you out. It's not really the store if you prefer DIY shopping, but it's ideal for the woman who wants to 'stay seven hours and buy her whole season's wardrobe'. Sizes go from 8 to 20 and there is an atelier within the shop which can cope with any alterations.

ZENTA, 6 rue de Marignan, 75008
Tel: 01 42 25 72 47
Métro: Franklin D. Roosevelt
Opening Hours: Mon: 11.00–19.00, Tue–Sat: 10.00–19.00
August: open
Credit Cards: Visa, Amex, Diners, MC, JCB
Price Range: suiting 3,500–25,000FF, knitwear from 1,000FF, evening dresses 3,500–20,000FF

GUERLAIN: SCENT

Now owned by LVMH, Guerlain has several stores around town although this is the original. It is worth checking out, not for its recent over-saccharine perfumes but rather for those classic and classy Guerlain fragrances which have retained a cult following. We're talking exotic and seductive scents such as Parure, Chamade and Vol de Nuit, all of which can be bought in wonderful golden bottle-holders (N.B. all men: this is the definition of a perfect gift). Another must-buy is the terracotta bronzing powder which is the secret to the 'naturally' glowing Parisian complexion. For men the original fragrances, such as Habit Rouge, are still the sexiest.

GUERLAIN, 68 avenue des Champs-Élysées, 75008
Tel: 01 45 62 52 57
Métro: Franklin D. Roosevelt
also at:
2 place Vendôme, 75001. Tel: 01 42 60 68 61
56 rue du Faubourg St-Honoré, 75008. Tel: 01 44 94 04 91
47 rue Bonaparte, 75006. Tel: 01 43 26 71 19
35 rue Tronchet, 75009. Tel: 01 47 42 53 23
93 rue de Passy, 75016. Tel: 01 42 88 41 62
Opening Hours: Mon–Sat: 9.45–19.00, Sun: 15.00–19.00
August: open
Credit Cards: Visa, Amex, MC, JCB
Price Range: Chamade soap 80FF, body cream from 235FF, perfume from 490FF, Habit Rouge from 305FF, terracotta powder from 185FF

SEPHORA: COSMETICS, PERFUME, SKIN-CARE

This is a gigantic spaceship-looking mega-store devoted to cosmetics and fragrances across every price range from Christian Dior and Chanel to the less expensive Bourgeois and RoC. Housed in 14,000 square foot of space are over 12,000 different products including a Sephora own-brand range of bath, body and cosmetic products which is reasonably priced and stylishly packaged. The display system is brilliant and original with products arranged alphabetically around the walls, allowing you to touch, look and smell in your own time without some pushy salesperson drenching you in unwanted scent. The future of fragrance and cosmetic shopping now.

SEPHORA, 70 avenue des Champs-Élysées, 75008
Tel: 01 53 93 22 50
Métro: Franklin D. Roosevelt
Opening Hours: Mon–Sat: 10.00–midnight, Sun: 11.00–1.00am
August: open until 2am
Credit Cards: Visa, Amex, Diners, MC, JCB
Price Range: Sephora own-range lipstick 50FF, nail varnish 19FF, eye pencil 19FF, shower gel 36FF

TARA JARMON: FASHIONABLE WOMENSWEAR
See 6th arrondissement for details.
73 avenue des Champs-Élysées, 75008. Tel: 01 45 63 45 41

FREE: FUNKY, WELL-PRICED TREND
A Sentier brand, Free makes sexy, fun clubwear and high fashion pieces at reasonable prices. Come show time it keeps its eyes peeled on every catwalk (more specifically Gucci, Miu Miu, Gaultier, Helmut Lang), churning out 'inspired by' pieces. Body-conscious is the only constant here, otherwise stock changes every few days according to new trends and once a month they completely change the whole shop stock. Some of the kit is a very skinny fit and kind of teenage, but they do some great summer clothes such as a stretch print long dress ripped straight out of a Gaultier style-book and sexy pieces for Ibiza clubbing. There's no guarantee on quality, but these are not clothes that are meant to last.

FREE, 84 avenue des Champs-Élysées, 75008
Tel: 01 43 59 19 59
Métro: George V
also at:
8–10 rue Montmartre, 75001. Tel: 01 42 33 15 52
32 rue du Four, 75006. Tel: 01 45 44 23 11
Opening Hours: every day: 10.00–22.00
August: open
Credit Cards: Visa, Amex, Diners, MC, JCB
Price Range: sunglasses 180FF, T-shirt 129–200FF, trousers 250–350FF, nylon shirts 200–350FF, ethnic-cyber print dress 379FF

LADURÉE: SALON DE THÉ/RESTAURANT
A new version of the quintessential Parisian tea room on rue Royale, this Ladurée has an altogether different scene and decor. It is designed by Jacques Garcia who has gone to town with lashings of gilt and velvet. Unlike the original it is open at night for dinner and is rather romantic with intimate salons à deux on the first floor. The evening opening hours mean that macaroon fans can now get their fix at night as well.

LADURÉE, 75 avenue des Champs-Élysées, 75008
Tel: 01 40 75 08 75
Métro: George V or Franklin D. Roosevelt
Opening Hours: every day: 7.30–1.00am
August: open
Credit Cards: Visa, Amex, Diners, MC, JCB
Price Range: starter from 75FF, main course from 125FF

LOUIS VUITTON: LUXURY CLOTHES, LUGGAGE

Since taking design power at the house of Louis Vuitton, American designer Marc Jacobs has transformed the brand from bourgeois predictability to the epitome of urban cool. What's so clever about Jacobs is that he mixes a downtown nonchalance with an uptown luxe sensibility. He slaps the logo on canvas coats, jackets and skirts, cuts a lean 1970s silhouette, makes some seriously desirable knitwear and uses luscious cashmeres, silk jersey and leather. It's a Midas touch which has the label looking jet-set and sexy once more and LVMH president Bernard Arnault grinning from ear to ear. Even the house monogram has had a new lease of life reappearing stamped on pastel patent leather bags. And not forgetting the shoes – from stiletto to loafer – they are now on every fashionable foot.

There are several stores in Paris but in terms of Marc Jacobs's ready-to-wear collection and his accessories this store has the best choice.

LOUIS VUITTON, 101 avenue des Champs-Élysées, 75008
Tel: 01 53 57 24 00
Métro: George V
Opening Hours: Mon–Sat: 10.00–20.00
August: open
Credit Cards: Visa, Amex, Diners, MC, JCB
Price Range: trousers from 2,000FF, sweaters from 3,000FF, canvas coats from 6,000FF, pastel patent bags from 3,000FF

Opéra

9TH ARRONDISSEMENT

There is a gritty glamour to the place de l'Opéra in the 9th arrondissement. Six roads collide here and the grands boulevards, bulging
Garnier opera house and runway of department stores are all testa-
ment to Baron Haussmann's dramatic town planning in the 19th century. The Opéra is open again after several years of surgery and now
shows mostly ballet, while opera performances are at the Bastille. You
can tour inside but, before you pay, make sure they are not rehearsing,
or you won't get to see Chagall's magnificent ceiling in the auditorium.

The 9th is a showgirl of an arrondissement. There are some 16 the-
atres here as well as the opera house, while to the north of the
arrondissement you break into the cabaret country of Pigalle and the
Moulin Rouge and over to the east is the Folies-Bergère. It used to be
dominated by big banks and businesses, but has increasingly become
a fashionable young place to move into. People are lured by the low-
ish prices and a chance of an apartment in a Haussmann building,
which means high ceilings and the Paris property oxymoron – space.
At night the club scene round Pigalle is hot. Not just sex-clubs but
nightclubs like Bus Palladium and Folies Pigalle, while for concerts
and dance nights, the Divan du Monde on rue des Martyrs is great.
Jean Paul Gaultier lives in Pigalle in a stunning private road, avenue
Frochot, where Toulouse-Lautrec had his last studio. Shoe designer
Christian Louboutin and actress Valérie Lemercier are Pigalle residents too. For a walk off the tourist track, wander round the quartier
of place St-Georges just below Pigalle, which is the area where artists
like Renoir, Bonnard and Gustave Moreau had their studios, and there
is a museum of Moreau's work at 14 rue de La Rochefoucauld.

For shopping the 9th is mainly known for the department stores
Printemps and Galeries Lafayette, bitter rivals and situated within
spitting distance of each other along boulevard Haussmann. If you're
only in Paris for the day, department stores are an easy way to get an
intensive fashion retail fix and leave you time to do some sights or a
museum. If you're here for longer they're a good way of orientating
yourself to the Paris fashion scene and prices. You'll find they stock a
great selection of less expensive high fashion, as well as their own
labels which can be classic Paris chic, but at realistic prices.

As well as the department stores in the 9th, the culture of ballet,
cabaret and theatre has prompted the opening of some wonderful supply shops such as Repetto for ballet kit on rue de la Paix. And don't
miss the big high street chain shops Zara, Célio and Mango in place de
l'Opéra.

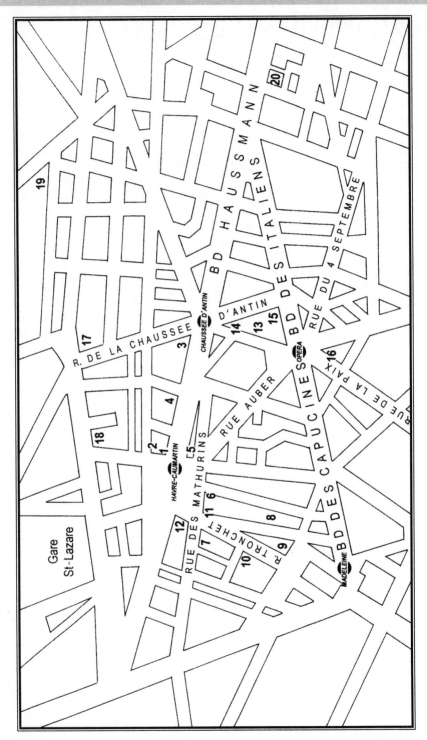

A shopper's Guide to Paris Fashion

1 PRINTEMPS
2 PRINTEMPS DE L'HOMME
3 GALERIES LAFAYETTE
4 GALERIES LAFAYETTE GOURMET
5 MUJI
6 DU PAREIL AU MÊME
7 DU PAREIL AU MÊME BÉBÉ
8 ANNEXE DES CRÉATEURS
9 ERÈS
10 PETIT BATEAU

11 CACHAREL
12 GUERLAIN
13 ZARA
14 CÉLIO
15 MANGO
16 REPETTO
17 SEPHORA
18 ANOUSCHKA
19 DETAILLE
20 L'ARBRE A CANNELLE

BOULEVARD HAUSSMANN

Quintessentially French in service and layout, Printemps and Galeries Lafayette were both built around the turn of the last century and Printemps in particular has a stunning Art Nouveau glass cupola of cascading colour. Both are constantly jostling for position, fighting for exclusivity of designers and putting on exhibitions and promotions which vary from interesting loan exhibitions from abroad to a chance to flog a load of cheap imported goods. They often have special offer days when prices are down by 10% and you can always pick up a free tourist map at your hotel or métro station which entitles you to discount at one or both stores.

PRINTEMPS: DEPARTMENT STORE

Until recently Printemps has always been better for homeware and furniture than fashion, but they have spent a cool 200 million francs on transforming a formerly dowdy store into the sleekest and most fashion-conscious department store in town. They've ripped out ceilings, floors and frumpy brands and in their place installed clean white decor, themed floors and hip fashion. There are still the three different stores: Printemps de la Maison, with a ground-floor perfumery and make-up hall, upstairs for furnishings and home decor; Printemps de l'Homme, for menswear; and the newly refurbished Printemps de la Mode. The Mode store ground floor is now pure accessories stocking brands from Burberry's to Jamin Puech. Then comes the brilliant Quartier du Prestige on the first floor selling Diptyque candles (great to know if you don't have time to make the trek to their boutique in the 5th arrondissement), J.P. Tods, Loewe bags and a mini version of the Ladurée tea room. Designer-wise the first floor has Helmut Lang, Dolce & Gabbana, Martin Margiela, Narciso Rodriguez, Jeremy Scott et al. Meanwhile, adjacent is the chic section for more middle-market brands such as Philippe Adec (good for workwear) and Ventilo. Then on the third floor is the mode section for younger, funkier, high street labels such as Zara, Mango, Tara Jarmon and Free.

Printemps offers a free short-stay nursery for children aged 2–9 available to parents (Wednesday and Saturday afternoons, 14.00–18.00), and there is also a free fashion and image consulting service.

PRINTEMPS, 64 boulevard Haussmann, 75009
Tel: 01 42 82 50 00
Métro: Havre-Caumartin
Opening Hours: Mon–Sat: 9.30–19.00 (Thu until 22.00)
August: open
Credit Cards: Visa, Amex, Diners, MC, JCB

PRINTEMPS DE L'HOMME:
MENSWEAR DEPARTMENT STORE

As part of its new fashion thrust, Printemps has also totally renovated its menswear shop, transforming it from a fairly frumpy, grey-slacks and slip-on-shoes store to what Printemps now calls an 'extreme shopping' experience. With six floors and 7,000 square metres of menswear, it basically aims to dress every breed of contemporary man. That means there is urban wear with Diesel, G Star, Helmut Lang Jeans, Mandarina Duck etc. on the first floor, while for preppier looks the third floor is devoted to 'leisure, travel, Fridaywear' with brands such as Tommy Hilfiger, Ralph Lauren and Aigle. For the fashion man check out L'Endroit on the second floor where you can find collections by Martin Margiela, Kostas Murkudis, Costume National and Martine Sitbon. As well as the clothes there is the World Bar up on the fifth floor, which is designed by Paul Smith, and downstairs is the Nickel male beauty salon where you can slip for a little pampering between purchases.

PRINTEMPS DE L'HOMME, corner of rue Caumartin and rue Provence, 75009
Tel: 01 42 82 50 00
Métro: Havre-Caumartin
Opening Hours: Mon–Sat: 9.30–19.00 (Thu until 22.00)
August: open
Credit Cards: Visa, Amex, Diners, MC, JCB

GALERIES LAFAYETTE: DEPARTMENT STORE

Galeries Lafayette is the most tourist-heavy of the department stores and still operates an archaic payment system which takes forever and involves scurrying back and forward between sales assistant and till. There are four buildings: fashion, sportswear, menswear and the gourmet section. On the ground floor of the main fashion building is the perfumery and at the back is a whole section devoted to Japanese make-up brand Shu Uemura, so if you cannot make it down to the store in St-Germain this is a good place to stock up on colour. You'll notice at both Printemps and Galeries Lafayette that they always load you up with testers when you make a purchase of perfume or cosmetics, and they'll do nice gift wrapping for free.

First floor is the shoe department, where you'll find Prada shoes, Michel Perry, Mosquitos, Free Lance and Patrick Cox as well as designer bags by Public Gaultier and 31 février. There is also a brilliant jeans department on this floor with brands such as Diesel, Liberto and Cimarron, a Spanish label which does jeans in Bardot-kitsch fabrics like pale pink gingham. Agnès b., Et Vous and Gap all have boutique spaces here.

Up on the second floor it's prime designer time with Donna Karan and DKNY, as well as Ann Demeulemeester, Yohji Yamamoto, ICB by

229

Japanese group Kashiyama, Galliano and Alaïa. There's also a turnout of the French brigade: Yves Saint Laurent, Montana, Jean Paul Gaultier, Sonia Rykiel, Inès de la Fressange and then mostly the diffusion lines of ready-to-wear from houses like Givenchy, Ungaro and Valentino. If you are looking for something more accessible in style and price, but still Paris sophistication, then check out brands Gérard Darel and Patrick Gérard on this floor. There is also a mixed corner of younger and newer designers, which gives a good overview of what's going on in the Paris fashion scene although there is only a limited number of pieces from each designer. After March if it's fine weather you can go right to the top on the seventh floor and walk out for the most amazing rooftop view of Paris and you'll also find a restaurant up there.

Galeries Lafayette hold regular free fashion shows (Wednesdays at

11.30, Fridays at 14.30 in summer, Wednesdays only during the winter). They also offer free of charge fashion shopping advice, a delivery service of packages to your hotel and hemline alterations (there is a charge for other alterations).

GALERIES LAFAYETTE, 40 boulevard Haussmann, 75009
Tel: 01 42 82 34 56
Métro: Chaussée d'Antin
Opening Hours: Mon–Sat: 9.30–19.00 (Thu until 21.00)
August: open
Credit Cards: Visa, Amex, Diners, MC, JCB

GALERIES LAFAYETTE GOURMET: FOOD

Galeries Lafayette Gourmet is a superior kind of grocery store located above MonoPrix, where smart Parisians do their version of the supermarket shop. Less of a cliché than Fauchon, it's got golden shopping trolleys and old blokes in berets and raincoats sitting around drinking coupes of champagne. You can come and perch at one of the fresh food counters for half a dozen oysters and a glass of Sancerre, fresh fruit juice of mango, banana and orange, or a plate of six cheeses with bread and salad. Expect friendly service. It's also the perfect place to buy foodie gifts – fresh coffee, foie gras, sugared Turkish delights and gob-stopper olives.

GALERIES LAFAYETTE GOURMET, 48 boulevard Haussmann, 75009
Tel: 01 48 74 46 06
Métro: Chaussée d'Antin
Opening Hours: Mon–Sat: 9.00–20.00 (Thu until 21.00)
August: open
Credit Cards: Visa, Amex, MC, JCB
Price Range: dozen oysters 90FF, fresh fruit juice 25FF, plate of cheeses with salad 76FF

MUJI: JAPANESE BASICS
See 6th arrondissement for details.
19 rue Auber, 75009. Tel: 01 43 12 54 00

DU PAREIL AU MÊME: CHILDREN'S CLOTHES
Situated just near Printemps department store, this shop sells funky French clothes for kids with groovy colours and extremely reasonable prices with the average price around 55FF for a piece of clothing. Prints, cut and detail of the clothes are all very French with navy sailor dresses, cotton salopettes, linen jeans jackets and pretty smocked dresses. France is a country where kids are still dressed to look like kids, rather than as members of the Spice Girls. Come collection time the shop is teeming with fashion editor mums who nip in between shows to get their kiddie fix. Stock tends to change fast and sizes go up to age 14.

DU PAREIL AU MÊME, 15–17 rue des Mathurins, 75008
Tel: 01 42 66 93 80
Métro: Havre-Caumartin
also at:
1 rue St-Denis, 75001. Tel: 01 42 36 07 57
168 boulevard St-Germain, 75006. Tel: 01 46 33 87 85
3 rue de la Pompe, 75016. Tel: 01 42 24 82 84
Opening Hours: Mon–Sat: 10.00–19.00
August: open
Credit Cards: Visa, MC
Price Range: average price for clothes 55FF

DU PAREIL AU MÊME BÉBÉ: BABY CLOTHES/KIT

The same concept as Du Pareil au Même but this store specialises in all things new-born (from clothes to Moses basket) continuing up to age one. In a fearfully overpriced market, this store gives good value with padded cot protectors in fresh prints such as lemons or cherries priced 240FF, tiny cotton navy sweaters with white crown motif priced 55FF and baby pyjamas 60FF. There are also good gift sets such as towel, flannel and booties all in towelling. Clothing stock changes twice a week, while designs for the bedroom change once a month. There is also a collection of clothes for premature babies.

DU PAREIL AU MÊME BÉBÉ, 23 rue des Mathurins, 75008
Tel: 01 47 42 63 32
Métro: Havre-Caumartin
Opening Hours: Mon–Sat: 10.00–19.00
August: open
Credit Cards: Visa, MC
Price Range: average price for clothes 55FF

ANNEXE DES CRÉATEURS: DESIGNER SALE SHOP

This is a designer solderie which means they sell designer clothing from the equivalent season of the previous year. All the clothing is new and prices here are cut by 40% to 70%. The nature of the solderie, which is often unsold stock from other boutiques or leftover stock from the designer, means Annexe des Créateurs always has a changing, if erratic, stock of names. But designers you can count on finding are Versace, Moschino, Montana and Thierry Mugler all for a dressed-up look and Helmut Lang, Westwood, Galliano and Dolce & Gabbana for a younger clientele. Service is helpful, which means you don't have to rummage for hours, but can ask for something specific in terms of a label or the kind of outfit you're looking for.

There are two stores divided between evening and occasion wear and, two doors down, a shop for daywear, with a small selection for men of designers like Versace, Montana and Romeo Gigli. They also have the odd wedding dress and lots of accessories with enormous sunglasses straight out of *Charlie's Angels*. Size-wise they are interesting, as owner Madame Accardo-Meister buys in stock from 8 up to 18. She also stocks Genny, Lagerfeld, Ferre, and some lesser known Italian and French designers. There is an alteration service which costs extra. It's a good store to include while you're doing the department stores.

ANNEXE DES CRÉATEURS, 19 rue Godot de Mauroy, 75009
Tel: 01 42 65 46 40
Métro: Madeleine or Havre-Caumartin
Opening Hours: Mon–Sat: 11.30–19.00
August: open
Credit Cards: Visa, Amex, MC
Price Range: prices are reduced by 40–70%, skirts from 350FF, dresses from 900FF, Sophie Sitbon suit from 1,650FF, Mugler suit 2,700FF

RUE TRONCHET

ERÈS: GREAT SWIMWEAR

Every fashion mag may now preach capsule wardrobe, but the Parisians have been doing it for years – investing in a limited number of key pieces, one of which is the Erès swimming costume. Well cut in quality fabric, the Erès swimsuit is desirable, flattering and does not come cheap. Every season there are new colours and designs to suit different-shaped bodies from the simplest low-back one-piece to a hipster bikini with belt. Designs follow fashion, but at a low-key French pace. The great advantage to Erès is that the tops and bottoms are sold separately so you can mix and match in different sizes and styles to suit your silhouette, i.e., big bottom, small top – no problem. However, the store has so many different shapes and styles it can be daunting, but this is where French service comes into its own. Staff here are knowledgeable and you just tell them if you're looking for a bikini or a one-piece and the shape of your body and then they'll pull out several suitable styles for you to try.

The look is very St-Tropez – colours are rarely flashy, and you're more likely to find bright white, aquamarine, dusty pink or pumice-stone grey with cream piping. The new collection of costumes starts to arrive in the store from November along with pareos, halter-neck tops, beach dresses and hot pants to match. Sizes are from 8 to 14/16 and customers aged 15 to 80. A great tip to know is that Erès hold their sale at the end of July when they sell off last year's designs at half price. It's all very discreet, with not even a sign up at the window, but inside Parisians run wild.

ERÈS, 2 rue Tronchet, 75008
Tel: 01 47 42 28 82
Métro: Madeleine
also at:
4 bis rue du Cherche-Midi, 75006. Tel: 01 45 44 95 54
6 rue Guichard, 75016. Tel: 01 46 47 45 21

Opening Hours: Mon–Sat: 10.00–19.00
August: open
Credit Cards: Visa, Diners, Amex, MC, JCB
Price Range: bikinis 500–1,150F, sarong in coordinating print 350FF, swim-suits 600–1,200FF

PETIT BATEAU: CULT T-SHIRTS

What started as a bourgeois little kiddies' shop – navy stripes and dainty smocking – has turned into a cult T-shirt store. Paris hipsters, club girls, gay boys and schoolgirls come here in search of plain cotton T-shirts, marked 'Age 14'. 'Upstairs,' inform the shop assistants before you even ask. There you will find the perfect T-shirt – round-necked or V, teeny sleeves and close-fitting and done up in baby-doll packaging. Start with the white V-neck which is softest cotton, dead simple and priced at 55FF. Jane Birkin lives in them. Two 17-year-old schoolgirls in their lunch hour explained Petit Bateau charm as 'a kind of little girl Lolita look, yet actually quite grown up'. Colours are lemon, pale blue or cream and for winter there is a great grubby green.

PETIT BATEAU, 13 rue Tronchet, 75008
Tel: 01 42 65 26 26
Métro: Madeleine or Havre-Caumartin
Opening Hours: Mon–Sat: 10.00–19.00
August: open
Credit Cards: Visa, Amex, MC
Price Range: plain white T-shirts from 38FF, ribbed vest with heart buttons 45FF

CACHAREL: FRENCH ROMANTIC

See 6th arrondissement for details.
34 rue Tronchet, 75009. Tel: 01 47 42 12 61

GUERLAIN: SCENT

See 8th arrondissement for details.
35 rue Tronchet, 75009. Tel: 01 47 42 53 23

PLACE DE L'OPÉRA

ZARA: FASHIONABLE, CHAIN STORE CLOTHES

If there's one high street chain where you'll to want to shop in Paris, it's Zara. A great source for this season's look at competitive prices, this Spanish chain has stores all over town. In a city where the high street fashionable chain is still a relatively new concept, Zara is riding a retail high. The rumour is they take 100 million FF a year in this store alone. The label targets three different looks: working women with classic suiting, weekend jeans and casual wear, and more fashion-foward, trend clothes. Prices are around M&S level, although quality is not as stringent. Suiting is very neutral, lots of trouser suits and dress-jacket combinations in navy, cream, black and beige. Be warned: the Zara beige can look very beige, and do check the fit on jackets before buying. Where Zara is strongest and extremely quick on the draw is in their versions of the season's essential pieces and 'translating the latest designer new look. The reality is you'll buy these pieces, wear them absolutely non-stop, then dump them after six months. They also do good basics like shell tops, winter coats, viscose knits and, in shoes, strappy sandals and wedges.

As a shopping phenomenon, Zara is fascinating: they never advertise but pull the crowds by word of mouth. They attract every single type of Parisian, from 16th arrondissement housewife to banlieue office girl, all of whom seem to find their style here. It's always full of international buyers during the collections and fashion trade shows, trying to figure out just how Zara does it. Weak points: the changing rooms are overcrowded so you often have to queue and the tills always seem short-staffed, so be prepared for another wait. Upstairs is kids' and menswear, but the men's department is not nearly as developed in fashion or as extensive as the women's. Men's suiting doesn't look a particularly great cut; you're probably better off going for casual shirting, priced around 199FF, and T-shirts and cotton trousers or weekend jackets.

ZARA, 2 rue Halévy, 75009
Tel: 01 44 71 90 90
Métro: Opéra
also at:
44 avenue des Champs-Élysées, 75008. Tel: 01 45 61 52 80
128 rue de Rivoli, 75001. Tel: 01 44 82 64 00
53 rue de Passy, 75016. Tel: 01 45 25 07 00
18 boulevard des Capucines, 75009. Tel: 01 42 68 31 10
45 rue de Rennes, 75006. Tel: 01 44 39 03 50
Opening Hours: Mon–Sat: 10.00–19.00
August: open
Credit Cards: Visa, Amex, MC, JCB
Price Range: jackets 550–670FF, skirt 250–350FF, coat 790FF, leather-upper mules 249FF

CÉLIO: CASUAL FRENCH MENSWEAR

Célio menswear looks like a Frenchified version of Gap and is less expensive. Suiting and city wear are down in the basement, but they are much better at doing competitively priced sporty basics. There's lots of weekend wear with long-sleeved white cotton waffle T-shirts, chinos and brightly coloured glazed cotton jackets. There are some nice sweaters inspired by the Canadian trekking and hunting outdoor life. A total Célio outfit could look a little Monsieur Average, but it's a good place to get your weekend basics. On the first floor is a café which looks straight on to the front of the Opéra and is a fine place to grab an eggs Benedict toasted sandwich with bacon for 35FF.

CÉLIO, 4 rue Halévy, 75009
Tel: 01 42 68 30 60
Métro: Opéra
Opening Hours: Mon–Sat: 9.30–19.00
August: open
Credit Cards: Visa, Amex, Diners, JCB
Price Range: jackets 750–850FF, trousers 350FF (suiting sold separately),
casual cotton shirts 199FF, canvas jacket 249FF, cotton trousers from 199FF

MANGO: FASHIONABLE HIGH STREET

A Spanish high street chain, Mango is great for young street and sportswear-inspired fashion. The look is teenager to twenties, with basics (rail upon rail of stretch trousers, tops, knits etc.) as well as suiting and more trend pieces. The shop concept is a more street-wise version of Zara with zipper fake-leather jackets, high-tech fabrics and masses of stretch. Prices are extremely competitive as Mango manufactures all its own product which also means new stock arrives every few weeks. There is also a line of shoes, bags and accessories which are nylon- and fabric-based. The store looks small from the outside with a narrow shop entrance, but inside it is huge and packed with Paris youth chicks.

MANGO, 6 boulevard des Capucines, 75009
Tel: 01 53 30 82 70
Métro: Opéra
Opening Hours: Mon–Sat: 10.00–20.30
August: open
Credit Cards: Visa, Amex, Diners, MC, JCB
Price Range: skirts from 229FF, jackets 299–659FF, coats about 900FF, dresses from 249FF

REPETTO: DANCEWEAR

This is one of those Parisian in-the-know addresses that are such a coup to discover. Yes, it's mainly a balletwear shop, but push your way past tantrums over tutus and you will find a fab selection of tiny cardigans and swimwear. Models like Carla Bruni are regulars not only for the dance kit, but also for the pretty cache-coeur cardigans in fleece or lambswool. Their range of swimwear features different shapes and styles for different physiques including gingham one-piece costumes, little triangles of lurex or a pretty two-piece costume with cache-coeur wrap top in pale pink Lycra. Nice surprise price-wise for all Repetto kit, with swimming costumes starting at 250FF. They've got everything for *Fame* wannabes: leg-warmers, point shoes and those nylon elasticated trousers that are supposed to make your legs sweat and shed pounds. Hillary Clinton's been in to buy ballet gear for Chelsea.

REPETTO, 22 rue de la Paix, 75002
Tel: 01 44 71 83 12
Métro: Opéra
Opening Hours: Mon–Sat: 10.00–19.00
August: open
Credit cards: Visa, Amex,Diners, MC
Price Range: swimming costumes 250–390FF, cache-coeur tops 240FF, body 270FF

SEPHORA: COSMETICS, PERFUME, SKIN-CARE

See 8th arrondissement for details.
66 rue de la Chausée d'Antin, 75009. Tel: 01 49 70 84 20

ANOUSCHKA: RETRO INSPIRATION

The apartment door swings open on to a hallway lined from high ceiling to floor with rack after rack, row after row, of original stilettos, kitten heels, square toes and 1920s perforated lace-ups. This is Anouschka's apartment of fashion which international designers use as a laboratory of ideas. A former model, Anouschka opted for a more abstract role in fashion ten years ago when she started filling an apartment with clothes, shoes and accessories from the 1930s to the early '70s. The majority of what she offers is excess stock which she buys up from closing down factories etc., so it's mostly unused and is all for

sale. 'Designers come not to copy,' explains Anouschka, 'but for inspiration. They may be looking for a print, a collar detail or a colour.' There are piles of tweed slacks, rows of raincoats, shiny raffia hats, a heavy crêpe black jumpsuit with plunging V-neck, 1950s summer dresses, 1960s men's mod suits. Donna Karan, Comme des Garçons, Dolce & Gabbana, Gucci, Jil Sander, Gaultier, Banana Republic all use it as a design playground, but the apartment is open to individuals too. Great place to find a mega cocktail dress or evening dress. Although there is masses of stock, it's quite easy to figure out as an assistant is there constantly folding up immaculate piles. When the Japanese design teams come into town they can take over the shop for days, so it's a good idea to ring before turning up.

ANOUSCHKA, 6 avenue du Coq, 75009
Tel: 01 48 74 37 00
Fax: 01 48 74 27 30
Métro: St-Lazare or Trinité
Opening Hours: Mon–Fri: 12.00–19.00, Sat: call for an appointment
August: open
Credit Cards: Visa
Price Range: 150–2,000FF, tweedy slacks 650FF, men's suits 1,500–2,500FF

DETAILLE: COUNTESS COSMETICS

This store ranks as pilgrimage point for the cosmetic junkie. Detaille started in Paris in 1905 when the Countess de Presle bought herself a car. She thrilled at the speed of whizzing round the country, but that nightmarish pollution was playing havoc with her skin and causing premature ageing. She asked a chemist friend to come up with a protective moisturising potion. He invented a formula which the Countess used herself and then went on to flog to the Euro-aristocracy. The shop still sells her Baume Automobile, made to the original recipe from natural ingredients including egg whites which separate in the bottle.

Detaille has a whole range of skin-care products like the Manudouce, a non-greasy hand lotion with lemon, mint and a touch of alcohol. All the flower essence toners, however, are without alcohol which makes them good for sensitive skins. Detaille customers include ancient dowagers from the 16th who arrive by taxi to buy a pot of powder, dancers and theatre people, Isabelle Adjani and Béatrice Dalle. Rei

Kawakubo swears by the moisturisers and sells them in her own store in Tokyo. In the back of the shop they still have the Countess's sales book, hand-written and recording all the orders placed at the beginning of the century from smart addresses in Biarritz, New York and Monte Carlo and from Queen Mary of Yugoslavia in Belgrade and Queen Astrid of Belgium. All products can be bought by mail order.

DETAILLE, 10 rue St-Lazare, 75009
Tel: 01 48 78 68 50
Métro: Notre-Dame de Lorette
Opening Hours: Tue–Fri: 10.00–13.30, 14.00–19.00, Sat: 10.00–14.00
August: open first week only
Credit cards: Visa, MC
Price Range: Baume Automobile from 195FF, Manudouce from 125FF, face mask from 110FF

PASSAGE VERDEAU, PASSAGE JOUFFROY, PASSAGE DES PANORAMAS

These are a series of old-fashioned shopping arcades which are far less fashiony and touristy than the nearby galerie Vivienne, but are charming for a walk and a cup of tea. They were all built in the first part of the 19th century, starting with passage des Panoramas in 1800 which is one of the oldest covered arcades in Paris. It's a strange and intriguing tangle of shops with stamp collectors, print dealers, old postcard shops and the establishment engraver Stern at No. 47. If you know Paris well or want a breather from Notre-Dame, this is lovely and off the tourist track. If you're in the 9th and want to walk back into the centre it's a nice way of doing it without using the main roads. You can hop from one gallery, across the main road and into the next, starting at passage Verdeau which is just down from the auction house Hôtel Drouot. Passage des Panoramas will spit you out in the 2nd, a ten-minute walk away from place des Victoires.

L'ARBRE A CANNELLE: TEA ROOM
Crumble in a colonial setting is what this lunch restaurant/salon de thé offers. During the time of Napoleon III it used to be a chocolate shop, so all the carved wood acanthus columns and painted panels of cocoa leaves, vanilla pods and boys shinning up trees to harvest the stuff are original. Sit outside in wicker Lloyd Loom chairs surrounded by tubs of bamboo plants. It's an unselfconscious scene which during the week is made up of workers from the auction house, Bourse, or the customers and shopkeepers in the passage. At the weekends it's Parisians du quartier. For lunch you can get a plat du jour (Friday's always fish) or tasty tarte salée like tomatoes, Cheddar, courgette and fresh herbs for 40FF. For a midday pick-me-up try a batik double: lots of smoked salmon, taramasalata, peppered smoked mackerel and blinis

served with a double shot of vodka. Teatime red fruit crumble or brownie served with a pot of crème fraîche is pleasurably wicked.

L'ARBRE A CANNELLE, 57 passage des Panoramas, 75002
Tel: 01 45 08 55 87
Métro: Rue Montmartre or Richelieu Drouot
Opening Hours: Mon–Fri: 11.30–18.00, Sat: 11.30–19.00
August: sometimes closed, call for exact dates
Credit Cards: Visa, Amex, MC
Price Range: pot of tea 22FF, batik double 108FF, crumble and cream 32FF

16TH ARRONDISSEMENT

In rue de Passy in the 16th arrondissement the air is always thick with the smell of Barbours. Situated in the west of Paris, the 16th arrondissement is perhaps best described in estate agents' terms as: '15 minutes from the centre of Paris ... attractive residences of grand standing ... just a minute's drive from the magnificent Bois de Boulogne.'

Inhabited by old ladies with candy-floss hair, bourgeois families and the nouveaux-riches, the 16th has a poodle parlour on every corner. As a shopping route it may not be a priority, but it is far from the fashion vacuum many assume.

The biggest draw of this part of town are the dépôts-ventes, which are prime hunting ground for cut-price designer wear. When the Parisian woman can't face wearing that Lacroix gypsy dress one more time, when last season's Chanel just looks so last season and when the Mugler vinyl bodysuit turns out to be a mistake, she takes the whole lot round to a dépôt-vente and gets them to sell it. Led by the biggest, Réciproque, these stores sell secondhand designer men's and women's clothes, handbags, silk scarves, shoes and costume jewellery and give the former owner a cut of the takings.

Apart from the nearly new, rue de Passy is the busiest shopping street in the area and worth walking for both designer and high street shopping without the crowds. There are branches of Zara, Joseph, Et Vous and Esprit along here as well as designer stores Victoire, Meredith and a great branch of A.P.C. round the corner in rue Franklin Roosevelt.

RÉCIPROQUE: SECONDHAND DESIGNER CLOTHING

If you are looking for secondhand, good-condition classic designer clothing – you'll find it here. Nicole Morel has an empire dealing in secondhand illustrious labels – from Hermès scarves to Saint Laurent suits – which stretches along the rue de la Pompe. She started up nearly twenty years ago and now has six stores. Don't be put off by the old-fashioned shop look; people come from all over Paris and out of town to shop here. Once a week there is a queue down the block of well-heeled, wealthy ladies waiting to consign suitcases jammed full of clothes. This is, says Nicole, 'a chance for them to clear a bit of space in their wardrobe, so they can go out and start buying again'. Nicole sells off their designer wear, often only a season old, shoes, scarves, accessories, rash buys, evening dresses they couldn't possibly wear twice, as well as non-designer sportswear. Prices are around half the original. She probably has the biggest selection of secondhand Chanel in Paris. She is obliged to remove all the buttons temporarily from Chanel jackets, as she has had such a problem with women coming in and stealing the buttons by cutting or ripping them off. Once you've made the purchase, all the buttons are sewn back on. As well as Chanel for day

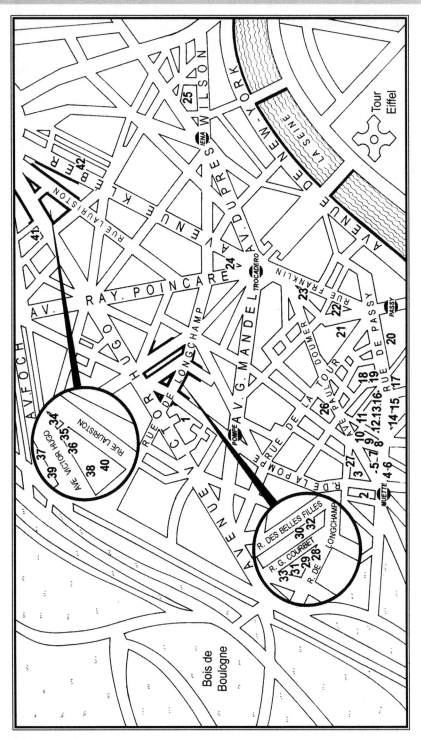

1 RÉCIPROQUE
2 DU PAREIL AU MÊME
3 MAXMARA
4 KENZO
5 FRANK & FILS
6 GUERLAIN
7 ET VOUS
8 BYBLOS CAFÉ
9 ERÈS
10 SCOOTER
11 PETIT BATEAU
12 MAC
13 SEPHORA
14 PASSY PLAZA
15 TARA JARMON
16 ANNE FONTAINE
17 JOSEPH
18 VICTOIRE
19 MEREDITH
20 REGINA RUBENS
21 DÉPÔT-VENTE DE PASSY
22 LAURENCE TAVERNIER

23 A.P.C.
24 CARETTE
25 MUSÉE GALLERIA DE LA MODE ET DU COSTUME
26 LES FOLIES D'ÉLODIES
27 VENTILO
28 LINDA WRIGHT
29 MELROSE
30 MOSQUITOS
31 CORINNE SARRUT
32 HERVÉ CHAPELIER
33 GROOM
34 CÉLINE
35 APOSTROPHE
36 CERRUTI
37 ROBERT CLERGERIE
38 YVES SAINT LAURENT
39 STÉPHANE KÉLIAN
40 GEORGES RECH
41 LOLITA LEMPICKA
42 HÔTEL RAPHAEL

and night you'll find, among the French designers, Hermès from scarves to overcoats, loads of Lacroix, Yves Saint Laurent, Montana, Givenchy, Mugler and Ungaro. Stock changes from week to week but international big names usually include Armani, Versace, Valentino, Moschino, Donna Karan, Calvin Klein and Ralph Lauren. There is less choice from the avant-garde designers, but you can always find pieces from Prada, Gaultier, Dolce & Gabbana and Martine Sitbon as well as less expensive basics from Joseph, Agnès b. and Irié. Downstairs at No. 95 is a non-designer, cheaper selection of suits and dresses. For shoes and boots there is usually quite a lot from the French designers like Clergerie, Maud Frizon and Kélian, as well as the odd pair of Patrick Cox, Louboutin and Manolo Blahnik. With so many stores and so much stock, you need to leave yourself a couple of hours to go through those rails. No problem with browsing.

RÉCIPROQUE, rue de la Pompe, 75016
Tel: 01 47 04 30 28
No. 88: accessories
No. 89: objets and homeware
No. 92: bags and scarves (Hermès, Louis Vuitton, Chanel), costume jewellery, lingerie, swimming costumes and beach towels
No. 93: women's evening wear with strappy sandals and evening bags
No. 95: enormous women's department on the ground floor with the Chanel counter and suits from other designers; downstairs there is a less expensive section of sportswear, dresses as well as fur, leather, shoes and boots
No. 101: menswear with suits from Boss, Dior, Armani, Versace
No. 123: winter coats, raincoats, hats (good in the summer for wedding hats)
Métro: Rue de la Pompe
Opening Hours: Tue–Fri: 11.00–19.30, Sat: 10.30–19.30
August: closed 25 Jul–23 Aug
Credit Cards: Visa, Amex, MC
Price Range: Chanel jacket 2,500–10,000FF Manolo Blahnik strappy satin evening shoes 660FF, spring coat from Hermès 1,320FF

DU PAREIL AU MÊME: CHILDREN'S CLOTHES
See 9th arrondissement for details.
3 rue de la Pompe, 75016. Tel: 01 42 24 82 84

MAXMARA: SLEEK ITALIAN FASHION
See 8th arrondissement for details.
100 avenue Paul Doumer, 75016. Tel: 01 40 50 34 05

KENZO: FRENCH DESIGNER FASHION
See 7th arrondissement for details.
99 rue de Passy, 75016. Tel: 01 42 24 92 92

FRANK & FILS: MEGA-STORE
Not so long ago a stroll around Frank & Fils was a bit like having a walk-on part in *Are You Being Served?* But ever since LVMH's Bernard

Arnault bought out the former family-owned department store in 1995 he's been working on transforming it into a 'mega-store'. Basically it's a scaled-down department store, so it makes a handy place to shop if you're staying around here or if you can't face the crowds at the other department stores. Christian Dior and Chanel both have in-store boutiques here, stocking accessories and clothes, and there is also a huge Bobbi Brown cosmetics counter. There is a great millinery department on the ground floor, which has smart and casual hats, and wonderful fake furs in the winter. The store has its own hat atelier with three milliners designing and making the hats. If you call up in advance, they do free tours for small groups around the atelier to watch hats being made.

Fashion is limited, but getting better. The first floor has more trend designers including Céline, Donna Karan, Givenchy and Cerruti 1881 as well as the French classics such as Sonia Rykiel. The lingerie department is strong with brands like Wolford, Hanro and La Perla – but make sure you don't get swallowed in a rack of padded velour dressing gowns. They used to have a wonderful tea room which was the local gossip stop for fur-trailing octogenerians. That's all been ripped out, refurbished and transformed into a 'fashionable' café – but you can't help missing the ladies and their pooches.

FRANK & FILS, 80 rue de Passy, 75016
Tel: 01 44 14 38 00
Métro: La Muette
Opening Hours: Mon–Sat: 10.00–19.00
August: open
Credit Cards: Visa, Amex, Diners, MC, JCB

GUERLAIN: SCENT
See 8th arrondissement for details.
93 rue de Passy, 75016. Tel: 01 42 88 41 62

ET VOUS: CONTEMPORARY WOMENSWEAR
See 8th arrondissement for details.
72 rue de Passy, 75016. Tel: 01 45 20 47 15

BYBLOS CAFÉ: LEBANESE RESTAURANT
This is a great lunch stop if you're shopping rue de Passy. The interior
is light and contemporary, the food is fresh and tasty and it's ideal for
when you've eaten one too many rich French sauces. There are two
sections, which means at lunchtime you can either go for a full restaurant menu or take a less expensive option and sit in the café, where
you can choose from a hot pitta loaded with crudités, falafel, chicken,
tabbouleh or hummus. There is a good choice for vegetarians and you
can also take away. In the evening it's sophisticated but relaxed with a
mix of locals, Carole Bouquet and Jane Birkin.

BYBLOS CAFÉ, 6 rue Guichard, 75016
Tel: 01 42 30 99 99
Métro: La Muette
Opening Hours: every day: 11.00–15.00, 18.30–23.00
August: open
Credit Cards: Visa, Amex, Diners
Price Range: hot pitta and filling from 26FF, lunch menu 96FF

ERÈS: GREAT SWIMWEAR
See 9th arrondissement for details.
6 rue Guichard, 75016. Tel: 01 46 47 45 21

SCOOTER: TREND JEWELLERY
See 2nd arrondissement for details.
12 rue Guichard, 75016. Tel: 01 45 20 23 27

PETIT BATEAU: T-SHIRTS & CHILDREN'S WEAR
See 9th arrondissement for details.
41 rue Vital, 75016. Tel: 01 45 25 55 19

M.A.C.: COSMETICS
See 6th arrondissement for details.
62 rue de Passy, 75016. Tel: 01 53 92 08 60

SEPHORA: COSMETICS, PERFUME, SKIN-CARE
See 8th arrondissement for details.
50 rue de Passy, 75016. Tel: 01 53 92 28 20

PASSY PLAZA: MALL
This is an American-style mall which is fairly unremarkable but you can find branches of Gap, Zara and Agatha in here. If you turn right out of the back entrance of the Plaza you will find yourself on a market street called rue de l'Annonciation and at No. 28 is the Brûleries des Ternes which sells the most wonderful fresh coffee.

TARA JARMON: FASHIONABLE WOMENSWEAR
See 6th arrondissement for details.
51 rue de Passy, 75016. Tel: 01 45 24 65 20

ANNE FONTAINE: WHITE SHIRTS
See 2nd arrondissement for details.
22 rue de Passy, 75016. Tel: 01 42 24 80 20

JOSEPH: CONTEMPORARY WOMENSWEAR
See 8th arrondissement for details.
27 rue de Passy, 75016. Tel: 01 45 24 24 32

VICTOIRE: CHIC DESIGNER WOMENSWEAR
Less fashion scene than the flagship Victoire at place des Victoires, this shop caters perfectly for the 16th arrondissement woman. She is, according to boutique director Carmen, either 'the femme objet – small-boned and size 10' or the professional woman. Translated into clothes the look is simple, chic and smart and does go beyond just size 10. DKNY and Mr & Mrs MacLeod are both store staples and there are pretty dresses by Yara, as well as the best of Lacroix's Bazar collection. It's also good for their own-label basics: linen shirts, knitwear, stretch satin shirts and stretch trousers.

VICTOIRE, 16 rue de Passy, 75016
Tel: 01 42 88 20 84
Métro: Passy
also at:
10–12 place des Victoires, 75002. Tel: 01 42 61 09 02
1 rue Madame, 75006. Tel: 01 45 44 28 14
Opening Hours: Mon–Sat: 10.00–19.00
August: closed
Credit Cards: Visa, Amex, Diners, MC
Price Range: hats 300–1,200FF, knitwear 800–3,000FF, suits 2,500–5,500FF, summer dress 1,000–2,500FF

MEREDITH: CHIC DESIGNER WOMENSWEAR

Owned by Madame Meredith and her daughter, this is a fairly formal boutique selling elegant designer fashion. As Mademoiselle Meredith puts it, 'we mix our own mayonnaise', meaning there is a mixture of designers and style with a little from Gaultier, Comme des Garçons' second line, Atsuro Tayama, Alexander McQueen and Zoran, but the main thrust here is in more classic suiting such as Apara. They have a great selection of Italian knitwear with lush cashmere sweaters as well as nice accessories like steel belts threaded with leather. One word of warning: Meredith sales assistants are the kind who notice the ladder in your tights before you're even through the door.

MEREDITH, 14 rue de Passy, 75016
Tel: 01 42 88 08 20
Métro: Passy
Opening hours: Mon–Sat: 10.00–19.00
August: open except Mondays
Credit Cards: Visa, Amex, MC
Price range: Apara suiting 2,700FF, cashmere knitwear 700–3,000FF, hats from 500FF, belts 150–600FF

REGINA RUBENS: FRENCH CLASSIC WOMENSWEAR

See 1st arrondissement for details.
15 rue de Passy, 75016. Tel: 01 45 20 56 56

DÉPÔT-VENTE DE PASSY: SECONDHAND CLOTHES

Another secondhand designer shop, this one is smaller than Réciproque and tends to concentrate on the ready-to-wear lines from the big-name French houses such as Chanel, Lacroix, Ungaro, Yves Saint Laurent and Alaïa, although they do often have suits from Karl Lagerfeld and Valentino dresses as well. Most of the customers are aged 35 and up and looking for smart suiting, cocktail dresses or wedding outfits. They get a younger customer popping by for the Chanel and Hervé Léger. There are masses of secondhand luxe accessories: Chanel bags, belts, costume jewellery, Louis Vuitton bags and Hermès scarves. According to owner Catherine Baril, when she set up in 1982 Parisians were coy about buying secondhand, then they discovered the joys of slipping into a little designer something from last season at a third of the price and now they're in twice a week to check the rails.

DÉPÔT-VENTE DE PASSY, 12–14 rue de la Tour, 75016
Tel: 01 45 20 95 21
Métro: Passy
Opening Hours: Mon: 14.00–19.00, Tue–Sat: 10.00–19.00
August: closed
Credit Cards: Visa, Amex, MC, JCB
Price Range: Hermès scarves 700FF, Chanel jacket around 4,000FF, Hervé Léger jacket 2,000FF

LAURENCE TAVERNIER: NIGHT AND HOUSE WEAR
See 7th arrondissement for details.
3 rue Benjamin Franklin, 75016. Tel: 01 46 47 89 39

A.P.C.: PERFECT DESIGNER BASICS
This branch of A.P.C. is bigger but less well known than the one in the 6th, which means you don't normally get the situation during fashion-show times of someone getting there before you and buying every item you want in your size. It's also beautiful and on the ground floor of a grand 16th arrondissement apartment block, which was the first to be built in reinforced concrete, in 1903. With friendly, non-pushy staff, this branch has mostly womenswear with just a little of the men's basics. It's in an unlikely location on a road just off the Trocadéro, so you can come here and do the Eiffel Tower afterwards. See the rue Cassette branch in the 6th arrondissement for full details and sale shop.

A.P.C., 25 bis rue Benjamin Franklin, 75016
Tel: 01 45 53 28 28
Métro: Trocadéro
also at:
(womenswear) 3 rue de Fleurus, 75006. Tel: 01 42 22 12 77
(menswear) 4 rue de Fleurus, 75006. Tel: 01 45 49 19 15
(general) 4 rue de Fleurus, 75006. Tel: 01 45 48 72 42
(sale shop) 45 rue Madame, 75006. Tel: 01 45 48 43 71
Opening hours: Mon–Sat: 10.30–19.00
August: closed for week of 15 Aug
Credit Cards: Visa, Amex, MC
Price Range: T-shirts 200FF, trousers 500–800FF, floral shirts 500–550FF, jeans 480FF

CARETTE: TEA ROOM
Over 70 years old, Carette is an old-fashioned salon de thé with a gorgeous view of the Eiffel Tower and a wicked way with mille-feuilles (Yves Saint Laurent and Pierre Bergé are Saturday afternoon regulars). It is still a family-run institution which also does a sideline as traiteur cooking up traditional French dishes. Christian Dior jewellery designer Victoire de Castellane swears by them and calls Carette for her every dinner party, ordering up delicacies such as langouste à la Parisienne which are then delivered to the door. Then it's just a question of discretion whether you choose to tell your guests or dispose of the tell-tale Carette bags before they arrive.

CARETTE, 4 place du Trocadero, 75116
Tel: 01 47 27 88 56
Métro: Trocadéro
Opening Hours: Mon–Sat: 7.30–midnight, Sun: 7.30–22.00
August: open
Credit Cards: Visa, Amex
Price Range: mille-feuilles 32FF, café crème 32FF

MUSÉE GALLERIA: MUSEUM

This is the Paris museum of fashion and costume and shows temporary exhibitions. The space is intimate and exhibitions are usually themed, with free guided tours at 2.30pm on Thursdays and Saturdays.

MUSÉE GALLERIA DE LA MODE ET DU COSTUME, 10 avenue Pierre
Premier de Serbie, 75116
Tel: 01 47 20 85 23
Métro: Iéna
Opening Hours: Tue–Sun: 10.00–17.40
August: closed from 4 Aug
Credit Cards: Visa
Entrance Fee: 35FF (25FF for under-25s)

AVENUE PAUL DOUMER

LES FOLIES D'ÉLODIES: LUXURY UNDERWEAR

Les Folies d'Élodies is a study in peachy femininity. One of Paris's most famous lingerie stores, it's a frothy confection of silk satin, chiffon and Calais lace with bras, teddies, slips and bodies stitched up in ivory, oyster pink or beige. In a boudoir setting of mirrored dressing tables and perfume spritzers, there are luxury short satin dressing gowns, black and white checkered bra and French knicker sets and satin corsetry. You can either buy off the peg, or choose demi-mesure, which means you pick your own colour combination from a choice of thirty different shades and they make it up for you at no added cost. For less expensive sex appeal, they also do a range of microfibre and Lycra bodies, bras and knickers at more realistic prices. Men, apparently, love it in here (Warren Beatty and Johnny Halliday are among those who have been in); they make up the majority of customers and are the biggest spenders. Demi-mesure takes ten days and can be sent on to you.

LES FOLIES D'ÉLODIES, 56 avenue Paul Doumer, 75016
Tel: 01 45 04 93 57
Métro: La Muette or Trocadéro
Opening Hours: Mon: 11.00–18.30, Tue–Sat: 10.15–19.00
August: closed 3–25 Aug
Credit Cards: Visa, Amex, MC
Price Range: bra and knicker set from 150FF for microfibre, up to 2,500FF in silk satin, slip 700–3,000FF, body 600–3,000FF, nightdress from 1,000FF

VENTILO: FRENCH CLASSIC WOMENSWEAR

See 2nd arrondissement for details.
96 avenue Paul Doumer, 75016. Tel: 01 40 50 02 21

RUE GUSTAVE COURBET

Rue Gustave Courbet's fashion is dictated by the huge secondary school, Lycée Janson de Sailly, situated nearby. It's one of Paris's most exclusive schools and full of screaming teenagers with mobile phones, cabriolet cars and an attitude to match. Both rue de Longchamp and rue Gustave Courbet are lined with stores like Kookaï, Mosquitos and Comme Ça des Halles – all hankering after lycée pocket money.

LINDA WRIGHT: CLASSIC, CHIC

Slim-set and elegant, Linda Wright worked for Ralph Lauren decor and as a fashion stylist before setting up as a fashion designer on her own and it shows. Both she and her clothes exude American ease and style, from her crisp white fitted shirt to what she calls her blue silk 'Audrey Hepburn' pants with no pleat, no pocket. American by birth, Parisian by choice, she does modern classic pieces with skirts, dresses, jackets, six different shapes of trouser and lots of knits, plus great plain shirting. She aims to 'take the chi-chi out of French dressing' with clothes which work for the office (such as a nice three-quarter-length single-breasted jacket) and the weekend with her summer staple of linen shift dress in sweet-pea colours.

LINDA WRIGHT, 3 rue Gustave Courbet, 75016
Tel: 01 44 05 11 10
Métro: Victor Hugo or Rue de la Pompe
Opening Hours: Mon–Sat: 10.00–19.00
August: closed
Credit Cards: Visa, Amex, MC
Price Range: trousers from 600FF, jacket 1,200–3,500FF

MELROSE: SMART FASHIONABLE SHOES

Melrose has a loyal following for shoes which are fashionable, not frightening. They are great for boots and do every length, height of heel and style from satin ankle boots to glossy leather calf boots. More questionable in taste are the thigh-highs – no matter what the trends, Parisians still love them. They manufacture their own shoes and so have come up with different-width boots to suit different calf shapes. There are some pretty wedge-heel leather mules and strappy evening sandals.

MELROSE, 5 rue Gustave Courbet, 75016
Tel: 01 47 27 21 32
Métro: Rue de la Pompe
Opening hours: Mon: 14.30–19.30, Tue–Sat: 10.30–19.30
August: closed for one week, call for dates
Credit Cards: Visa, MC
Price Range: high-heel ankle boots 890FF, boots from 1,700FF, shoes from 700FF

MOSQUITOS: FUNKY FOOTWEAR
See 6th arrondissement for details.
12 rue Gustave Courbet, 75016. Tel: 01 45 53 36 73

CORINNE SARRUT: PRETTY FASHION
See 7th arrondissement for details.
7 rue Gustave Courbet, 75016. Tel: 01 55 73 09 73

HERVÉ CHAPELIER: SMART NYLON BAGS
See 6th arrondissement for details.
13 rue Gustave Courbet, 75016. Tel: 01 47 27 83 66

GROOM: LIGHTWEIGHT NYLON AND LEATHER BAGS
Organic shapes and minimal but striking detail make Groom bags priority dressing for modern women. Made from leather or lightweight matt nylon, they are intended for city life and start in price from 365FF. Beyond trend, these bags are more about a way of life – architects love them, as does Lauren Bacall. The best-selling shape is a roomy nylon backpack, the bag part of which ties in a fat knot before separating into straps. Groom designer Corinne Geffrey comes up with two collections a year, one in nylon, the other in leather, and there are purses and wallets as well to go with every bag. All the bags contain a metal sail clip inside to attach your keys.

GROOM, 17 rue Gustave Courbet, 75016
Tel: 01 47 27 02 77
Métro: Rue de la Pompe
also at:
13 rue du Cherche-Midi, 75006. Tel: 01 45 48 49 36
Opening Hours: Mon: 12.00–19.00, Tue–Sat: 10.00–12.30, 13.30–19.00
August: closed
Credit Cards: Visa, Amex, MC
Price Range: shoulder bag from 365FF, backpack 525FF (nylon), 1,635FF (leather)

AVENUE VICTOR HUGO

There are quite a few good stores down this street which tend to stock the more classic items from their ranges.

CÉLINE: FRENCH DESIGNER CHIC
See 8th arrondissement for details.
3 avenue Victor Hugo, 75016. Tel: 01 45 01 80 01

APOSTROPHE: FRENCH CHIC WOMENSWEAR
See 8th arrondissement for details.
11 avenue Victor Hugo, 75016. Tel: 01 45 01 66 91

CERRUTI 1881:   SMART, CLASSIC WOMENSWEAR
See 8th arrondissement for details.
3 avenue Victor Hugo, 75016. Tel: 01 45 01 80 01

ROBERT CLERGERIE: ELEGANT DESIGNER SHOES
See 6th arrondissement for details.
18 avenue Victor Hugo, 75016. Tel: 01 45 01 81 30

YVES SAINT LAURENT: FRENCH DESIGNER
See 6th arrondissement for details.
19 avenue Victor Hugo, 75016. Tel: 01 45 00 64 64

STÉPHANE KÉLIAN: TREND AND CLASSIC SHOES
See 7th arrondissement for details.
20 avenue Victor-Hugo, 75016. Tel: 01 45 00 44 41

GEORGES RECH: FRENCH CHIC
See 1st arrondissement for details.
23 avenue Victor Hugo, 75016. Tel: 01 45 00 83 19

LOLITA LEMPICKA: FRENCH DESIGNER
See 8th arrondissement for details.
46 Avenue Victor Hugo, 75106. Tel: 01 45 02 14 46

AVENUE KLÉBER

HÔTEL RAPHAEL: HOTEL
Distinguished and utterly discreet, the Hôtel Raphael has always been a grand address in town. Marlon Brando, Ava Gardner and Ingrid Bergman all used it as their Paris pied-à-terre. You can either stay here or do what Parisians do and use the bar as a hide-away to hole up in. With an open fire and wood panelling, it's a gorgeous setting for afternoon tea or apéritifs in the winter.

HÔTEL RAPHAEL, 17 avenue Kléber, 75016
Tel: 01 44 28 00 28
Credit Cards: Visa, Amex, Diners, MC, JCB
Price Range: double room from 2,340FF per night

Destination Shopping

DESTINATION SHOPPING

Destination shopping is about those areas of Paris which may not have enough fashion shops to justify a chapter, but nevertheless have some must-see, select stores worth getting on a métro for. They are arrondissements or areas that are not dead central but are all within a 20-minute métro trip from the centre of Paris.

FLEA MARKETS

Doing les puces or flea markets is a quintessential Paris weekend pastime. The laid-back atmosphere, the mix of treasures and tat, the people-watching, throw in a lunch of moules and frites and red wine, and it's worth getting out of bed early at the weekend. There are two flea markets that count:

MARCHÉ CLIGNANCOURT

When you get out at métro stop Porte de Clignancourt you will see stacks of stalls selling dodgy-looking T-shirts and almost-Nike sports gear. Ignore this. The Clignancourt puces is in fact made up of masses of tiny markets adjacent to each other; to get to the best you want to walk north and then cut into the market and look for the following: Marché Paul-Bert, Marché Serpette, Marché Jules-Vallès, Marché Vernaison and Marché Biron. This is where you'll find what you are looking for – jewellery, furniture, glass, paintings, luggage, textiles, garden furniture, clothes and hats plus all the other extraordinary bits and pieces you find at the puces. For lunch or coffee try any bar/bistro that takes your fancy or go to Chez la Mère Marie at 82 rue des Rosiers or Chez Louisette at 130 avenue Michelet for the Edith Piaf singing impersonations and greasy-caff ambience. Bear in mind that Clignancourt is open to the public on Saturday, Sunday and Monday only.

Opening Hours: for the public Sat/Sun/Mon: 7.00–19.30
Métro: Porte de Clignancourt

MARCHÉ DE VANVES

A hit with the fashion crowd, the Marché de Vanves is smaller than Clignancourt and deals in smaller pieces – objets, mirrors, textiles, clothing, handbags and glass, although there is some furniture too. Be warned: unlike at Clignancourt, many of the stalls pack up and go home around lunchtime. Other than the early start this is a great market, less touristy, less populated, more compact and therefore easier to shop than Clignancourt.

Opening Hours: Sat/Sun: 7.00–19.30 (many stalls pack up at lunchtime)
Métro: Porte de Vanves

LATIN QUARTER

DIPTYQUE: **SCENTED CANDLES**

The Diptyque candle is a Parisian classic. It is a perennial fashion item and is burned in every self-respecting Paris interior. Others may now have caught the trend and started trying to compete, but Yves Coueslant has been creating dreamy-smelling candles in a glass for over thirty years and the original is a must. Candle fans spend hours deliberating over their choice and it isn't easy with 43 different scents to tempt you, plus charming sales assistants who talk about each scent in vivid terms of 'it's the smell of an English country house, a Greek Orthodox cathedral, a leather club chair, a summer's evening'. Scents range from a smoky musk or heady lily of the valley to hawthorn and newly mown hay, while Diptyque fans are similarly diverse and include Karl Lagerfeld, Tom and Nicole, Kristin Scott Thomas and Donatella Versace. The candles burn for 60 hours and, unlike some interior candles you come across, Diptyque scent is never cloying.

DIPTYQUE, 34 boulevard St-Germain, 75005
Tel: 01 43 26 45 27
Metro: St-Michel
Also on sale at Printemps; see 9th arrondissement for details
Opening Hours: Tue–Sat: 10.00–19.00
August: open
Credit Cards: Visa
Price Range: candles are all priced 160FF

10TH ARRONDISSEMENT
JAMIN PUECH: FASHIONABLE HANDBAGS
French accessory designers Benoît Jamin and Isabelle Puech wince at the thought of the over-stuffed tote. They shudder at the mention of the utilitarian body bag. Their design mantra is instead uncompromisingly Parisian and that means hand-held feminine. Isabelle's bottom line: 'A bag should never cover the hips.' Hooked on flea-market finds and exotic travel (Isabelle spent her childhood sailing around the world on a boat with her mother), Jamin Puech have established a deliciously quirky, Agatha Christie-goes-glam aesthetic. They do giant sequins and hand-dyed crochet, paisley beading, tattoed leather and rattling fringes of horn. Fashion-wise there is not much else in this neighbourhood but it is worth getting your taxi to stop by the boutique on your way back to Gare du Nord.

JAMIN PUECH, 61 rue d'Hauteville, 75010
Tel: 01 40 22 08 32
Métro: Poissonnière
Opening Hours: Mon–Fri: 9.30–18.30, Sat: 10.00–19.00
August: closed
Credit Cards: Visa, MC
Price Range: raffia bag 500–1,300FF, leather bag from 995FF, sequin bag from 750FF

ANTOINE ET LILI: HIPPIE, FUNKY KIT
This is a cute hippie-feel brand which makes well-priced ethnic-inspired kit to bring out the love child in you. They have several stores around Paris, but this is more of an Antoine et Lili commune – they call it the Village. It's all about turquoise and scarlet knitted ponchos, kooky hairgrips, dresses made from furnishing fabrics, bindis, incense, cut-plastic rainbow curtains, it's kitsch goes Goa Paris-style. As well as clothes there is furniture, plant pots, brocante (old bits of furniture for sale) and a salon de thé. You never knew the French could be this laid back.

ANTOINE ET LILI, LE VILLAGE, 95 quai de Valmy, 75010
Tel: 01 53 38 55 55
Métro: Gare de l'Est

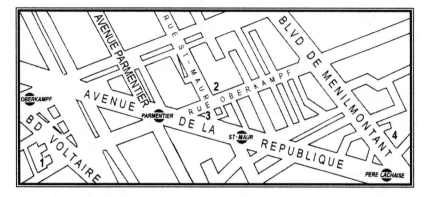

1 URSULE BEAUGESTE
2 CAFÉ CHARBON
3 LA VILLE DE JAGANNATH
4 ZAP SPIRIT

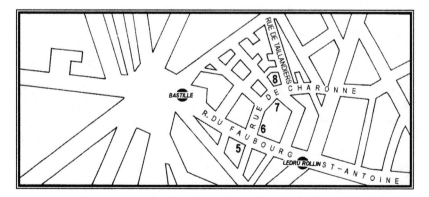

5 JEAN PAUL GAULTIER
6 ISABEL MARANT
7 MOD'EMPLOI
8 TOSCA

also at:
90 rue des Martyrs, 75018. Tel: 01 42 58 10 22
87 rue de Seine, 75006. Tel: 01 56 24 35 81
Opening Hours: Mon–Sat: 11.00–20.00
August: open
Credit Cards: Visa, Amex, MC, JCB
Price Range: from 10FF for a hairgrip to 2,000FF for a coat

OBERKAMPF

A working-class, cosmopolitan neighbourhood with a gritty feel, Oberkampf has turned bohemian and downtown over the last few years with an influx of artists, young designers, musicians and photographers. At night the rue Oberkampf heats up with a cool, young crowd hanging out at the bars and restaurants that line this street from Le Kitch at the bottom of the street at No. 10 right up to Le Robinet Mélangeur at 123 boulevard de Ménilmontant which also does a great weekend tea.

URSULE BEAUGESTE: HANDBAGS

Designer Anne Grand-Clément makes bags which are functional with a bohemian charm. She stamps and engraves leather for a fringed hippie kind of saddle bag and in the summer she turns out the perfect raffia holiday basket or a pale mauve leather dainty bag. Her design basic is the Safari-feel 'Fever', a many-pocketed, highly practical hand-held bag which in winter comes in tweed or felt and in summer in brightly coloured canvas. You can find the kind of bag here that is not swinging from every other wrist in town.

URSULE BEAUGESTE, 15 rue Oberkampf, 75011
Tel: 01 49 23 02 48
Métro: Oberkampf or Filles des Calvaires
Opening Hours: Mon–Sat: 11.00–19.00
August: closed for two weeks, call for exact dates
Price Range: purses from 280FF, most bags 900–1,700FF, large size Fever bag 1,790FF

CAFÉ CHARBON:
HIP CAFÉ

When you're tired of idyllic cafés with idyllic views over Paris, it's time to slip over to Café Charbon for a little action. One hundred years old, this establishment has seen life as a ballroom, café-theatre, cinema, and has reopened as a café once more. Located in a working-class, cosmopolitan part of town, it is used during the day by locals for espresso and lunch. At night, a DJ moves in and the pace heats up. Food is only served during the day and they do a brunch on Saturday and Sunday. The setting is bohemian bistro, with original tiled floor and dusty metal lamps, plus a slice of now in cool clientele and music. But watch out for those frightening pissoirs – they're just a little too historic.

CAFÉ CHARBON, 109 rue Oberkampf, 75011
Tel: 01 43 57 55 13
Métro: Parmentier or Oberkampf
Opening Hours: every day, all day: 9.00–2.00am
August: open
Credit Cards: Visa
Price Range: weekend brunch 75FF, bottle of house Bordeaux 65FF, espresso 8FF

LA VILLE DE JAGANNATH:
VEGETARIAN INDIAN RESTAURANT

This is a Hindu vegetarian restaurant where fashion people such as Mario Testino, Rei Kawakubo and Christian Lacroix all come by. Run by former model John Armstrong, it serves fragrant and delicious food, and the service is charming. The menu features the traditional Indian thali which is a stainless-steel platter containing several different dishes and can be ordered in different sizes, small, medium or large. The decor is kind of exotic and laid back with garlands of dried jasmine hanging at the windows, low-slung seats and wonderful Indian fabrics draped around. They used to operate a 'no stimulants' policy of no smoking, no alcohol, no coffee, but the French were predictably so outraged that one by one these rules have fallen and today you can even get a caffeine-loaded espresso.

LA VILLE DE JAGANNATH, 101 rue St-Maur, 75011
Tel: 01 43 55 80 81
Métro: St-Maur
Opening Hours: evenings only, Mon–Fri: 19.30–23.30, Sat/Sun: 19.30–00.30
August: open
Credit Cards: Visa, Amex, MC
Price Range: thali small 90FF, medium 130FF, large 160FF

ZAP SPIRIT:
MOROCCAN RESTAURANT

Downtown and Moroccan, this restaurant is decorated to look like a salon; the food is great with tajines of lamb cooked with prunes and almonds, crumbly couscous and pistachio patisseries. The scene is casual and multicultural: diners perch on stools or gold satin cushions, oriental and African beat music plays on the sound system and there's a scent of cinnamon coffee in the air.

ZAP SPIRIT, 84 boulevard Menilmontant, 75020
Tel: 01 43 49 10 64
Métro: Père Lachaise
Opening Hours: every day: 12.00–2.00am
August: open
Credit Cards: Visa, Amex, Diners, MC, JCB
Price Range: starters from 48FF, main course from 85FF, bottle of wine from 85FF

BASTILLE

Check out the Bastille for bars, cinemas and the new opera house. For fashion you'll find the largest Gaultier store sandwiched between truly bad-taste furniture shops. It's lively and fun around here at night, with bars like the What's Up Bar in rue Daval good for music and the China Club in rue de Charenton still a local favourite. The rue de Charonne is lined with contemporary art galleries, a couple of clubwear boutiques and the odd interior shop, as well as the quartier's favourite fashion cafés and restaurants like Chez Paul and the Pause Café. One of the best things about Bastille life is the fresh food market held on Thursday and Sunday mornings (closes at 1pm) along the boulevard Richard Lenoir. It's a classic neighbourhood market, with the most fantastic fresh seafood, fruit, cheeses and wines. You can buy yourself a hot picnic lunch of paella or spicy sausages and sauerkraut, sit by the fountains and listen to the banjo band.

JEAN PAUL GAULTIER: FRENCH COUTURIER

In 1996 Jean Paul Gaultier decided to launch his own haute couture collection and ever since both he and his creativity have been on a natural high. After a fall from fashion and being swept up as a media darling on the TV programme *Eurotrash*, he has learnt to discipline his prolific output, giving up all other distractions (the television presenting, film costumes, videos and records) to concentrate fully on his house. And boy does it show. Not only is he enjoying a design renaissance, but the house of Hermès announced in 1999 that it had bought 35% of the company and was planning to build the brand, open more stores and generally take Jean Paul Gaultier from small independent house to reach its global potential.

Fashion-wise Gaultier's limitless imagination continues to see everything, feel everything, absorb every influence – television, video, film, music, cultures, street-style, sexuality – then he re-mixes it all like some daring, iconoclasic DJ of fashion. And his couture training with

Pierre Cardin means that there is always technical brilliance and tailoring to his originality. He cuts an elegant trouser suit, drapes a sexy halter-neck dress from a horn choker and makes the consummate Paris chic trench-coat. But what's great about Gaultier is he mixes his couture sensibility with a funky sense of humour giving us tops and ruffled dresses in stretch sheer knit with ethnic prints and sweaters with graphic Nordic patterns done out in shimmering sequins.

This store sells the whole Gaultier universe, meaning the ready-to-wear, the Jean Paul Gaultier Classique line (around 20% less expensive and good for suiting), JPG jeans, jewellery, bags, eyewear and his fragrances, which are among the best-selling perfumes in the world.

JEAN PAUL GAULTIER, 30 rue du Faubourg St-Antoine, 75012
Tel: 01 44 68 84 84
Métro: Bastille
also at:
6 rue Vivienne, 75002. Tel: 01 42 86 05 05
Opening Hours: Mon/Sat: 11.00–19.00, Tue–Fri: 10.30–19.30
August: closed for two weeks around 15 Aug, call for exact dates
Credit Cards: Visa, Amex, Diners, MC, JCB
Price Range: suit from 6,000FF, jeans from 700FF, JPG jacket from 1,500FF, dress from 1,200FF

RUE DE CHARONNE

Now that much of the Bastille has been taken over by kebab street vendors and football supporters, rue de Charonne is holding out as the fashionable artery of the quartier. It is lined with bars, restaurants and clubby and street kit stores such as Jelly Pot, while Rough Trade records at No. 30 is a hot music source.

ISABEL MARANT: BOHEMIAN DRESSING

La Melting Mode is how designer Isabel Marant describes her style which is a fusion of layered, often floor-length silhouette with Asian and African influences. A young designer, she has made her niche in Paris by dressing the eastern Paris bohemian girl who smokes Camel before breakfast and drinks mint tea on the rue Oberkampf. They come in search of her rough-edged khaki satin dresses, short pareos in sari material worn over pin-striped trousers and her chunky-knit calf-length cardigans which close with a giant safety pin. Isabel started her design career in jewellery which she still does mainly in enamel and burnt copper with decorative grips for the hair, strands of necklaces as well as leather bags and notebooks.

ISABEL MARANT, 16 rue de Charonne, 75011
Tel: 01 49 29 71 55
Métro: Bastille or Ledru Rollin
Opening Hours: Mon–Sat: 10.30–19.30
August: closed for two weeks, call for details
Credit Cards: Visa, Amex, JCB
Price Range: trousers 900–1,100FF, jacket 2,000FF, jumpers 800–1,000FF

MOD'EMPLOI: HIPPIE FASHION

Wild colours, hippie tie-dye and Asian influence are what sells here. Many of the clothes are made up in Nepal and Tibet and the look is yellow satin padded jackets, tiny knitted dresses for kids, embroidered fuschia tunics for you. Once a month they hold a happening here which could be tarot card reading, body piercing or a hairdressing night. This store is not for you if the word minimalism is still your mantra.

MOD'EMPLOI, 30 rue de Charonne, 75011
Tel: 01 43 14 06 39
Métro: Bastille or Ledru Rollin
Opening Hours: Mon: 12.00–19.00, Tue–Sat: 10.30–19.30
August: closed for two weeks
Credit Cards: Visa
Price Range: hairgrip 20FF, skirt 500FF, jacket 1000FF

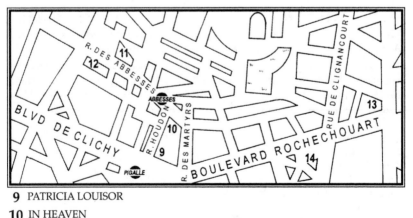

9 PATRICIA LOUISOR

10 IN HEAVEN

11 BONNIE COX

12 TÊTES EN L'AIR

13 TATI

14 GUERRISOLD

TOSCA: PERIOD SECONDHAND WOMEN'S CLOTHING

This is a treasure of a boutique jammed with period secondhand clothing. It is not old designer, it is not old couture, it is just lovely clothing
from 1900 through to the 1970s at reasonable prices. Owner Tonia is a
singer and actress with a lifelong passion for hunting at the puces. She
opened up in this street five years ago because it's next to where she
rehearses. She's there in the afternoons reading novels and cuts a
glamorous Paris pose dressed in a beret and black and silver Chinese
opera coat.

Tonia has an enormous stock of clothes which she keeps at home,
changing what's in the shop according to fashion trends. Her choice is
eclectic and subjective, from a hand-embroidered Lyon silk shirt to a
crêpe georgette black evening dress. There are always '50s silk jersey
petticoats which Tonia wears as dresses, as well as one-off pieces like
a wondrous maxi silk skirt in horizontal bands of purple, orange and
emerald green. Accessories are good value, with hats from 100 to
600FF including a gold lamé turban at 200FF. She keeps the more
expensive beaded pieces and wedding dresses at home; you can look
at photos in the shop and view them by appointment.

TOSCA, 1 rue des Taillandiers, 75011
Tel: 01 48 06 71 24
Métro: Bastille or Ledru Rollin
Opening Hours: Tue–Sat: 14.00–19.00 or by appointment
August: closed
Credit Cards: none
Prices: satin '50s suit 650FF, slips and petticoats from 120FF, silk hand-
embroidered shirts from 300FF, black halter-neck party dress 350FF

MONTMARTRE AND PIGALLE

Drop down from the tourist throngs around Sacré Coeur and there is
a village feel to the streets of Montmartre. Here you can find the last
remaining two windmills of the quartier, steep cobbled roads, artisans
at work, artist ateliers and hookers on the corner. Both the market
street of rue Lepic, where Van Gogh once lived, and rue des Abbesses
are great to wander or linger in restaurants and bars (check out the
Club Club at 3 rue André Antoine for funky nights including poetry on
Tuesdays). Shopping-wise it's for you if you enjoy groovy, individual,
well-priced fashion as there's a set of talented young Montmartre
designers who are doing their own fashion thing. Slightly over to the
east is a small fabric district, Marché St-Pierre, where you can pick up
dress and furnishing material at nice prices.

PATRICIA LOUISOR: WOMENSWEAR

This boutique is the favourite fashion source of every Pigalle hipster.
Three sisters, Patricia, Caroline and Monique, run it and they've figured

le photo-shoot

out what fashion-conscious Parisians want right now is an individual look at cheap prices. What they sell has two styles. Patricia's own label is very easy to wear, relaxed clothes with wide-legged trousers, full-length cotton coats and jackets. It's quite a bohemian but well-dressed style and you can't walk down a street in Pigalle without seeing some girl dressed in a flowing full-length Patricia Louisor coat. The second style is glorious 'victim' pieces by other young Paris labels: lots of high shine, kaleidoscope colours, clubwear and peacock-blue sheer shirts with *Come Dancing* ruffles. The shop counter is covered in crazy paving, the changing rooms in cardboard flying angels and new stock arrives every week. This is not just clothing for clubbers – they've got daywear, fluffy knits and summer dresses too.

PATRICIA LOUISOR, 16 rue Houdon, 75018
Tel: 01 42 62 10 42
Métro: Pigalle or Abbesses
Opening Hours: every day: 11.00–20.00
August: open
Credit Cards: Visa
Price Range: nylon shirt with ruffles 200FF, T-shirt 100FF, prices usually not more than 800FF

IN HEAVEN: FUNKY FASHION AND CHANDELIERS

English designer Lea-Anne Wallis sits in a back room of her boutique with a sewing machine, literally sewing up the stock herself. It means some pieces are one-offs, others are available in small series and stock changes every day. The look is individualistic and pretty, as Lea-Anne tends to make quite dressed-up, nostalgic clothes – the sort of thing you used to dress your Sindy doll in. Not Barbie doll kit, but padded matinée jackets made from shiny upholstery material or sparkly party dresses. Her boyfriend, Jean Christophe, works downstairs making wonderful lamps and chandeliers from glass bead droplets and gold metal wiring. They are delicate and colourful, some with an Eastern influence, others with more of a '30s twang, and each piece is a one-off.

IN HEAVEN, 83 rue des Martyrs, 75018
Tel: 01 44 92 92 92
Métro: Abbesses or Pigalle
Opening Hours: Mon: 14.00–19.30, Tue–Sat: 11.00–19.30, Sun: 14.00–19.30
August: closed
Credit Cards: Visa
Price Range: dress from 800FF, coat from 1,850FF, Uskudar lamp from 550FF, chandelier from 890FF

BONNIE COX: TREND WOMENSWEAR

This is a funky boutique with batik hipsters by hippie dudes Cosmic Where?, stretchy op-art tops and crochet bonnets. There are always quirky, sometimes inexplicable accessories, like a brown paper grocery

Montmartre

bag painted with green poster paints and covered in plastic. Owner Ludovic is turning the shop into more of a cyber-boutique by getting plugged in on the Internet, so now you can commune with W. & L.T., watch the fashion show on screen, design your own T-shirt and send it through to Walter. Newish labels here are Diesel and Bridget York.

BONNIE COX, 38 rue des Abbesses, 75018
Tel. 01 42 54 95 68
Métro: Abbesses
Opening Hours: every day: 10.30–20.00
August: closed approx 8–25 Aug
Credit Cards: Visa, Amex, Diners
Price Range: 100–1,000FF

TÊTES EN L'AIR: DASHING HATS

Anana makes hats for Têtes en l'Air which are glamorous and dashing. They are neither classic bourgeois, nor unwearably wacky – they are hats which make an entrance. 'I much prefer shape and colour to trimmings,' says Anana, who trained with an atelier making hats for haute couture before setting up alone. She waited an age to get this location as she'd always wanted the glorious view on to the windmill. She loves colour, hates black and for winter there are lots of felt and flannel everyday hats in saffron, deep plum or absinthe green which start from 150FF for something casual. For weddings and high days there are lilac straw top hats, Napoleonic shapes in pale straw with satin edging or floppy brims caught up with a satin button. You can either buy off the peg or have a hat made to measure for the same price, which takes three weeks during the summer, a week during the rest of the year. The clientele is totally mixed, ranging from old ladies to circus people, wedding guests, opera divas and even a clown.

TÊTES EN L'AIR, 65 rue des Abbesses, 75018
Tel: 01 46 06 71 19
Métro: Abbesses
Opening Hours: Mon: 14.00–19.00, Tue–Sat: 10.30–19.30
August: closed
Credit cards: none
Price Range: 150–1,500FF, wedding hat usually around 900FF

TATI: DISCOUNT DEPARTMENT STORE

There is nothing aspirational about shopping at Tati. In a city held hostage to luxe and good taste, Tati champions the cheap, tat and tacky. Great big bins of knickers for 2FF90 (they sell five million pairs a year), tights for 1FF90 (the price hasn't changed since 1950), T-shirts for 10FF, wedding dresses from 600FF (they sell the most wedding dresses in France) and everywhere frantic crowds of people shoving for bargains.

Tati was founded in 1948 by Jules Ouaki, whose intention was to sell clothing cheap like potatoes on a market stall so people could rummage, touch and feel. His target customer was the immigrant community and the poor, and for years Parisians viewed Tati discounting with disdain. Then a combination of the recession and grunge made Tati thoroughly desirable. Fashion mags started doing total Tati clothes shoots, Tati opened a store on the Left Bank, launched a perfume and suddenly those distinctive pink gingham plastic bags could be seen all over town. Now they have 14 stores in France, a turnover of well over 1.7 billion FF and have recently opened in Switzerland and South Africa.

Tati is for you if the word 'bargain' makes your pulse race. Stock stays on the shelves for three weeks only; if it hasn't sold by then prices are slashed. Expect to find: the cheapest espadrilles that ever walked, cotton zip-up cardigans 60FF, net curtains, Tippex-type nail varnish, Miu Miu-look beige bodies for 15FF and breath-takingly bad-taste ornaments. This is another store where the assistant needs to write you a chit before you pay at the caisse. If you think you've seen Paris when you've sipped café au lait in St-Germain, take a trip up here and see the other side.

TATI, 4 boulevard de Rochechouart, 75018
Tel: 01 42 55 13 09
Métro: Barbès Rochechouart
also at:
13 rue de la République, 75003. Tel: 01 48 87 72 81
Opening Hours: Mon: 10.00–19.00, Tue–Fri: 9.30–19.00, Sat: 9.15–19.00
Credit Cards: Visa
Price Range: from 1FF90 for a pair of tights

GUERRISOLD: SECONDHAND TAT

Guerrisold makes Tati look like Harvey Nichols. This is a chain of stores selling men's and women's secondhand mass-market clothing mostly from the '70s and '80s. A concept that started as a way of selling real cheap clothing in a poor part of town has been hijacked by the alternative fashion pack. This is not for you if you like your nylon with a designer label inside. But it is for you if you're a stylist or fashion student, love jumble sales or are committed to trash fashion and a bargain. Jean Paul Gaultier and Jean Colonna are regulars. Guerrisold bad news: the smell from the clothes can be off-putting (whatever the price add the cost of dry-cleaning), and some days you find absolutely nothing. Guerrisold good news: it's dirt cheap, well organised and sorted into skirts, tops etc. for easy shopping and some days you find your dream item – like when you walk in to see a zip-up A-line chestnut-brown leather maxi coat, price 50FF, begging to be bought.

There are seven Guerrisolds in Paris, the best are at 33 avenue de Clichy – good to do if you are up around Montmartre or Pigalle – and the store at 17 boulevard de Rochechouart which is enormous with a special retro area. According to a Guerrisold groupie the best days to go are Wednesday and Thursday as that's when the 'new' stock arrives – Monday is a write-off as there's no stock left after Saturday.

GUERRISOLD, 17 boulevard de Rochechouart, 75009
Tel: 01 45 26 38 92
Métro: Anvers
also at:
19, 29, 33 avenue de Clichy, 75017. Tel: 01 53 42 31 31
Opening Hours: Mon–Sat: 9.30–19.30
August: open
Credit Cards: Visa
Price Range: womenswear 19–200FF, wedding dress 500FF, menswear 19–300FF

INDEX

In this index, designers are listed alphabetically according to their full name (Yves Saint Laurent is under Y, not S, for example) if that is how they are commonly known, or it is the official name of their label, or they have an own-name shop which uses their full name. Other designers, for instance Delphine Véron who designs for the shop Fifi Chachnil, are listed in the normal way – Véron, Delphine – as their first names are perhaps not widely known.